JIMMY
THE GREEK

JIMMY
THE GREEK

by Himself

with the editorial assistance of
Mickey Herskowitz & Steve Perkins

P❦P
A Playboy Press Book

Published simultaneously in the United States and Canada by Playboy Press, Chicago, Illinois. Printed in the United States of America. Library of Congress Catalog Card Number: 74-33558. ISBN 87223-424-X. First edition.

PLAYBOY and Rabbit Head design are trademarks of Playboy, 919 North Michigan Avenue, Chicago, Illinois 60611 (U.S.A.), Reg. U.S. Pat. Off., marca registrada, marque déposée.

For Joan and the kids, who helped me beat the odds.

Contents

Prologue

The island of Kios kept rising out of the blue-green Aegean Sea as the boat moved slowly closer, lurching and rolling through the rough water. The boy held onto a stanchion and threw up on the deck. Pop had said not to lean over the side to throw up "or you'll throw yourself up and over and feed the fishes." This was the longest part of the trip. This was forever, coming from Piraeus on a boat that could have fit on the deck of the big boat that had brought them from America. He was too sick now to think about why they were coming to Kios. He didn't want to think about that anyway, or he would cry again. A grown-up boy of ten, in Greece, didn't cry. Throw up, yes. Cry, no. All he knew was that Kios was "home." This had been drilled into him all the way over by his father and by Uncle Stanley. Even though he had never been there before, even though home to him had always been the house in Steubenville, which he was not going to think about now. That and the telephone pole by the front yard with a bullet hole in it.

He had always heard of Kios, the magical island, on Sundays in the house in Steubenville, when all the cousins and the friends of cousins would come from far away to eat and talk and laugh and sometimes sing. On summer Sundays they would put chairs under the big tree in the backyard, and the men would dance in a line with their arms stretched across each other's shoulders. Back then, Kios seemed no farther away than the end of the street-car line. Grandpa was always "going to the island" and coming back.

Grandpa had started it all, bringing Pop and his brother Tom and his sister Maria to Steubenville when Pop was six years old. In school, the boy had subtracted Pop's age and decided this happened in 1904. They all came to Steubenville because that's where the other villagers of Kios had gone. Nobody could remember who were the first Kions to live in Steubenville, but everyone else from the island followed because they were there. Grandpa opened the biggest food store in town, the White House Meat Market, and in a little while he went back to Kios and got the baby son, Anthony.

One time when everyone was talking about Kios, the boy asked Uncle Stanley—who was really Pop's cousin but seemed like an uncle—why everyone loved the island. "If they like it so much," the boy said, "why do they come *here?*" Uncle Stanley treated the question seriously, as he always did. "Because," he said, "the *living* is good there, but the *money* is good here. Blessed be the man who can have both."

He knew that the home village was Kalamote, or "the good eye," and the island's language was his language. They were never allowed to talk English in the house. "You will learn to talk American in school," Pop said, "and you'll learn from your playmates. Here you will talk the language of your people."

Now all he cared about was that the island didn't move—though it seemed to move even after he had stepped ashore. Uncle Stanley kidded him about walking straddle-legged, but all the boy wanted was a bed, and then he slept around the clock. In the morning he came downstairs to find Grandpa alone in the house. Everything was strange and familiar at the same time. All the furniture, the beds and the chairs and the tables, was just like Steubenville, but everything else was different. The walls and the floors and the windows. Everything clean, but different. This was some goddamn faraway place, all right. After the big ship had left America he had had a fine time crawling in the lifeboats and going down to the kitchen. No, the galley. Then the first sight of land, which he thought was Kios, turned out to be Portugal. *Poor-too-gal*, they told him. Then Naples. Then Piraeus, with a trip up to Athens where Pop had bought him a .25 rifle. Finally, Kios.

"Grandpa," the boy said, "where's Pop and Uncle Stanley?"

"Men rise early and children sleep abed," Grandpa said. "Your father is in the field with his gun, where the quail flutter. As he did at your age."

The boy hurried back upstairs to get his precious .25 and came down again. "How do I get there?" he said.

"Your car awaits you at the front of the house," Grandpa said.

Okay, the boy thought, *I can handle that. Hot-damn, a real car.* But what he discovered in front of the house was a jackass. Then he remembered coming up from the boat the night before, through streets too narrow for a car or even a good-sized wagon. He went back to the house. "What am I supposed to do with that?" he said.

"If you want to get anywhere," his grandpa said, "and you don't want to walk, that's what you're going to ride."

He never did find his father that morning. The jackass had its own ideas: a jaunt through the fig trees. When the animal stopped of its own accord, and the young rider was sampling the ripest fruit from the low-hanging branches, a deputy appeared from nowhere shouting, "You, boy! What are you doing here stealing fruit? Little bastard. You'll come with me." He grabbed the rope bridle and led them through the orchard and into town, past laughing villagers, to the office of the constable. "I've got a very serious case of theft here," the deputy said. "He's been eating figs." The constable was laughing, and for the first time the boy ceased being scared.

"Well," the constable said, "if he's stealing, he's stealing from himself. This is Demetrios, grandson of Synodinos. And that acreage is what his grandfather means for him to have."

For the first time in his life, little Jimmy Synodinos realized what it meant to have the heritage of his family.

The pride of that moment carried him through the next few weeks, miserable every one. There were no electric lights; you had to light a match to a lamp. No radio, no telephone to talk to your buddies.

Hell, no buddies. And you had to crap through a hole in a board in the backyard, like the outhouses of early America. But gradually Kios began to take hold of him.

Mainly there was pride, and the sense of who he was. For one thing, there was Grandma. A tough cookie. She ruled the island women. The well was drawn at 7:00 A.M. and at 5:00 P.M., and the women would stand around waiting for Grandma to make her appearance. She would draw the first water. Woe be unto the woman who stepped in front of her. Grandma would lower the boom. The same procedure was followed at Sunday mass. Grandma was the first to enter church. If she was a moment late, the women would wait upon her. Her name was Kyraki, or "Sunday," and she was as peaceful as her name, until she was crossed. *This* was a Synodinos.

Jimmy learned the rituals of the island. He learned how Turkish tobacco was grown, dried, packed, auctioned off. "*Turkish* tobacco?" he said, and learned that Kios was only a quarter of a mile off the coast of Turkey. He had always taken it for granted that the land mass over there was Mother Greece.

Gradually, he made friends with the village boys and learned to gamble drachmas on the toss of a stone. The boys loved to set their game on a bridge that spanned a creek near Kios, which was also the name of the town, each putting a coin on top of a stone and each tossing at the other's stone. Jimmy had spent three days searching for the right stone, a small stone, one easier to control. Jimmy won most of the drachmas, and his friends said he won because he didn't need the money. He was rich; that's why he could throw so easily. The truth was he loved the game and didn't think about the drachmas.

There was a school in town for all the children, but this wouldn't do for the son of George Synodinos, grandson of John Synodinos. This heir, this paragon, should have a private tutor. The daughter of Dalma was hired to instruct him. That was how she was known; Jimmy never learned another name. The family name was enough, and the affiliation was identity. Dalma was a very old lady, Jimmy was aware, in her late twenties, and she was strict in demanding him to complete assignments—in Greek, mathematics, and English. They would go for long walks, or ride jackasses and do the lessons under an olive tree.

This was in the spring of 1930, and Dalma had packed a fine lunch, with an emphasis on desserts for the sweet tooth of her student. They were high in the Kios hills and could look down and see the coast of Turkey. For the first time the world seemed right. "Dalma," he said, "do you know what happened to my mother?"

And he told her how he had been playing with a friend outside his father's store that early evening in March. His mother, Sultania, and his aunt, Theano, were there, and little Marika was being pushed in her baby carriage by Mary, another aunt. "Hey, Mom," he said, "can I wait and go home with Pop?" She said no at first, and then she said, "Well, why not?" And Mom and Aunt Theano went on. The walk home was only about four blocks. Theano had been living at her sister's house since breaking up with her husband a few weeks before.

Jimmy went on playing sidewalk "tennis" with his friend Johnny in front of the store, even though it was eight-thirty and they had to play by the streetlights. At nine o'clock he heard the clang of a paddy wagon leaving the police station down the block. Then a policeman was into the store, and Pop was walking out fast behind him yelling, "Demetrios, come with me!" He followed him into the police station and heard the sergeant tell Pop that Mom and Aunt Theano had been shot dead. Theano's husband had killed them and then turned the gun on himself. He was a war hero, with a battlefield commission and a chestful of medals. Plus battle fatigue. When Theano, a great beauty at age twenty-six, had left him, it shoved him over the edge. Jimmy's mom was twenty-nine.

"The guy was at the house waiting for them," Jimmy told Dalma. "He had all kinds of guns he saved from the war. He had a German gun. A Luger. And when I went outside the next day, my buddies were digging in the telephone pole for a bullet he shot."

Then the daughter of Dalma hugged him in her arms and he let it all out, cried as he had never cried before, though he thought he had cried as much as a human being could. They stayed together a long time, looking out over the water, and when they started back for

home Jimmy sighed the deepest sigh—as if a part of him was gone
forever.

It was about this time that Pop and Uncle Stanley began including
him in their quarter-mile journeys across to Turkey. Uncle Stanley
had come to Kios with four hundred American dollars and it hadn't
run out yet. Pop had done even better, selling his big store months
before the Black Friday of the stock market crash. In the two years
they were in Greece, the prosperity spilled over to young Jimmy; and
a twelve-year-old in Turkey who had ten American dollars in his
pocket was a force to be reckoned with beyond his years. The men
had a cold, yet soft, regard for the boy. He had lost his mother. Now
he was a man. Far ahead of the years to be a man, but a man
nevertheless. They saw nothing wrong as he naturally gravitated to
the company of eighteen-year-olds. And this was how young Jimmy
got laid, at age twelve, in Smyrna, Turkey.

Smyrna is the largest Turkish town within the purview of Kios,
across that narrow band of water and inland a few miles. So it
happened that a pair of eighteen-year-olds from Kios had Jimmy in
tow one night when he said, "Hey, isn't there anything to do in this
place?" And they said, "If you got the money, yes."

"I got the money," said Jimmy, and away they went. For two U.S.
dollars he and both of his friends were treated to the ultimate
mysteries of the Smyrna night. Jimmy's woman he was to remember
as a *Turkala*, meaning a Turkish beauty, and the most gentle—given
the circumstances—that he would ever know. The experience
immediately filled him with a sense of importance. When he came
out of the alcove of delight, he told the madam, "Put those other two
guys on my bill."

It was quite a comedown from breaking your maiden in Smyrna to
being a stepson in Kios, but that's the way Pop had it figured. Her
name was Agnes. And it made Jimmy think of all the things his *real*
mother was. She had been a big woman. That's why he was big.
Nobody on Pop's side was tall or heavy. Mom had been big, but she
had small feet. She had to have her shoes made to order because they
hurt so much if she bought them right off the shelf. That's why all her
kids had to have their shoes made to a last.

If you'd ask Mom if you could do something you knew was

wrong—like, "Can I go swimming in the river?"—she'd say, "Why don't you do what's in your heart?" Jimmy often wondered, "How can you beat that?" Mom had wanted Jimmy to be either an attorney or to play the violin. Mom was warm. That's why she was killed.

All the eligible young girls of Kios were after George Synodinos. They knew whoever married him would go back to America with him, which offset the fact that he came with three small children. He selected Agnes, the brightest and the prettiest, and the one who had shown an interest in the children.

Jimmy gave Agnes hell. For one thing, he stole the money out of her piggy bank. Four dollars and twenty-five cents. Agnes confronted him with the theft—softly. "I won't tell your Pop," she said, "but I want you to promise me you won't do this again." Jimmy thought this was an eminently fair deal, and he settled. (Six years later, when Jimmy sent Agnes on an expense-paid trip through Europe back to Kios, she said, "Well, that interest in the four dollars and twenty-five cents really mounted up, didn't it?")

When he returned with the family to Steubenville in 1932, Jimmy wasn't so little any more, and in later years he was to say, "I was never a child after my mother died. I became a man." However, the illusion of being a man was greater than the reality. There were no more ten-dollar bills from Pop. To Jimmy the Depression meant he had trouble promoting a two-bit piece. Pop had taught him, "Go first class or don't go." They had dined in the finest restaurants, stayed in the best hotels, with money that cashed in four-for-one, and now he was broke in Steubenville without even a jackass for transportation.

He began doing business at the junkyard, scrounging the back alleys for old newspapers and bottles and anything else he could lay his hands on. When the junkman let him have a discarded bicycle frame, Jimmy offered a proposition: "Help me get the pieces for this thing, and I'll go all over town getting stuff for you." The junkman laughed and sold him two wheels at half price. Piece by piece Jimmy put the bike together, then spent the last of his capital on a paint job, blue trimmed in white. Every kid in the neighborhood wanted to borrow it. After a few loan-outs, Jimmy stopped the free rides. "You can have it all day for twenty cents," he said. Inside of four months he had eight more bikes and was netting $1.60 a day.

That was the trouble with going back to school—it cut into a fellow's working time. The classes were no problem, especially arithmetic. He could add up a column of seven three-digit numbers so fast the teacher thought he was cheating somehow. He never told her what he was doing, but he tried to explain it to the kid across the aisle, "Don't start with the numbers on the right. Add up the hundreds first, then the tens. . . ." But the kid couldn't get it.

Just about the time Jimmy's bike business went sour because customers kept disappearing with the rental property, there was a sales meeting at the Eastman Kodak Company that was to change his life forever. A salesman complained, "We can't *give* these damn things away," and another one said, "Oh, yes, we can!" The idea was to give every seventh-grader in Steubenville a box camera free, post a twenty-five-dollar prize for the best photo, and see what happened to sales of film.

Jimmy made up his mind to win that twenty-five dollars. He sought professional advice at Miller's Camera Store. Mr. Miller told him that, in his experience, all photo contests were won by "nature studies," and then explained what the hell that was. So Jimmy took fifty-five pictures of the big tree in his front yard, morning, noon, and twilight. One day Mr. Miller said, "You go home for lunch every day, right? You pass right by the Ace newsstand. Do me a favor. On your way home tomorrow, pick me up a *Racing Form.*"

"A *Racing Form*," Jimmy said. "Sure." After that, Mr. Miller showed him how to use a darkroom and charged him nothing for the three dozen prints he made of the big tree. Jimmy won the twenty-five dollars. By now he was hooked on photography and good friends with Dan Miller. On the way home for lunch he would deliver *The Racing Form*, and on the way back to school he'd deliver Dan's bets to the back door of Money O'Brien's Academy Pool Room, where the gambling was. Jimmy's Uncle Mike had a barber's chair in the front of the poolroom, which is why Jimmy used the back door. What the family didn't know wouldn't hurt *him*.

Steubenville was a wide-open town, a steelworker's town, forty thousand citizens including the employees of eleven bookmaking establishments. On Water Street, Boys Town, you could get laid for two dollars, and that was expensive stuff. Every candy and cigar store had a pinball machine that paid off, and punchboards with a big gold seal. To Jimmy, Money O'Brien's place was just a bigger punchboard.

It didn't take Jimmy long to realize that Dan Miller's action was mostly one way, into O'Brien's pocket. Miller loved parlays and horses listed at twenty-to-one in the morning line. By this time Jimmy was reading the form himself and lingering at O'Brien's to see what the other bettors were doing. He started holding out some of Miller's bets. Hell, he might as well have the donation as O'Brien. Now and then he would slip in a one-dollar-show parlay of his own. He was fourteen, going on fifteen, almost six feet tall, and he didn't dress like a school kid. He also didn't ask a lot of dumb questions. He listened, at least until he found out what was going on.

All the talk was about the Kentucky Derby. Two days before the race, Jimmy picked out his horse and decided to make his first "real" bet. He had sixty-two dollars of Miller's and O'Brien's money, and he had another eighteen dollars in the school savings account. He forged his pop's name to get that out and he bet everything, eighty dollars, on the nose. "Jesus Christ!" O'Brien said. "Miller's rich uncle musta died." Jimmy's horse, Cavalcade, won easy. That Saturday night Jimmy knew he was the smartest fourteen-year-old horseplayer that ever lived. It caused quite a stir in the back room of the Academy when O'Brien complimented Dan Miller on his Derby score and Miller said, "Whaddya mean? I had the horse that ran second, Vanderbilt's horse, Discovery."

That summer Jimmy started running O'Brien's bets against other bookmakers. The tall, sandy-haired Irishman was raking it in with his own book, a crap table, some poker, and a Big Six wheel at the Academy. But he wanted to beat the horses, too. And never learned. When O'Brien tipped him five dollars, Jimmy turned it down. "I don't want a tip," he said. "I'll just take two and a half percent of what I carry." He was soon running bets from one book to another all over town. Some months he was the only winner. O'Brien and the rest didn't realize how two and a half percent could mount up.

O'Brien had two partners in the Academy, Tom Griffin and Harry Cooper. Griffin and Cooper also owned a nightclub casino on the edge of town, the Half Moon. It was a popular place, and Jimmy

invented a new business for himself, parking the customers' cars. The
Half Moon paid him ten cents a car. He soon had four helpers doing
all the work. They got the dime and Jimmy took all the tips.

During the day at the Academy, Jimmy began watching the dealer
at the Big Six wheel, an ancient geezer named Paul Dunkel. Half the
time, when Dunkel raked in losers, he would miss the bets on the
number under his left elbow and the money would ride free. Jimmy
started playing this number. O'Brien had never seen Jimmy show any
interest in the Big Six and it made him curious. After a few plays
O'Brien's face lit up with a grin and he came over. "Dunkel," he
said, "go help on craps. And you," he pointed at Jimmy, "you can get
behind there and handle the wheel." Within a few weeks, Jimmy was
dealing craps and learning to stack chips. On his dresser at home he
kept stacks of chips to practice cutting one stack even with another,
developing a smooth, fast "feel" for the counters that a dice dealer
has to have if he's going to keep the game flowing.

By the time he started high school that fall he was dealing craps at
the Half Moon. He went out for football as a sophomore, but some
stupid son of a bitch stepped on his hand and Jimmy decided he
couldn't afford the sport. He was getting from seven to fifteen dollars
a night with those hands. Everyone at the Half Moon thought he was
twenty-one. He wore Triple G suits, Kuppenheimer's at seventy
dollars a copy, from the Hub or Denmark's clothing store. He wore
special-ordered Bostonian shoes, thirty dollars. He never wore a hat.
There was still a depression on, but not if you picked fast horses and
played for the house.

One night the next spring Jimmy came home late and found his
pop waiting up for him. Pop thought he was still parking cars at the
Half Moon.

The old man said, "Where have you been, you bum?"

"Working," Jimmy said.

"Working what?"

Jimmy took out his bankroll, fourteen hundred dollars, and fanned
it. He knew he was making more money than Pop, and Pop owned a
grocery store.

Pop slapped him across the face. "Where did you steal it?" he
demanded.

A month later, Pop needed a thousand dollars to buy a freezer to store a product new to the market, called Birds Eye frozen foods. Jimmy gave him the money. It was about this time that he stopped calling his father Pop. From then on he called him George.

PART
I

GAMBLING MAN

CHAPTER
1

Payoff at the Half Moon

They say education is the basis for a fruitful life. Considering where my life was going to take me, I went to the right school, Steubenville Prep. It was a farm club for Las Vegas, a rough training camp for dealers who would become the great casino operators in the boom years after World War II. The Facinto boy, Mokie, would run the casino at Caesar's Palace. Paradise Island in the Bahamas would import Bob Sasso. Joey Tamburo would wind up in Reno. Pre-Castro Cuba would belong to Dino Cellini. And there was another kid, Dino Crosetti, the Romeo dealer at the Rex, an Italian joint. He later changed his name to Dean Martin, and never made it as a gambler.

I was attending high school during the day, and this elite postgraduate school at night, where the action was sometimes designed to move faster than the players' eyes. I learned about percentage dice that are shaved to favor an ace-six—and a plenitude of snake eyes and boxcars. I learned that a "marked wheel" was a roulette table rigged to activate a pin under a heavy number. I couldn't prove it yet, but I sensed that all the bastards who ran their games that way would stay forever in the minor leagues.

(With all of this going on, I was content to work with Money O'Brien at the Academy and deal for Cooper and Griffin at the Half Moon. Griffin, the quiet Irishman, was fascinated by the way I handled chips—"checks" in dealers' slang. "Let me see you take twenty, Greek," he'd say, and I'd lift twenty off the top every time, never nineteen, and sure as hell never twenty-one. Little Cooper was Griffin's opposite, talking with his hands and jabbing fingers, lapsing into Jewish dialect, a banty rooster sure of his turf.

It was Cooper who first started calling on me when high rollers crowded the crap table: "We need your speed, kid. Give us a fast two furlongs." When money is on the line, the faster the play the quicker the house percentage. Cooper took a liking to me. I could tell, because he was always challenging me on something.

Cooper said, "Greek, O'Brien tells me you think you can read a form."

"I can read it a little bit," I said.

"What? What? Speak up, Greek, you're not in church. I notice you always talk soft until somebody tells you you're wrong. I got a proposition for you."

"I'm listening."

"You pick a horse the night before, any goddamn horse in the U.S.A., and I'll lay you two-to-one."

"You were born dead," I said.

"Against a horseplayer, maybe. But against a *schmageggy* who ain't out of high school, I will do all right."

I looked at Cooper's bet as a license to steal. Of course, I had to pick the horse out of the overnight entries and before any odds were listed, but even so . . . in a month I had seven hundred dollars of Cooper's money.

"Greek . . ." Somehow Cooper could stretch that into three syllables. "Greek, you are nickel and diming me to death. When are you going to make a *bet?*"

"I got one for you at Saratoga," I said. "Merry Lassie in the feature. I like her for seven hundred."

"Let me remind you, keed, if Merry Lassie is scratched, you lose."

"I don't bet scratched horses," I said. I knew the filly would be, like, one-to-two in the morning line.

The next day I was at the Academy listening to the call: "At the quarter it's Merry Lassie by three . . . at the half it's Merry Lassie by two . . . in the stretch Merry Lassie is on top by one. . . . There is a photo in the seventh at Saratoga. . . . The winner is Clodian." That call will linger with me forever. It was one of many instances that led me to give up horse racing as a serious betting proposition altogether. But not for now.

"You want some more, huh, Greek?" Cooper said.

"Hell, yes, I want some more." To myself I said, "I got you by a hundred-forty percent."

Until the night Johnny Tatos came down with his people from Little Washington, Pennsylvania, Cooper never knew I had a temper to match his own. Tatos's group was what the Half Moon regarded as "good players," that is, both sharp and heavy. Cooper took a look at the action and said, "Pay them off in twenty-five-dollar checks." I didn't say anything. He thought the bigger chips would increase their play. I knew different. Too many people have a tendency to rathole twenty-five-dollar checks and cash them at the cashier's cage. Ones and fives they would continue to buck against the house. Besides, I felt I could keep the flow going with the smaller checks.

In fifteen minutes Cooper was back at my elbow. "What are you, deaf?" he said. "I told you to use the twenty-fives."

I turned and faced him nose to nose. "Stick the twenty-fives up your ass!" I yelled. "Deal 'em yourself." And I walked out. That was the last time I was ever going to work for someone else.

I was back in greater downtown Steubenville before I realized how bad my timing was. It was pay night at the Half Moon. I was tapped out—fillies that fade in the stretch will get you that way. But I was too pissed off to go home. I went to the Fort Steubenville Club on Market Street, a walk-up, after-hours sanctuary with private membership. I only had some pocket change, but I could sign the tab and play the slots. My first nickel hit two cherries and a bell. I moved to the quarter machine, and hit a ten-dollar jackpot. They were selling policy in the club, so I put the ten dollars on a "lucky number" I'd been playing for weeks, 807. The next day 807 was the final number in the stock exchange volume, and I collected six thousand dollars. To hell with the Half Moon.

That winter I quit high school. I had a brand new 750-dollar Plymouth and about 500 dollars left in reserve. Cecil (Skeeter) Gallagher was a horseplayer I knew from around the Academy, and he said to me, "You know, of course, why we are not cashing any bets. Because we are not *on the scene*. You got to look them babies in the eye. Move around at night and pick up inside information."

"Not only that," I said, "but we are up to our ass in snow." So Gallagher and I headed for Florida. We had nine hundred dollars between us and we were going to devote all of January and February to bringing Tropical Park to its knees. This was the beginning of a ritual with me, hitting Miami Beach for the winter. There was more than fun and comfort involved. It was also a badge of the big time for a fellow who bet money. In Steubenville in the winter, when a guy was busted, his friends would needle him, "Hey, Jake, when you going down to Florida?" And he'd say, "Oh, in a week or two, after the slow players get cleared out."

Gallagher and I took a suite at the Causeway Apartments. That was the way we liked to put it. What we did was rent two rooms that shared a connecting bath at fourteen dollars a week, and we moved the furniture around so all the beds were in one room and all the sofas and chairs were in the other.

In three weeks we were busted. I had twenty-two dollars and Gallagher had a few dimes. I gave him twenty dollars for bus fare and sent him north, 1026 miles back to Steubenville. He promised to raise the dough to bring *me* home. That night I met Cornelius J. Jones, another dealer from Steubenville, outside the Hickory House Restaurant on Twenty-third Street where all the gamblers hung out. Jonesy would later run the most exclusive casino in Cleveland and the Desert Inn in Las Vegas, but at the moment he didn't look like a winner either.

"How's it going?" he said.

"My rent's paid," I said, "and I just sent a rescue party north."

We added it up and we had six dollars between us. Jonesy poked a thumb at the restaurant. "We can go for the beef ragout for two-fifty," he said. "If we don't take dessert, that leaves a buck tip for the waiter."

The Hickory House had a Greek busboy who liked to swap some

of the old language with me. He came over now and said, "Tomorrow I go to the track. Have you got a horse for a fellow Greek?" I told him I liked a horse named Red Rain and he made me repeat it three times and write it down.

Things were slow at the Causeway Apartments, sitting around all day reading old racing forms. That night I met Jonesy at the restaurant again. He had promoted ten dollars for the big beef dinner, this time with dessert. As soon as we went in, Popkin, the owner, rushed up and said, "A guy's been in here asking for you. He didn't know your name, just said 'the tall Greek.' "

"That's okay," I said. "When he comes in, send him over. If he doesn't know my name, he isn't a bill collector."

Before we got to our table the busboy wanted to embrace me. "Ah, my friend," he said. "The horse you gave me I bet him six across and I win eighty-four-fifty." Naturally, my fellow Greek thought I had the horse, too. What I had was indigestion.

When we were on our cheesecake, an expensively dressed midwestern-looking guy walks up and introduces himself. It turns out he owns a meat-packing company in Pennsylvania, F. W. Alexander, Inc. "I want you to know," he said, "that I couldn't help overhearing you last night when you gave that horse to the busboy. When the race came up today I was down three thousand. . . ." Jones gave a little twitch in his chair when Alexander mentioned three thousand dollars. In 1938 this was a ton of money for your average meat packer to be betting. "I bet five hundred dollars across on Red Rain," Alexander went on, "and I feel I owe you something. Please take this." He pointed a sheaf of bills at me.

I said, "Oh, no, I can't do that," and Jones almost broke my shinbone with a kick under the table. Alexander insisted, I got kicked again. On the third offer I took the bills and shoved them in my coat pocket. When I looked later I counted five one-hundred-dollar bills and my first thought was, "Now I can play."

Alexander insisted that I come to the track with him the next day. This was Tropical Park, which is why Tropical Park was my favorite racetrack to the day they stopped racing there. Alexander, with his wife and mother-in-law, was staying at the new Vanderbilt Hotel on Collins Avenue, and he offered to pick me up in his car. I didn't want him to know I was staying in the Causeway Apartments, so I arranged to meet him outside the Vanderbilt.

Alexander had brought down his own limousine and driver, and before I had settled back in the cushions he wanted to know who I liked in the first race. "I don't like anything in that one," I said, "so you're on your own. I like a horse in the fifth race and another in the eighth. Other than that I don't like a thing."

When the fifth came up, Alexander bet six hundred dollars across—win, place, and show—and I bet fifty dollars the same way. That fifty dollars was a third of my bankroll. The horse ran second, so Alexander netted twelve hundred dollars and I netted one hundred.

My pick in the eighth race was the morning-line favorite at two to one, a horse named Flag Unfurled, a late finisher. Tropical Park had a short home stretch and my only concern was that the horse couldn't make up ground before getting to the wire. Alexander said, "How strong are you on this?" I told him it was a better bet than the one in the fifth. He bet a thousand dollars across and I went a hundred dollars across.

Flag Unfurled broke out of the starting gate last and Alexander yelled, "He's left at the post!"

I said, "Sir, that's the way he runs. When he hits the turn at the backstretch he'll be in stride, and when they come for home he'll be passing horses." The script went just the way Jimmy wrote it. Flag Unfurled was eighth, then seventh, then sixth, running past horses like they were sixteenth poles, and Alexander was going crazy. The horse was three lengths behind entering the stretch, running third—and won by two lengths drawing away. Alexander was slamming me on the back. "You're a genius!" he yelled. "Nobody . . . nobody knows more about racing than you do." I was feeling good, but not that good.

On the way back to the hotel, Alexander added up the day's winnings and said, "Here, partner, this is yours." He had forty-eight hundred dollars and wanted me to take half. I told him that wasn't how it works, that he should keep the forty-eight hundred dollars together and we would go at them again tomorrow. He pressed two hundred dollars on me for my "daily expenses." This was an overlay of 194 dollars, but I took it.

When I went by the Vanderbilt the next day to meet Alexander, his room didn't answer. I was stunned. I had him paged in the dining room, no answer. Finally, I asked if there were any messages. And there was. "My mother-in-law wanted to go to Cuba today and there are some things a married man has to do. This is one of them. Will see you when I get back.—Alex."

That day the three horses I liked all ran out of the money. On top of that I had to listen to Jonesy tell me what nine kinds of fool I was not to grab the twenty-four hundred dollars when I had it. He said, "It's a long price you will never see the guy again." I was thinking that if Alexander hadn't gone to Cuba this day would have been a real disaster with the dogs I had picked.

Every night we ate at the Hickory House, the only place Alexander knew where to reach me, and for a while there it looked like Jonesy was right. On the fourth night, I got a message to meet him Saturday at the Vanderbilt in time for the races. But when I showed up I found out he hadn't checked in. I figured it was another missed connection, probably the last one, so I went back to the Hickory House to pick up Jonesy. I was standing in front of the place when the limousine pulls up and Alexander yells, "Come on, let's go! We're late." At that time, it was amazing how much suspense twenty-four hundred dollars could create.

I only had one horse in the Saturday races, a horse named Middle Watch, I think. Again Alexander said, "How strong?"

"As strong as we can go," I said. "The whole forty-eight." Then I had second thoughts and told him to hold out two thousand dollars until we saw what the place and show pools did. There wasn't anything there, so we had twenty-eight hundred dollars to win on Middle Watch when he was leading by five lengths in the stretch. It was an overcast day, and suddenly a shaft of sunlight hit the track right in front of the horse. Middle Watch jumped the rail.

I never knew what happened to the horse, whether they had to destroy it or not. I know if I'd had a gun I would have helped. Alexander surprised me. He put an arm around my shoulder. He said, "That's the way life is, Jimmy, but that's what makes life so interesting."

He had to go back to Pennsylvania on business the next day. He split what was left of the pot, a thousand dollars each, and we said good-byes.

I've never exactly forgotten Middle Watch, but by the following Tuesday I had put him out of my mind. I was interested in a horse named Many Stings, who figured to be the favorite in the Tropical Park Handicap that Saturday. My ex-boss Harry Cooper was coming down with Jack Nolan, the political boss of Steubenville, and Nolan bet big. On Tuesday Many Stings got away badly, then put on a tremendous rush to win a match race. It reminded me of Flag Unfurled, but that wasn't this horse's style. I turned to Jonesy and said, "This horse is absolutely dead now. He won't do a thing in the handicap and he'll be a heavy favorite, at least three-to-five."

"I hope not," Jonesy said. "Nolan will be here and he'll probably make a big bet on him."

"If he does," I said, "whatever he bets I want part of it."

On Saturday we were all together—Cooper, me, Jonesy, and Nolan—in the box seats with the Tropical Park operators, Charles Wolf and Joe Tobin, who were old friends of Nolan. This Irishman was such a big bettor, especially for 1938, that he couldn't put his money into the mutuels. It would drive the price down to nothing, and he was always betting short-priced horses, anyway. So Cooper and Jones were there to "take him off," book his bets. Wolf and Tobin knew what was happening, but they didn't mind—Cooper or Jones would put a token five hundred or thousand dollars into the machines on each of Nolan's bets.

When they posted the numbers for the big race, Many Stings was put up one-to-two, and right away Nolan tells Cooper, "I want ten thousand dollars to win and twenty thousand dollars to place." Cooper nodded, accepting the bet. Then he started fidgeting. The little guy was naturally nervous anyway, and now he was in anguish.

"I can't refuse Jack," he said, "but I'm in a jam. This horse is a cinch."

"Don't worry about it," I said. "Let me lay some of this horse, any part you don't want—or what you'll trust me with over the money I've got." I was riding a streak. I had sixteen hundred dollars when Alexander left town, and in just a few days I'd built it to over six thousand dollars. I felt like I could do no wrong. I said, "Go tell Nolan you want him to press his bet," and Cooper almost jumped out of his skin.

Five minutes later Nolan came back to Cooper and said, "I want five thousand dollars more to win and ten more to place on the favorite." I couldn't help laughing at the look on Cooper's face. A bookmaker named Jockey Lightning came over and relieved some of the pressure.

"You got anything you want to lay off, Coop?" he said.

"Yeah, I'm giving you two and four on the four horse." Many Stings was four in the program.

When the ex-jock walked away, I said, "Whatever you're giving away, cut it down. I want some of it."

Cooper said, "How much money have you got?"

I told him. "And I want to lose every penny of it, plus. I got some ability to make money. Trust me."

"All right, Greek," he said, "you got three thousand dollars to win and six thousand dollars to place."

I told him again to stop worrying, that Many Stings was guaranteed to run out of the money. I hate to see a man suffer.

"If you don't like the favorite," Cooper said, "who *do* you like?"

"The eight horse," I said. "Dolly Vall."

Cooper said, "Okay, let's you and me bet ten dollars on Dolly Vall." He was a strange guy. He would take a horse for a lot of money, but he would never bet himself more than ten dollars. He had a simple explanation for it: "I don't believe any of them can win."

Many Stings ran a staggering fifth, and Dolly Vall won and paid eighty-four dollars. All of a sudden I had a real bankroll, over sixteen thousand dollars, and in a few weeks I would have new and bigger ideas, none of which had anything to do with horse racing.

Five years later when my name had begun to mean something—I mean, I was "Mr. Greek" and living *high*—I was sitting in the boxes at Aqueduct when a slender fellow in a gray suit walked over to me and said, "Jimmy, do you remember me?"

I said, "Do I remember *you!* Come on, Mr. Alexander, let's you and me go have a drink together."

And he said, "Fine, Jimmy, but first—who do you like in the third race?"

CHAPTER
2

Jimmy from Steubenville

I was still a punk kid, not even nineteen, but I had seen enough to decide a guy can't challenge the dice and the cards and the horses and the ball games all at the same time. To have any kind of edge he'd have to concentrate on one and stick with it. For dice and roulette he'd have to be on the house side of the table, and I was sick of casinos. I hated them, and still do. I didn't want to spend my time in places where naked anxiety and naked greed go hand in hand.

Cards were out, too. Playing poker on a big scale demands a lot of physical stamina when a game goes twice around the clock. I noticed all the poker players I knew looked a little fagged out.

And except for the big races, I discarded horses. There were too many variables. I could never feel I was in *control* of a bet, and a bettor who thinks he is in control is a fool. A racetrack is a fun place, unless you want to make a killing at it and have to wait around all day for an overlay in the place and show pools.

That left one thing: sports, minus the king of sports, mainly the team games. This was an area a guy could research, form an opinion, then stake his judgment against another's. Besides, at least I would be betting on people. My bankroll had slipped since I got home from Florida. I had taken six thousand dollars—which I still thought of as a separate bundle from the time I hit the 807 number at the Fort Steubenville Club—and bought Reynolds Metal stock at fourteen and seven-eighths. Years later, when I got a divorce, I had to sell it at thirty-five. Reynolds later went to 250, so that's another thing I don't like to think about.

But now I had less than three thousand dollars in the bank and only four-hundred fifty in my pocket on the night of the second Louis–Schmeling fight. I went up to Bob Sasso's place and asked him, "What have you got on the fight?"

"It is nine-to-five," he said. I thought it would be a lot more than that. In fact, I thought Louis was a cinch. Schmeling had knocked him out in the first fight, but the German had put in two hard years since then, and now he was thirty-three. Louis was in his prime.

"I want to lay it," I said.

"If you want Louis, you got to lay two-to-one," Sasso said. We went around and around about that until I got it back to nine hundred dollars to five hundred. I gave Sasso my four-hundred fifty and said I would go get the other half. My sister Mary was holding five hundred dollars for me.

Sasso said, "Don't worry about it. Bring it up after you lose."

"I'll bring it up before I lose," I said, "because I ain't going to lose."

I didn't get home because I ran into Tom Griffin by the corner of the Green Mill Restaurant, where everybody loafed around and drank coffee all night. I said, "I just bet Sasso nine hundred dollars to five hundred on the fight. You want half of it?"

Griffin said, "If you like it, why not?" He reached in his back pocket and gave me five hundred-dollar bills. Just then somebody yelled that the fight was on and we went into the Green Mill to hear it. Clem McCarthy was screaming, "He's out! It's all over!" Louis had stopped him in two minutes. I turned to Griffin and said, "Tom, we win it!" But he said, "Naw, I can't take that. You never got my half down." I went back and collected from Sasso, and Griffin still wouldn't take his two-hundred fifty. Finally, he said, "Tell you what.

I'm going down to Hot Springs for a few weeks. Keep our money together and go ahead and play with it, whatever you like."

He came back about thirty days later and I went in to see him at the Academy. I handed him twenty-two hundred dollars. He said, "What's this?"

"That's our Schmeling money," I said. "I ran it up to forty-four hundred dollars."

"My God," he said. "You got to be kidding. Nobody ever gave me money back. What do you want to give it back for? Just keep going with it, play better, play higher."

I said, "You know what I'd like to do? I'd like to rent an office." Griffin said anything that suited me tickled him to death. I took the smallest available space in the National Exchange Bank Building, right across the hall from Jack Watson's stockbroker office. There were days in the years ahead when I moved more money than Watson did. The sign on my door read "B & F Commissioner," as in *Baseball* and *Football*. Griffin and I remained partners for ten years with all my expenses, living and everything, coming off the top. Later I took a salary. The bankroll eventually reached into six figures. Griffin never said anything about what I bet. To him this was all gravy.

From my new office, with a filing cabinet and a desk and two phones, I decided I had outgrown Steubenville. Around town you could bet good money on big events, but in day-to-day betting it was hard to get down more than two or three hundred dollars. At the Imperial Restaurant on Sixth Street I met a guy named Natie Farber who bet in Pittsburgh, and he said he'd give me an introduction to his bookmakers, Aces and Kelski. They were the first two big bookmakers I ever did business with. I could bet them a thousand dollars on the phone on anything.

They also contributed to my education. They were laying what you call "a wide line." If the odds were eight-to-five and I liked the favorite, I had to lay two-to-one. That's a twenty percent spread, and it will grind you down if you stay with it.

The first bet I made with them, Pittsburgh was a three-two favorite over Nebraska, and I won fifteen hundred dollars on

Nebraska. In those days, football was all odds. The bookmakers didn't start posting point spreads until 1941 and '42, and even then a lot of people stuck with the odds or played both. After I had a reputation with Aces and Kelski, I got an okay to phone bets into the Amorita Club, where two bookmakers named Tucker and Brown took the calls. In a few weeks I was twenty-five hundred dollars ahead and drove to Pittsburgh to collect.

The Amorita was on the iron mountain overlooking Pittsburgh and had a peephole in the front door. A few moments after I punched the button a voice came through, "Get away, kid!"

I said, "I want to see Mr. Tucker."

"I told you," the guy said, "we don't let kids in here."

"Tell Mr. Tucker that Jimmy from Steubenville wants to see him."

After a long wait the door opened, and a tall, handsome guy stared at me. "For God's sake," he said, "are you the one we owe money?" It turned out that I may have looked old in Steubenville, but I was still young in Pittsburgh. Tucker took me inside and introduced me around. Milton Jaffe, who then owned the Bachelor's Club a few blocks away, and later a piece of the Stardust in Vegas, was a patron of the Amorita. I also met another partner, Slim Silverheart, and that made it my lucky day. I came to learn that Slim had a national reputation for integrity. He was the final arbiter for any gambling dispute that developed. For instance, when Leo Durocher came along and began the strategy of starting a left-handed pitcher and replacing him right away with a right-hander, it caused a big controversy all over the country. A lot of people made their bets specifying "if so-and-so starts," because a change in pitchers could make a big change in the odds. Durocher, of course, was making the opposition load its lineup with right-handed hitters. But gamblers were arguing about who was the *actual* starting pitcher in that situation. The appeal went to Slim. "If the man throws one pitch," he declared, "he is the starting pitcher." That was that, as if it had come down from the U.S. Supreme Court.

When the guys at the Amorita Club noticed how I was winning, they paid me the compliment of favoring the side that I liked. That is, they would move the line. Early. The next winter when I was in Florida, Slim introduced me to the big bookmakers—Mel Clark in

Chicago, Billy Hecht in Minneapolis. I intended to bet a lot of big money someday, and these were the people I had to know. Hecht created the Gorham Press and became the first to sell a betting service around the country for twenty-five dollars a week—the famous "Minneapolis Line." Hecht and his partners were the first to put executive ability into bookmaking. Hecht had three handicappers working for him full time. And they learned early that if a guy was a continuous winner they'd have to go toward his number. Big bets didn't faze them. It was *who* bet that mattered. When a guy they respected took six, they'd drop the line to five or five and a half. In later years, they'd give me the line on Monday and let me bet into it even money. Then they'd adjust it.

The B & F Commissioner's office was making steady progress when the first Joe Louis–Billy Conn fight came up in 1941. This one almost broke up my partnership with Griffin, which by now showed a net of ninety thousand dollars. Conn was from Pittsburgh, right in our backyard, and he was Irish. So naturally Griffin was in love with him. I liked Louis, especially when I could beat the odds in Steubenville and Pittsburgh where there was a lot of Conn money. In New York it was eighteen-to-five, but I was giving only five-to-two, and in some cases two-to-one.

The week of the fight Griffin came up to the office. He said, "Who do you like in the fight?" When I told him Louis, his red face got redder and I thought steam was going to come out of his ears. "By how much?" he said.

"The whole thing," I said.

"Well, I hope you lose your ass!" And he slammed the door on his way out.

This was the biggest bet I'd ever made, and I would feel it the night of the fight. Cornelius Jones, the fellow who had shared his beef ragout with me in Miami, was running the casino in the Mounds Club at Cleveland, the most fabulous place in the country at the time. But he kept his home in Steubenville and he had two beautiful daughters, Betty and Babe. I was dating Betty, but I was sweet on Babe, and that's why I kept coming around the house. Finally, Jonesy told me, "I know you're kind of soft on Babe, but one gambler in the family is enough." I went out to listen to the broadcast with the girls and they were going crazy rooting for Conn because he was winning the fight. It sounded like he would take a decision. For the first time I actually felt a pull in my stomach over a bet. I said to myself, "My God, am I going to lose this, lose two years of work in just one night?" I promised myself I'd never do this again, put up the whole bankroll.

It must have shown on my face. "You're white as a sheet," Betty said. Suddenly, in the thirteenth round, Louis caught Conn and knocked him out, and color came back to my cheeks. "You were pulling for Louis," Betty said. "How much did you have bet on the fight?"

"Four hundred."

"Well, I was rooting for the other guy, because that wouldn't hurt you."

Griffin wouldn't speak to me for a month.

Betting a championship fight comes down to a matter of opinion, because everything about the fight is laid out for you in the papers every day. Betting college football was a different proposition, especially in those days when communication and publicity were comparatively primitive. I hit on an idea to give myself an edge. I went to the Penn Station in Steubenville where the railroads came through east-west and north-south, and I talked to the porters on the trains. I told them to collect every newspaper they could get their hands on along the line. I tipped them fifty cents or a dollar per paper. Pretty soon I had papers from all over the country, and I had them the day after publication most of the time. The St. Louis *Post-Dispatch*, the Nashville *Banner*, the Atlanta *Journal*, *The New York Times*—all of them were loaded with college football stories by good solid writers. Fred Russell in Nashville, Furman Bisher in Atlanta, Dave Condon in Chicago, Allison Danzig for *The New York Times*, Shirley Povich of *The Washington Post* and Al Abrams in Pittsburgh were writers who could tell you what you needed to know when you were trying to evaluate a team's chances.

The important advantage was to know more than anybody else *before* the season started. It would take several weeks every season before the handicappers would get their lines adjusted to shade down false favorites and upgrade surprise teams.

There was a Steubenville kid, a cousin of mine, Mike Paidousis, whose way I helped pay to the University of Tennessee. Mike was the first of a series of great athletes—the number would eventually reach seventeen—I helped steer to colleges across the country. I would call him from time to time to talk about the Southeastern Conference. This was in September, and I had been getting a lot of good information about Wake Forest, which was in the Southern Conference. I asked Mike if he knew anybody there and he said no, but he had a cousin playing football for Virginia Tech. I called the cousin and asked him what he thought about Wake Forest playing North Carolina the following week, not telling him which side I liked.

The kid said, "We played them both practice games."

I said, "You did?"

"Yeah. We beat North Carolina four or five touchdowns, not keeping score, but like you do in practice scrimmage. And Wake Forest kicked the hell out of us."

I could hardly wait for Monday to get the number. I called Billy Hecht in Minneapolis. I was doing business there and in New York, Chicago, and Pittsburgh. They gave me eight-to-five. Wake Forest was the underdog because North Carolina had won the year before. My limit at the time was a thousand dollars per bet, and I took it at every spot. I went back later and they had it at seven-to-five and I bet them all again. I bet them each seven times for a total of twenty-eight thousand dollars—the bankroll again. So much for a promise made while listening to Conn and Louis.

I was also putting out a football card around Steubenville which ended up being distributed in four different states. There were seven cards around, and six of them were the same because they used the Minneapolis line. Mine was different because I thought my numbers were better. When Cornell opened the season against Ohio State, all the cards had one side favored by six and I put it six the other way. Common sense told me I should have made it even and been all right, but I was arrogant. My team won by three and I lost about nine thousand dollars. (The player had to pick at least three teams on those cards, giving or taking points. The listed payoff of five-to-one was actually four-to-one because it included the player's original bet. The correct odds on a three-team parlay are seven-to-one.)

So now when I come out with Wake Forest a six-point favorite over North Carolina, everybody thinks I made a mistake again, and they jumped on it.

It came up a muddy day in Carolina—not just bad conditions, but atrocious conditions, a rainstorm for four quarters. A Wake Forest guy tried to field a punt and it went through his hands into the end zone, where North Carolina fell on it to win the game, 6–0.

I was totally busted. My bankroll was gone, and I still had to pay off the cards. I called Slim Silverheart and told him what happened. He said, "Well, Greek, it happens to everybody. You've got to show what kind of man you are now."

I knew exactly what he meant. Your credibility, your word, that's all you've got as a gambler.

Slim said, "I'm going to help you. What you owe here, I'll let you carry. You don't have to worry about this one. Pay five hundred dollars a month or something. Call Billy Hecht and tell him how much business you're doing on the cards."

Billy reacted the same. "Tell you what," he said. "I'm going to let you play, but you got to promise me that whatever you do you'll pay as you go along. I'll leave this thirteen thousand dollars go and you pay a thousand dollars a month."

I paid off New York and Chicago. I didn't even bother to call. And I paid off on the card, which turned out to be a bonanza the rest of the season. Because I had everybody paid off, the next week we did eighteen thousand dollars. Mine was the pink sheet, and everybody looked for it.

I not only made a killing on the cards, next week Wake Forest was playing Duke and was a fourteen-point underdog. I had to go easy because I was low on cash, but I did call back and bet two thousand dollars. Wake Forest won the game straight up, and never failed to beat the point spread the rest of the year. North Carolina bettors never cashed another ticket. I paid Slim and Billy off within three weeks and ended up having a great season.

Wake Forest was an example of why gamblers hate bad-weather games. The football takes enough crazy bounces on a dry field. A mud-bath day in New Orleans made me do something I've never done before or since—pray for a win. It was the 1942 Sugar Bowl between Fordham and Missouri. Fordham had opened at nine-to-five and I laid eighteen hundred dollars to a thousand. When it dropped to eight-to-five, I laid another sixteen hundred dollars. Then a story broke that one of Fordham's top backs, Jim Blumenstock, had a bad ankle. Helen O'Connell, the blonde singer with Jimmy Dorsey's band who made "Green Eyes" famous, was a Steubenville girl I had known growing up, and I had heard she was dating Blumenstock. I phoned her, and she started laughing. "There's nothing wrong with his ankle," she said. "He chased me all over the room last night."

When I phoned Pittsburgh I found out the Blumenstock rumor had knocked the odds down to seven-to-five, so I pressed my bet. I ended up with eight thousand dollars on the game.

And it rained in New Orleans. Fordham went ahead 2–0 when Alex Santilli blocked a punt through the end zone. I was listening to the game on the radio. Blumenstock played every down. A kid named Harry Ice gained 102 yards for Missouri but never could get into the end zone. In the final minutes Missouri got close enough for a field goal. I looked up at the ceiling of my room. "If You're up there," I prayed, "now is the time to come to the rescue of Your boy Jim."

The field goal was short and my eight thousand dollars was safe, but I didn't like the feeling that remained. That was one promise I've kept. No more prayers on bets.

CHAPTER
3

Grantland Rice
Wouldn't Listen

George's marriage to Agnes had produced another brother and sister for me, John and Angela. Since I was fourteen years older, and more, than they were, the kids thought I was only a half step behind the Almighty. Ever since we had come back from Kios, Agnes had always treated me as her own. I still called her Agnes, but in my mind I thought of her as "mother." And John and Angela, they weren't a *half* brother and a *half* sister; we were all one close family, with never a conflict once George understood I was going to go my own way. Everything was laid on for me. They'd call me at the office and want to know what I wanted for dinner, what time to put it out. And it was there, on the minute. The clothes I was going to wear that night were laid out on my bed, shirt freshly ironed, and a suit just back from the cleaners. Anything that I owned was sacred. I can't describe the way my little brother and sister would say, "That's Jimmm-meee's." It was like a prayer.

I think mine was typical of Greek family life. If I had stayed in that environment—gone home to Kios, claimed an old-country bride, apprenticed at the grocery store—I could be sure of living to a ripe old age. My Uncle Anthony died in a plane crash in 1954, but my other Uncle, Tom, went back to Kios when he retired and died there at the age of 90. My great-grandmother lived to be 116, my grandmother 103, grandfather 96. I won't lay odds on my number, but it's tempting.

Because I had this feeling for my family, a series of small bets I made in 1943 meant more to me than a dozen big scores that followed later. I cleaned out Meyer Pearlman and Slim Neal, who were making book together in Steubenville.

As I got more and more into studying college football, I learned that the odds posted by bookmakers weren't necessarily correct. In fact, there were many times when I thought my number was closer to it than their number was. Pearlman and Neal would take no more than five hundred dollars on a football game from me. Nevertheless, that season I hit them for twenty thousand dollars, which was their whole bankroll. Pearlman quit and opened a men's clothing store. He made a mint and was eternally grateful for my assistance: "If it hadn't been for you, I wouldn't be so successful."

Slim Neal should have opened a clothing store, too. He wanted to keep booking my bets, even though he was out of cash. "I got my house," he said. "You want to play against my house on Sunset Boulevard, up on the hill? It's worth twelve thousand five hundred dollars."

"I don't want to take your house, Slim."

"Goddamnit, you tap me out and you're gonna stop betting? Give me a chance."

"If you insist."

In another two months, he had to give me the deed. I turned around and gave the house to George. He and Agnes lived downstairs and rented the upstairs. It gave them a little income, and they had a nice place.

One of the games that sank Slim and really made my season for some big money was Notre Dame versus Great Lakes Naval Training Station. Notre Dame was unbeaten and had outscored opponents 326 to 50. The Irish had a great team, with five All-Americans—John Yonakor, Jim White, and Pat Filley in the line, quarterback Angelo Bertelli and halfback Creighton Miller. Johnny Lujack was backing up Bertelli. They were knocking off college kids like running through a picket fence.

But they weren't going up against college kids this time. In the war years, service teams were often good enough to play the collegians even-Stephen. Notre Dame opened as a seventeen-point favorite, and the odds straight up had to be tremendous. What the bookmakers didn't realize was that Great Lakes had some great players, too—Steve Lach, Steve Juznik, Emil ("Six-Yard") Sitko, who would be All-American for Notre Dame in 1949, Dewey Procter, Lou Saban. And they had a truly great coach, Paul Brown. He would take a lot of those Great Lakes sailors with him when he started the Cleveland Browns.

For some reason, if you really liked an underdog you went to Philadelphia. You could always get a half point more on the long side. I guess Philadelphia just liked favorites. The top bookmakers in Philly were Sam Litt and Slame Glassman. I called and said, "Slame, if a guy liked a seventeen-point underdog, what price would you give?"

"Oh, hell," he said, "that's a ten-to-one shot."

He knew and I knew that it was really fifteen to one.

"Well, maybe it is," he said, "if it's Notre Dame playing or something."

This was a bartering situation. We settled on thirteen, but he wouldn't book two thousand dollars. I settled for five hundred dollars at thirteen and five hundred dollars at twelve. Then I called Litt and got the same bet. I finished up around the country betting thirty-five hundred dollars with odds and eighteen thousand dollars with points. Notre Dame was leading 14–13 until the last thirty-three seconds when Lach hit a forty-six-yard touchdown pass.

Suddenly, I was famous. Walter Winchell had a note in his column: "The smart bookies are singing the blues in Philly. A young Greek in Steubenville, Ohio, hit them for half a mill backing Great Lakes over the Irish." What happened was Slamey told a guy in Atlantic City, who told a guy in Pittsburgh, and the score inflated at every stop.

It was this game, and Winchell's publicity, that forced me to start keeping records for the IRS. I had a guy in my office mark down every transaction, wins against losses. On my income tax form I listed my profession as "speculator," and I paid off on the net.

I was doing other things for Uncle Sam in those years, too, promoting war bond raffles and rallies everywhere I could help. It helped take the pressure off. When I'd reported for my induction physical I'd learned I had a congenital—that is, from birth—defect in my stomach wall. The doctor said, "You're going to have to have that taken care of. You can't lift anything heavier than ten pounds." I told him I had never lifted anything heavier than a telephone. Years later in Vegas, the thing almost did kill me. But here I was, a tall, stud-looking guy and out of uniform. From time to time I'd get an anonymous letter, I guess from somebody who had a son in service. What the hell could I do? So I helped sell war bonds.

I did another bit to boost America about this time, and also to help my good friend Harold Salvey in Miami Beach. Among the top gamblers, there were some beautiful men, and Salvey was my favorite. He was a little guy, five-foot-eight, pug-nosed, good dresser, originally from Detroit. He was one of six in a syndicate that handled bookmaking up and down the Beach, including the top hotels. You could lay in a cabana and bet every track running. That's where the term *syndicate* originated, though it came to mean something more ominous than what Salvey and his partners were doing. Salvey was the political man in the combine. He talked to the councilmen. He was the ambassador to the politicians, and that kept the whole thing going.

He kept me going on occasion, too. Once I called him from Steubenville and said, "Harold, I need some money."

He said, "I'll get a package off to you today." He meant by registered mail. A couple of days later it arrived, a cigar box wrapped in brown paper. Inside the cigar box was fifty thousand dollars in cash. A beautiful man.

Now he was on the phone complaining about the blackouts along the Florida coast. "Damn," he said, "I'm getting the hell out of here. All these stories about German submarines lining up on our lampposts. I don't need this aggravation. I'm getting the hell out."

"Harold, I'm going to give you some advice." Here I was, at twenty-two, counseling my elders. But to me it was strictly an odds proposition, and I was never shy about declaring my odds. "You're nuts, just point-blank nuts."

"Shut up, Greek. What the hell do you know about it?"

"I know this—you had a bet on the U.S. and now you want to get off."

"What are you talking about?"

"Everybody down there is selling at a distressed price right now, and if I had the money I'd buy up every piece of property I could get my hands on. It's a no-lose proposition. If we lose the war, what good is it, anyway? If we win it, you're rich. All you're doing is betting on the U.S. to win the war. What better bet can you get than that?"

"I'll be goddamned," Salvey said. So that's what he did. With every dime he could get up. After the war he became a millionaire over and over. If I had told Salvey that pepper was white and salt was black, he would have bet on it.

In the years right after the war, I started building my own investments—because college recruiting suddenly came to be the cutthroat business we all know and love today. It so happened that my section of the Ohio River Valley, which included southern Pennsylvania and rock-hard West Virginia, was a mother lode for great high-school football players. I knew most of these kids personally. A lot of them I would help get summer jobs, either at a strip mine I had an interest in or through friends who owned companies. It got so our Penn Station looked like a coaches' convention, and almost all of the coaches would end up seeing me.

"Tha's a boy up in Pennsylvania who is a monster—ah mean, a monster—tackle, and that boy tells me ah got to see Mr. Snyder about him coming to Yale." This was Herman Hickman, and the start of an enduring and loving friendship.

I would help all the coaches, when I could, when it was best for the kid. Some of them could handle the studies at Yale and Tulane and Georgia Tech, and some had to go where there was a lenient phys.-ed. department. This way I came to know about half of the assistant coaches in the Southeastern Conference. And I soon had kids I knew at just about every one of the thirteen schools down there.

I would send the kids fifty or a hundred dollars from time to time.

At Christmas I'd help them get train fare home. One kid who was five-foot-four I helped the whole way through Georgia Tech because I liked him, and he's mayor of Steubenville today. When there was a game I liked, believe me, I knew who was injured and who wasn't, and what kind of player the backup man was.

One week during basketball season, I called Mike Paidousis at Tennessee, just to chat and ask him how things were in general. Tennessee was going to play Dayton the next night, and it happened that I had an opinion Dayton was severely underrated at the start of the season. Mike said the kids at the dorm were laughing about the basketball captain: "His girl gave him the shaft today, and they've been steady for three years." This kid was Tennessee's leading scorer. Naturally, I took Dayton very strong and cashed a big bet.

That time my followers picked it up, and the number on Tennessee, an eleven-point favorite, dropped to seven by game time. Dayton won, 57–38. The next day, when I called the Gorham Press for the line on the games that night, Leo Hirschfield got on the phone. Billy Hecht's office took the bets, but Hirschfield sent out the line. "Greek," he said, "after last night Tennessee has been barred. No more Tennessee in this office."

If Leo made a mistake, he had to blame somebody else. But Tennessee remained barred.

My contacts worked in other wondrous and innocent ways. When Hickman was coach at Yale, I went up to visit him in early summer at his Connecticut cabin. He lived in New Haven, but he had this shack in the mountains. He loved the mountains; he had a cabin down home in the backwoods of Carolina, too. While I was with him, Granny Rice came up to visit. Rice was full of Vandy, his alma mater, coming off a great year. He was telling us Vanderbilt might even be national champion this coming season. I started pointing out some things to him—such as the fact that Vandy had lost its coach (Red Sanders moving to UCLA) and that the new coach, Bill Edwards, was coming off the Cleveland Browns staff to change Vandy from single-wing to T-formation. He wouldn't hear any of it. No, Vandy was going to be the greatest. Then I caught myself. "What am I doing arguing with this guy?" I thought. "He's going to tout Vandy as a world-beater when he writes that big preseason piece in

Collier's. His syndicated column is the most respected in sports. Let him alone."

Later that summer, Hickman invited me to the annual college coaches' convention at Evanston, Illinois. But Edwards was there, and he started popping off about how he was going to teach the Southeastern Conference what the "T" was all about. Bobby Dodd of Georgia Tech was standing nearby, not with Edwards, but close enough to hear what he said. Dodd was sort of tossing a football from hand to hand, and in his slow southern drawl, he said, "Yes, and he gets to teach us first."

I mean, I wanted to rush to the phone and see if anybody had a line on the game yet.

The week of the game, Vanderbilt opened a fourteen-point favorite. I didn't use the phone. I *flew* to Chicago and went to Mel Clark's office to see Charley McNeil, his top handicapper. I said, "Mac, I got a proposition for you."

He said, "I knew you would, Greek boy."

"Vandy is playing Georgia Tech and I want a straight price on the game, and we both know what it figures."

Mac said, "A fourteen-point favorite in other games is one thing, but at Grant Field against Bobby Dodd it's another."

I thought to myself, "Well, why the hell don't you make it seven then?" Aloud I said, "Professor, I agree with you, but you got to give me a fair price." I thought this was a lock-mortal cinch, so I didn't mind taking his offer of five-to-one. I bet him four thousand dollars at that price, and I took the fourteen points for twenty-two thousand dollars' worth.

Georgia Tech didn't need any points. Dodd's team won, 12–7.

The next week I bet again, the following week I bet again . . . that year I didn't do much of anything else except bet against Vandy. Those twenty-nine returning seniors Grantland Rice was so proud of never did learn the new formation. I won a packet. And Edwards didn't last long.

I enjoyed my contacts with college coaches, and I admit I benefited by the friendships in accumulating details that influenced my handicapping. But rarely did I ever get anything that I could surely put in the bank. One exception was a conversation I had with

Hickman, bless his memory. I would have had to be friends with Hickman, that big Falstaffian giant of a personality, Latin scholar, poet, bon vivant—even in the unlikely event that he had been a hardware merchant down the block. He was one lovable guy.

I was thrilled for him one season when he went out to Wisconsin and got Yale a victory over the Big Ten. That's the team that had Levi Jackson. I called him up to congratulate him. "Save your breath," he said. "I haven't had those bums out of the clouds in two days. They're still celebrating. The goddamn band met the train, and there's been nothing but parties ever since. And we're playing Vanderbilt this week. Nobody knows this hardly, but Vanderbilt is probably the number one football team in the United States."

I had the same notion. This was the season before Edwards came in, and indeed Red Sanders was loaded. I couldn't resist picking Herman a little more. "Vandy is a strong team," I said, "but you'll hold your own with them, won't you?"

Hickman said, "I would if they'd practice. But they don't give a damn about Vanderbilt, some chicken-shit school down south. They're thinking about playing Harvard and Dartmouth and all these other pushovers up here."

I commiserated some more with my friend and then, let me say, I made my first hundred-thousand-dollar wager. I won it easy, something like thirty-five to nothing.

I had just about stopped betting on anything except the Southeastern Conference. On Saturday afternoons in Steubenville, all you could get were broadcasts of Notre Dame and Ohio State games. I had all my money down south, so I would go to the movies every Saturday to get my mind off of it. I saw some lousy movies, but I made a lot of money.

Only once did my friendship and counseling with young athletes cause me any embarrassment. This came about from accepting bets on high-school games. Steubenville High had a fine team and everybody in town wanted to bet on them. I always had an opinion, and when the big game came up against Canton McKinley I said it was Steubenville by six. Some two thousand dollars in bets was forced on me, against Steubenville. No sentiment in my town, baby.

A bartender at the Fort Steubenville Club was the only loyalist.

He backed the home team for two hundred dollars. Okay. This "book" was overloaded to hell and gone.

Steubenville had a great athlete on its team, a black kid named Gilliam, who was already starting to get offers from colleges all over the country. He came up to see me, because he'd heard about all the other kids I'd helped. We talked for about a half hour. I recommended him to Bo McMillan at Indiana, where he became a standout, one of the first black athletes I helped get to college.

But Gilliam had a bad moment against Canton. He was running for a touchdown and the strap on his pants broke. When he grabbed for the strap, he fumbled the ball, and Steubenville lost the game. I also lost eighteen hundred dollars.

The next day, Jack Watson, the stockbroker across the hall, walked in to see me. He had been sent by the editor of the *Herald Star*, Steubenville's daily newspaper. He and the editor were on the school board together. He got to the point right away. He said, "Did you have Gilliam in the game?"

"Did I *have* Gilliam?" I said.

"It's all over town that Gilliam was up here the other day, talking to you. I saw him. Did you do anything wrong with him?"

My first inclination was to get pissed off. Chee-rist! I was betting thousands of dollars around the country every weekend, and I was going to get bollixed up for a few hundred on a high-school game. Sometimes, however, I can control my temper. "Jack," I said, "look at these slips—I lost eight bets and won one."

"Who did you win from?" he said.

I mentioned the guy's name. I forget it now, but he had an Italian name, I remember that.

"That's the guy who's screaming," Jack said.

It taught me a lesson—I haven't made a number on a high-school team since, or gotten involved in a game in my own hometown. That's why I won't to this day make a number on the University of Nevada at Las Vegas for football or basketball. They have good little teams, but it's too close to home. I can be associated too easily. I don't need that.

My conscience rests easy. An example of how I could be a force for *good* was the case of the most highly sought prospect in the annals of the Steubenville valley. This was a raw hunk of a great person named Bob Gain who played for Weirton (West Virginia) High School not far from our town. I knew he was a prize, a can't-miss, but I hadn't realized until then how pressurized college recruiting had become.

One night my front doorbell rang. It was eleven-thirty, and that startled me. I had a glass door on my front porch, and you had to get through that before you got to my front door. I had an intercom hookup to talk to callers. I also had some intricate half-fail-safe arrangements inside the house. I had two "plants," one that had 3400 dollars in it, and one that had 180,000 dollars. Even the first one was hard as hell to get to—the whole damn closet practically came out, false doors flew up. If push came to shove, I would oh so reluctantly divulge its secrets. I had to protect the Greek.

The guy on my doorstep I had never seen before. He said, "You don't know me. My name is Mike Balitsaris; I'm an assistant coach at Kentucky."

I said, "Well, you got the right kind of name." Balitsaris is no more Greek than Socrates.

"I'm from Pittsburgh," he said, "and I got a favor to ask of you."

I let my fellow Greek in and furnished him a Scotch. He said, "I got to get Bob Gain or I'm fired. I went to Bob and he told me he wouldn't go anywhere unless you okayed it."

I knew this. Bob Gain was one of my strip-miners in his off season. I said, "Mike, you know there's a hundred schools after Bob."

"I don't give a damn if there's a thousand. You got to help me. Bear Bryant says I get him or my ass is out."

Mike stayed at my place that night. I knew Kentucky was one of the schools Gain should consider. He had to go to either Kentucky or Georgia, because I knew he was only going to major in football. I didn't make any deal with Mike that night, but a couple of weeks later he came back with another Bryant assistant, Carnie Laslie. Laslie had a mountain of snow-white hair. He looked like a Roman senator, and he had warmth. After a half hour with Laslie and Mike, I wanted to send the whole Weirton team to Kentucky.

There was a problem. Gain's mother was a widow, and the family had no money. Another school had offered to give Mrs. Gain a whopping bonus if her boy went their way. Bob told me about this.

Now this was a terrific kid, straight shooter all the way, and I cared about him. I said, "Bob, put the money deal out of your mind. Whatever it is, I want you to remember this, the school is not giving you any money. This is a friendship situation between you and me, not because you're going to Kentucky. I'll give you the money, anyway, no matter where you go. You don't have to be obligated to anybody."

But I honestly thought his career would be in the best hands with Bryant and Balitsaris and Laslie. So he signed with Kentucky.

Do you think I'm going to miss the next spring practice at Kentucky, when Bob Gain first starts to put it on with the varsity? I was there. And it so happened that a prominent bookmaker I knew from Lexington was also present, Ed Kurd, as we watched the boys in their annual Blue-White scrimmage.

I said, "Ed, what kind of odds would you give me that I could pick out one of those freshmen and bet you he was going to make All-America by his junior year?"

Kurd was a big, heavyset fellow with a voice that sounded like it came up from his ankles. "Oh, hell," he said. "That's a prohibitive price, you know that. A million things can happen to him. He could get hurt, he could flunk out, he could get killed. Shit, Bryant might kill him if he looks at him wrong. It would have to be a real big price."

"Fine, just for a hundred dollars, give me the real big price."

"I'd have to say twenty-five-to-one on that, Greek, twenty-five-to-one."

I thought, How many times have I been through this? These sons of bitches are all alike. I said, "Wait a minute, you said a *big* price. Don't insult my intelligence."

"All right, you get fifty-to-one for a hundred dollars, but it's got to be a legit All-America team."

"I want either the AP or UP. If he's picked on either one, I win it."

"First team only," he said.

"Absolutely, but one more proviso. If he makes it as a sophomore, I win it, too."

"All right. Which kid do you want?"

"His name is Bob Gain, and remember that name because it's five thousand dollars if you lose it."

I'll always remember it, too. Bob made second team All-America as a soph, then he made Associated Press, United Press, and Football Writers' All-America as a junior.

The five thousand dollars from Kurd got me even on his recruitment. Or so I thought. After he retired from his eleven-year career with the Cleveland Browns in the early sixties, Bob got word from home that I was in financial trouble. He didn't call. He didn't write. He just sent a check for twenty-five hundred dollars.

CHAPTER

4

The Marriage Wager

Strolling through the Central Park Zoo in New York one spring, just killing time, I made an important biological discovery. Turning to a friend, I pointed at the cages and said, "You know, there must be *something* to it. There's a he and a she in every one."

For starters, that isn't a bad game plan. It has a way of leading to the biggest bet most of us ever make—getting married. I lost my first bet, but I won the second. Won big.

Looking back, I lost the first because I violated one of my own rules. I didn't research the situation properly. This was one time when I should have kept my mind, and my field glasses, on the tote board. I was in a box at Tropical Park, on a mild March afternoon in 1942, when I noticed a lovely, blue-eyed blonde in the next box.

"Who," I asked one of the people with me, "is that?"

"Sunny Miles," he said. "Her father is J. H. Miles."

I knew about her father. He was a big truck farmer in Indiana, a millionaire. He owned some racehorses himself. But, for once, I wasn't interested in getting information on horses. I wanted to know more about Pauline (Sunny) Miles. I arranged for someone to introduce us.

She was engaged, but we dated that night. We went out the next night, too. The night after that we were married in Fort Lauderdale. How, or why, it happened so fast I could never explain. I wasn't drunk or any other socially acceptable excuse. I was twenty-two, the bride was twenty-six. We just drove up the coast to Fort Lauderdale with Sunny's mother and two of my Steubenville pals, Cans Jones and Cecil Gallagher. We found a justice of the peace, and a half hour later were headed back to Miami Beach.

It was the sort of impulsive, romantic thing people were doing a lot that year, in the early months of a spreading war. Jonesy turned to me, in the backseat of the car, and grinned. "Well, Greek," he said, "you'll remember March twenty-eighth for a long time."

It was like drawing a curtain over a window. "I'll *never* forget March twenty-eighth," I said. "I'll never forget that date." For a moment I started to get mad. March twenty-eighth meant only one thing to me. It was the day my mother was killed. The anniversary of my mother's death. I felt a knot in my stomach as big as a fist. My God, I hadn't even realized what day it was. Out of respect for my mother, I never would have chosen that date to be married. One more day, two more, a week, would have made no difference.

I'm not usually superstitious about anything. But the month of March upsets me. I once counted eight members of my family who died under the sign of Aries, including my mother, aunt, and uncle by the gun, and another uncle in a plane crash. I'll take two-to-one that when I go, it will be in March. But when I mentioned that I hadn't researched Sunny enough, I didn't mean that ironic choice of wedding days. We just didn't know enough about each other to bet a marriage on it. Two days. Some people take that long to select a magazine off a newsrack.

There may be couples who have won that bet, but we were not among them. Our first year wasn't too bad. Then our daughter, Victoria, arrived. Sunny had to stay home now, and that cramped her style. She liked to go out and, even in Steubenville, there were bright lights and music. But Sunny had to take care of Vicki, and she wasn't the type to enjoy changing diapers and heating bottles. Not that I was the perfect husband. But, on the sly, she had been seeing another guy. One day a friend of mine phoned.

"She's with him right now."

"I don't believe it," I said.

"Then go look for yourself."

He gave me the address.

I saw red. I mean a flaming, matador red. I kept a .38 in those days. With the money I carried, I had it for protection. But that day, at that moment, I took it to use. I didn't care what she was doing, because she didn't mean that much to me any more, but she was the mother of my child. I was going to kill them, her and him. I jumped into my black Chrysler and I was tearing down Market Street hill when the car started wobbling.

Flat tire.

It was the luckiest flat I ever had. In the time it took me to get the tire changed, I had cooled out. There is just no way you can commit homicide after you have been in the sun, loosening lugs with a wrench, sweat rolling down your face, your hands filthy and grease smeared across your shirt. I realized that the best thing to do was divorce her. That's what I did. But as lucky as I was with the flat tire, I was as unlucky in the divorce settlement. She got everything, including the thousand shares of Reynolds Metal I bought with the idea of holding it for ten years. As I mentioned, I had bought it at fourteen and seven-eighths. It had climbed to thirty-five, but I had to sell to pay off Sunny. Ten years later the stock, after splits, would have been worth nearly two million dollars. I would never have had to work again.

But there was one thing Sunny didn't get. I kept Vicki, who meant a helluva lot more to me than Reynolds Metal. The settlement wasn't so bad, after all.

The next time I married, my instincts were just as swift, but I researched it much better. I had checked into the Kenilworth Hotel in Bal Harbour for the first North-South college football game in 1948, Christmas night. My man, Herman Hickman, the Yale coach, had the North squad, and a few days before the game we were heading to Joe's Stone Crab Restaurant for dinner. My room at the

Kenilworth was on the ninth floor, Herman's on the second. I was coming down in the elevator when it stopped at eight. When the doors opened this beautiful brunette, in a classy white evening gown, looked at me.

"Are you the elevator boy?" she said.

"Yes, ma'am," I said, alertly. "What floor are you going to?"

"Are you *sure* the elevator is working?"

"Yes, ma'am," I said. "I'm sure it is."

"It has come back three times, up and down," she said, suspiciously. "But there hasn't been an elevator boy on it and I won't get on."

"Where are you going, ma'am?"

"To the lobby."

"I'll take you there, ma'am."

I knew what had happened. When the elevator boy had his dinner hour, the elevator was put on automatic. I pressed the "L" button and down we went.

"Thank you," she said.

"You're welcome, ma'am."

In the lobby she was met by her date, a college boy I recognized as one of Herman Hickman's players, Jack Geary. I rode the elevator back to the second floor and walked into Herman's room with an announcement.

"I just met the girl I'm going to marry," I said.

Herman and his wife, Helen, laughed. I couldn't blame them. I had been divorced for a few years and I was dating maybe a dozen different girls. Look, I weighed about 175 then, with decent looks, plenty of money, a Cadillac convertible. I had the world by the chain.

"Who are you kidding?" Herman said.

"I mean it," I insisted. "I really mean it."

"What's her name?"

"I don't know."

That broke it for Herman. "You're going to marry her," he said, his eyes almost watering, "but you don't know her name."

"I'll find out."

The next day I checked her out. Her name was Joan Specht. She and her sister, Marge, were on Christmas vacation from St. Mary's of the Woods College in Terre Haute, Indiana. Their father owned the Hercules Manufacturing Company in Evansville, Indiana. George Specht was one fine human, and my strategy was to get to know him first. I have always gotten along well with older people. One night, when he was with her in the lobby, I sidled over and whispered, "Who is that young lady next to you?"

"I'm sorry, Jim," he said. "I didn't introduce you. This is my daughter, Joan."

I took it from there. She was spending most of her time with the Yale football player, but I had an edge. The Yale student manager was in charge of travel arrangements. I knew him from having visited Hickman's practices, and had once done him a helluva favor.

"When are the players leaving?" I asked him.

"Some leave on the twenty-eighth, some leave the twenty-sixth."

"When's the Yale tackle leaving?"

"He leaves on the twenty-eighth."

"You mean the twenty-sixth," I said, slipping him twenty dollars.

"Yes, sir, the twenty-sixth," the manager said.

The day after the game, several players were in the lobby with their bags. Outside a bus waited to take them to the airport. The kid from Yale was there, talking to Joannie, while I positioned myself in a corner. I was watching the manager make sure that everyone got on the bus who was on the list. When the bus pulled out, Joannie walked by me on her way to the elevator.

"Miss Specht," I said, "now it's my turn."

She glared at me and kept on walking. But my plan didn't call for me to make a big play for her right away. I had become quite friendly with her father and, earlier in the day, had invited him to dinner.

"That's fine, Jim," he said. "I'll have the family."

I had hoped he would say that. We went to one of the fine gourmet restaurants on Miami Beach, with the captains hurrying around, pouring the wine, lighting cigarettes, the whole number. I laid it on pretty strong. I could tell that Joan enjoyed herself, and I could tell that impressed her father. It went on that way for the rest of the week, without my making any kind of move on Joannie.

But I wanted to take her to the Orange Bowl game on New Year's Day. I had tickets on the fifty-yard line, up high, where you're supposed to sit to watch a game. When I mentioned it to her on New Year's Eve, she asked if her father could go, too.

"Well, yes," I said. "I do have another ticket."

"He has to sit down low," she said. "He has a heart flutter. He's not allowed to walk up steps."

I swallowed hard. "I don't know if I can change my seats," I said.

"I'm sorry, but if he can't go, I can't."

I looked at my watch. It was two in the morning, twelve hours to game time. *Twelve* hours. I drove Joannie back to the Kenilworth, then I hurried down to Twenty-third Street where I had my contacts. Painfully, I parted with my fifty-yard-line seats, up high, for three that were field level. It was the worst possible place to watch a game, with the exception of from the bench, but I couldn't complain. I was with Joan, and I had Texas and seven points against Georgia. Texas won big, 41–28.

"Well, you won your bet," Mr. Specht congratulated me.

"Yes, sir," I said. "I won ten thousand dollars on Texas."

"Ten thousand!" he repeated, shocked by the amount.

"I try to win my vacation expenses," I said.

Actually, I had won fifty thousand dollars, but I had cut down the amount so his heart wouldn't flutter. I didn't want a heart attack on my conscience. It was funny, in a way. Here was a prosperous businessman who often threw around fifty thousand dollars in his business, but he couldn't imagine anyone betting that kind of money on a football game. As it turned out, he couldn't imagine anyone betting ten thousand dollars on one.

Joan returned to school and I began commuting to Indiana. St. Mary's of the Woods was a strict Catholic college, whose rules did not allow students to leave the campus during the week. So when I drove up in my Cadillac convertible I brought a sack of sandwiches with me. We'd drive around and park and talk and eat the sandwiches and drink Coke and then I'd return her to the dorm. It was the purest, most innocent time of my adult life, a change of pace after my having dated some of the top models in New York. We had to toast each other with Coke, because if those nuns had caught her drinking anything else, she would have been expelled. And if that had happened, Mr. Specht would have expelled Jimmy Snyder.

In the years I courted Joannie, while she was in college, I lived in Florida and got involved with Ray Ryan in oil. As with Sunny and the Reynolds Metal thing, Joannie on one occasion, indirectly, cost me a fortune.

At an engagement party for her sister, Marge, and Dr. Owen Slaughter, later a prominent Evansville surgeon, Joan and I had a riot of an argument. I have no recollection of what it was about, except that it ended with one of us telling the other, or maybe simultaneously, "Go to hell!" I stalked out.

I chartered a private plane and carried my temper that night to New York, where I was supposed to sign the papers to start drilling an oil well on some Indiana property. The next day, one of my drilling partners, Bob Tulley of Tulley and Carter, called.

"Jim," he said, "you're due to start drilling in two days. Did you forget?"

"The hell with it," I snapped.

"What are you talking about?" he said.

"I'm not interested in the well," I said, not thinking clearly, still brooding over my split with Joan. "Take the property if you want it. You can have it all."

"Are you serious?"

"Send me the papers. You can do anything you want with it."

"If you say so," he said.

I hate to remind myself of it, but that lease produced eleven oil wells. I would have been a wealthy man. I kept the property around it, but the five wells we drilled there were dry. That's what happened to me whenever I mixed my women with my money.

Not that I'm complaining. I made up with Joan and we were married in 1952. Oil and money are passing things, but the love of a good woman will see you through blocked punts and wild pitches. Joan has had to put up with more than the average suffering housewife. In the years when I was gambling, I wasn't the most consistent husband in captivity. Three months after we married, she left me. She couldn't understand how I could be going so good one day, and so bad the next. She hadn't heard about the IRS filing a lien against people. It didn't last long, that separation. But while we were apart, and I was trying to forget how Joannie had walked out on me, I flew to Paris, after settling with the government. If you wished to be distracted, this was not a bad place to begin.

One night in Maxim's, I noticed I was being observed by two gentlemen at the next table. I judged them to be from the Middle East. Finally, one of them moved his chair around and spoke to me.

"Pardon me, sir," he said, "but His Highness is very impressed with the suit you are wearing. May we ask where you purchased it?"

"Thank you," I said. "It was made in Los Angeles. My tailor there is Tony DiGrandis. It's a midnight-blue mohair."

I don't believe this was your standard Paris-nightclub dialogue. But they invited me to join their table, and I was curious to see if His Highness was on the level. He turned out to be Prince Fahid Ibn Abdul Aziz, the sixth son of King Saud, who ruled a chunk of real estate known as Saudi Arabia. This young man had a nice pension, but there was nothing pompous about him.

"Call me Freddie," he said.

After dinner I invited them back to my hotel. I had just picked up a half dozen new suits in New York, and the prince and I happened to wear the same size, "perfect" 38s. I opened the closet and handed him a couple. You would have thought I had given him the offshore oil rights to Texas. For the next two weeks, we were inseparable.

Every night at five, his secretary would usher into Freddie's suite six of the most exquisite girls you had ever seen. The ratio was always the same—four to two, blondes to brunettes. We were to select our dates for the evening.

It was out of the Arabian nights. All we needed were the big satin pillows and the belly dancers.

Freddie was the perfect host. He always let me choose first. But his secretary had tipped me off that His Highness preferred blondes. So, as the perfect guest, I always picked a brunette. That way I never got in Freddie's way. Even though there were four blondes, I didn't want to risk picking the one that most caught his fancy.

It went that way every night. We would go driving off to the fleshpots of Paris, and later, with our blonde and brunette of the moment, drift gently into that great boudoir in the sky.

One night we went to a gambling house in the Paris suburbs, where the big attraction was a no-limit *chemin de fer* game. I knew nothing about the game, but I had to take a shot at it. I bought a hundred dollars' worth of francs and sat at one of the smaller tables to study the rules. After a few hands, I left and bought another three thousand dollars' worth of francs. I figured I might blow it, but I was going to get a run for my money.

In *chemin de fer*, you play with six or eight decks of cards in a box known as a shoe. That night, a burly, wealthy plunger from Switzerland was dominating the game. He kept saying, *"Banco,"* meaning that no matter what anyone put down, he booked it all.

Not for long. My first turn, I laid out the whole three thousand dollars' worth of francs. I got lucky. I won six times in a row. I swept up nearly five million francs and, with Freddie cheering me on, bought champagne for everybody. One of the people in the club that night was a man named Jack Chrysler. Yeah. *That* Jack Chrysler. I owned one of his cars once.

We met again not long after that, on the *Queen Elizabeth*, returning to New York with Prince Fahid and his secretary–talent scout. The second night out, we bid on how many knots the boat had done in the last twenty-four hours. Chrysler, at the next table from us in the dining room, bid two or three times and lost, I noticed.

The next night out the bidding was about to begin. "Jack," I asked, "how high you going?"

"I can't, Jimmy," he said. "I'm out of money."

"Beg your pardon?" I said. I mean, this was Jack Chrysler talking.

"They won't cash a check on the boat," he said.

What are strangers for, if not to help the rich? "What do you need?" I said.

"No, thanks," he said. "I'll survive."

"I'm serious," I said. "I happen to have some cash on me. Tell me what you need."

"Well, if you have two thousand dollars, I'll give you a check."

I reached into my pocket, peeled off a five-thousand-dollar package and handed it to him. "I don't want a check," I said. "I'll stop by your office in New York."

Naturally, I wasn't doing this entirely for humanitarian reasons. I had in mind getting to know Jack Chrysler better. You never knew when you might need someone with his assets. When we docked, I moved into the Madison Hotel, where I had taken an apartment. A day or two later Jack phoned.

"When are you coming by?" he asked.

"I'm going away for the weekend," I told him, "with the Prince. I'll see you Monday."

On the boat, after hearing me recite one of my tales of the oil frontier, Freddie had mentioned an Arabian oil deal he thought I might help put together. That weekend he explained it in more detail. My mouth watered. It sounded like a sure thing. But it was going to take a tidy sum, a hundred million dollars, to get it going. You do not produce that kind of money fishing for dimes through manhole covers. This was where Jack Chrysler would come in. When I dropped by his office—to get my loan back—I slid it into the conversation.

"Tell me more," he said.

He had an office the size of a ballroom in the Chrysler Building, carpeted, paneled, tasteful paintings, his own stock ticker flashing against one wall. And the more I talked of the oil deal, the farther he leaned across his desk.

"See if you can get me in on it," he said.

That was all I wanted to hear. I flew to Saudi Arabia with the Prince and sat in on half a dozen meetings. I taped them all, carrying a Webcor wherever I went. Back in New York, I played the tapes for Jack in his office. His interest grew even warmer.

"Look," I said, "as far as I'm concerned, this is out of my league. If it goes through I'll get a finder's fee and a little stock, but that's all."

Which was all right with Jack. All right with me, too. The finder's fee would come to five million, plus 2½ points of the stock. For me. Just for me. All that had to happen now was for Jack Chrysler to put it together—raise the money, organize the board of directors. That looked like a cakewalk. I was a big favorite now. But all of a sudden I was informed that the whole thing had collapsed. I phoned Freddie. Except it wasn't Freddie any more. He was the Prince.

"What happened?" I asked.

"Your man made a mistake," he said.

Among the board of directors, Jack had selected a wealthy New York real estate man, a wealthy *Jewish* New York real estate man whose recent two-million-dollar donation to Israel had been well publicized. It killed the deal on the spot. No second chance. When the Arabs saw that name, it was kaput.

So nearly was I. Every cent I had I'd spent trying to tie up the deal. The day it collapsed I didn't even have cab fare from the Madison Hotel on Fifty-third and Madison to the Chrysler Building, a dollar ride in those days. I walked the mile; at least, it seemed like a mile. For a fellow who had been a big favorite to collect a five-million-dollar finder's fee, that was some letdown.

Even though I had made Jack Chrysler a loan on the voyage to New York, I wasn't about to borrow money from him. It was against my code to show weakness. I had an apartment at the Madison and I wore a two-hundred-dollar suit. I didn't look like a guy who was busted, and there was no way I would admit that I was.

As an old gambler, I knew I could get money somewhere else. I went to a friend who owned the Hickory House restaurants, in New York and Miami, both hangouts for gamblers. I found my man, Pops Popkin, a horse lover and a work of art. He lent me three thousand dollars to fly to Paris to plead my case with the Prince. It didn't work. If he had been in it alone, I might have had a chance. But there was no way he could persuade the others to change their minds, short of tanks and jet fighters.

But all my luck wasn't bad. Joannie met me when I returned to New York and we patched it up again. She took me back when I was busted, on my ass. Despite myself, I somehow won the marriage bet.

It worked out. I became a fairly respected citizen in Las Vegas, an oddsmaker, public relations consultant, tolerable husband and adoring father. Joan and I have three children—Jamie, the oldest, eighteen as this was written, Stephanie, sixteen, and Anthony, eleven.

Jamie struggled against ill health most of his life, overcame it to become a state archery, bowling, and chess champion. He has the mind of a future nuclear physicist.

Stephanie is my sweetheart, a charmer, graceful and sufficient, a copy of her mother.

Anthony is the one who challenges the world, the one with the gambler's mind. An incurable Rams fan, he once took me for a sucker bet the last game of the 1970 season, when the Rams had to beat the Giants in New York to keep their play-off chances alive. Los Angeles was a seven-point favorite.

We watched the game at home in our den, on one of the two color sets I always keep going on football weekends. The Giants kicked a field goal early. "I want to bet a dollar on the Rams," Anthony said.

"You sure?" I said. "They're behind, three–nothing."

"I'm sure," he said.

"Go get the money," I said.

A little later the Rams scored to go ahead, 7–3. Anthony disappeared into his bedroom and came out moments later: "I want to press my bet on the Rams," he said, holding a five-dollar bill.

"You're on," I said. Now in real life, there was no way I could take that bet. But I was so impressed with the little scoundrel for thinking ahead, and for taking advantage of the situation, I couldn't resist.

The Rams won, and when I paid off that night at the dinner table the other kids started to beef. "How come Anthony gets all that money and we don't?"

"Because he thought of it," I said, "and you didn't."

I want my kids to know about life, how to play cards, how the point spread works, the value of money. Let me tell you, there is no faster way known to man to teach a kid good math.

With this know-how they learn scruples, too. The hardest I have ever swatted Anthony was when I saw him shuffling a deck of cards during a game with Jamie, and he peeked at the bottom card. "I thought you could do that," he yelped.

"Now you know that you can't," I said.

I don't claim it will make scholars of them, but it won't hurt. If they want to understand how odds work, they'll learn to concentrate, and to react.

The year after Riva Ridge won the Belmont, we were in a limousine driving home from the track with Dave Johnson, the track announcer. The next day was the Brooklyn Handicap, and I commented to Dave, "If the track is fast tomorrow, Riva Ridge is a cinch."

When they posted the field for the Brooklyn Handicap the next afternoon, Anthony handed me thirty dollars and said, "Dad, would you bet ten dollars across for me on Riva Ridge?"

"That's a lot of money," I said.

"Please."

"Okay," I said, and I put the bills in my pocket.

Anthony stood there, shifting his feet. "Dad," he said. "I want the tickets."

"All right, young man," I said. "Tickets."

I had planned to just pay him out of my winnings, if the horse came in. But, obediently, I marched off to the pari-mutuels. Riva Ridge won.

Later, driving across the bridge, I turned to my ten-year-old prodigy. "Young man," I said, "do you mind telling me what made you put down ten dollars across on Riva Ridge? I don't recall you betting that much before."

"Dad, do you remember saying yesterday that if the track was fast, Riva Ridge was a cinch? Well, I checked the board before the race, and it said 'fast.' Any time you say something is a *cinch*, I got to go all the way."

No device was ever invented that will spot a phony faster than a child. They are walking truth machines. Without them, we would have no excuse ever to poke around the toy department.

We had two others who died of cystic fibrosis, one we didn't know, Florence, our first-born, who died in 1956 at three weeks. She never left the hospital. We lost Christina in 1968, when she was two and a half. A beautiful child, Tina spent eight hours on an operating table when she was one day old.

I still think of her often. The night she passed away, I went back to my house on South Sixth Street and wrote my column in the Las Vegas *Sun* about her. It was the saddest, most agonizing time of my life.

When the column appeared, Joannie was hurt. It was as though I had exposed something very private, and painful, to strangers. She didn't feel our family losses belonged in the newspaper. But in the next few days, we received over fifteen hundred letters of sympathy from people all over the country, many of whom had been mailed a copy of the column.

The letters changed Joannie's mind. It taught us both something. "I didn't realize," she said, "that so many people would care."

CHAPTER
5

"Your Money, Your Watch and Your Ring"

From the time I was a teen-ager, I lived for years where the fast money flows. In big chunks. This is the kind of atmosphere that attracts people who want to get some of it for themselves with a minimum of work—such as pulling a trigger or swinging a baseball bat. I learned to spot these types early, when I first started working nights at the Half Moon. There was a big guy named Shannon, built like a linebacker, yellow hair clipped to a half inch. He had muscles bunched on the back of his neck like ridges on a washboard. One night I noticed he was throwing money around at the bar, buying drinks for everybody.

I said to Harry Cooper, "Shannon must have had a lucky day. What'd he bet on?"

Cooper said, "He doesn't bet. He charges people to let them live."

Thereafter I would cultivate Shannon and many of his friends. I would say, "How are you holding?" The friend would say, "I ain't," and I would say, "Let me lay a hundred on you until you turn it around." Or maybe a couple of hundred if I'd heard any interesting bulletins recently about broken teeth or fractured jaws. I counted on the word getting around that Jimmy was an okay kid. It was my own program of crime prevention.

This worked fairly well until the 1940s when I began getting a reputation far and wide as a man of big transactions, the transactions usually going from somebody else's bankroll to mine. That's when I found out a fellow could get tossed in the Ohio River if he wasn't careful.

When I flew into the Pittsburgh airport from Florida one night, two guys I knew happened to be there. Anyway, I thought they happened to be there. I was returning to Steubenville to attend the funeral of a good friend. Later I wondered if they had learned when I was coming and set me up. They offered me a ride home and I accepted. When we got close to Steubenville the guy driving pulled the car over to the side of the road overlooking the Ohio River. It was a very scenic view, if there had been a moon out that night. The other guy in the front seat turned around and pointed a gun at me. "What's this all about?" I said.

"We want you to give us some money, Greek. We know you got a big roll and we want some, like all of it."

"I don't have that kind of money," I said. I didn't, at least not that day. That was my first mistake. Getting in this goddamn car was the second.

The driver was smoking a cigar. He grabbed my arm and put the cigar out on the back of my hand. "I got three hundred dollars on me," I said. "Take it."

"We want ten thousand dollars, Greek."

I told them the three hundred dollars was it. The driver got out and walked to the trunk. He came back with a big brown blanket. He said, "Come up with the money or you go in the river."

I knew these guys weren't fooling. I could see it in their eyes. A strong-arm guy who gets in motion is like a train on rails. His eyes glaze and you can see he's disconnected from the real world. It's a kind of sight that can cause a man to lose control over his bladder. The next thing I knew, I was wrapped in the blanket and I could hardly breathe.

"You gonna give it up," one of them said.

"What the hell can I give up?" I said, trying to get my message through the blanket. "I'll give you anything I can get my hands on."

"We want ten thousand dollars."

"That's out. Go ahead, throw me in. If I could get ten thousand dollars, I'd use it myself." I knew if I said I could get any kind of big money real quick, they'd think I had more. "I'll try to get a thousand dollars for you, but that's all I can promise. If you want me to try that, I will. I'm not going to the law, I'll guarantee you that."

They untied the blanket and dumped me on the slope leading down to the river. It was that close. "All right," the gunner said, "we'll call you tomorrow." They knew I'd be staying at the Fort Steuben Hotel. "And we don't want any more talk." They charged me my three hundred dollars for the ride into town.

I knew they didn't have respect for anything, especially my life, but I knew also that I had to take a stand or I'd have a regular greeting committee every time I came back to Steubenville. I made them come up and get the money—five hundred dollars. Period. "Not only is that all," I said, "but I'll never give you guys a dime after this. If you needed five hundred dollars you could've got it by asking, you know that. You didn't have to take me to the river."

"We thought you were in real good shape."

"Even if I was, you wouldn't have got it."

"We should've thrown you in the river."

"Yeah, and get nothing."

I was always a target. The trick was not to have it all on you. A little, but not all. In Steubenville, I often bet with Billy Griffith in Barberton, Ohio, outside Akron. He was a great bookmaker, because, one, if you hit him you got paid and, two, he would give you a price on anything you wanted. We always checked out at ten thousand dollars, whoever owed whom. I usually had it coming. I'd drive up there to collect and I'd take a big manila envelope with me. I had a smaller envelope inside the big one. I'd slip my money in the smaller envelope, put it inside the big one and address it to myself. Outside Billy's poolroom there was a mailbox. I'd drop the package in the slot. At the time, the U.S. mail was better than a team of bodyguards.

But one day when I drove up to Barberton with a kid I had working for me, Paul Marsh, I forgot the envelopes. I collected my money, eighty-three hundred dollars this time, and I told Paul, "Let's go to the men's room."

Paul had a wooden leg from the knee down, and I was one of the few people who knew it. In the men's room I locked the door. "Unstrap your leg," I said, keeping my voice down.

Paul looked at me like I had made an indecent proposition. "What for, Jimmy?" he said. "What the hell for?"

"Because I forgot the damn envelopes," I said, "and we got to stash this money." I kept out three hundred dollars and put the eight thousand inside his leg. I didn't want to leave right away, so I shot some nine-ball with Billy's son, Jackie, and as usual dropped a hundred dollars. When Paul and I walked outside, I pretended to put something in the mailbox outside.

A few miles outside of town a car drew alongside us and forced us to the side of the road. "Keep quiet," I told Paul. "They don't know where the money is."

"All right, Greek," one of the guys said. "We know you picked up a big package from Billy. Let's have it."

"I got two hundred dollars on me," I said. "I dropped the package in the mailbox like I always do."

"The hell you did. Out." They searched us, digging in all pockets, but they didn't go near Paul's leg. Then they searched the car, slashing the upholstery, looking in the trunk and under the hood, inside the visors, everyplace.

"Do you believe me now?" I said.

"I guess you did mail it, Greek."

If you're heisted, the worst thing is not to have any money on you, which is what happened to me that winter in Miami Beach. I stopped by the Cavendish Club, a bridge club, on my way to a dinner dance at the Surf Club. I was spiffed out in white tie and tails and not twenty dollars in my pocket. I had stopped at the Cavendish to pick up a couple of thousand I had won from Jule Weiss, a bookmaker, earlier that day at the racetrack.

I used to play at the Cavendish myself. Not good. I was just learning to play, but some of the best bridge players in the world were there, and I've always believed if you want to learn a game, play with the best. Tommy Abdu, another gambler, liked to play bridge. He'd take a master player and I'd take one, sort of like a bridge pro-am, and we'd play for fifty cents a point.

That night, I was standing around waiting for Weiss when four guys with stockings over their heads came in carrying sawed-off shotguns. "Everybody up against the wall!" was the order. It was like you stirred a tank of minnows with a stick. There were fifty people on the main floor, and another couple of dozen on the balcony level watching a TV fight. In the confusion, everybody was trying to stash money. Midgey, a little gambler I knew, stuck his roll in a water pitcher. Moe Manus slid his money into a sandwich. Slim Silverheart was there and he crammed five thousand dollars into an air conditioner. In the middle of the room one of the robbers spread out a big white tablecloth. "All your money," he said. "No jewelry, just cash. Walk up single file."

I was behind a bridge player named Harry Harkaby, one of the best. I had left my money home, thinking I was going to get the two grand from Weiss. I didn't want to stiff anybody with a sawed-off shotgun. "Harry," I whispered, "can you loan me something?"

Harkaby looked around at me dumbfounded. He held out his money clip. "Take what you want, Jimmy. What difference is it?"

I took two hundred-dollar bills from him, and when I got to the tablecloth I threw it on the floor.

"Is that all you got?" the guy said.

I pulled my pockets out. I took off my coat. "I was waiting for a guy to bring me the money he owed me," I said. "That's all I got on me."

"You sure?"

"I'm sure."

He stared through that stocking mask for a full ten seconds. Then he made me drop my pants. Finally, he waved me away. "All right, Greek. Go ahead."

Meanwhile, one of his confederates was watching the clock, calling out the time. It was a regular countdown. He just sang it out: "It's eleven-forty . . . eleven forty-one . . . eleven forty-two . . . eleven forty-three. . . ."

Finally, he said, "Okay, it's eleven forty-four *and a half.* Let's go!"

With that they were gone, backing out of the room and through the door. No more than forty seconds had passed—I mean, I was still buckling my belt and zipping my fly—when Jule Weiss breezed in, as if nothing had happened. I told him he had just missed a helluva floor show. He handed me the two grand he owed me and I decided that, all things considered, this was a good time to leave.

As I headed for the front door I heard Harkaby yell, "Hey, Greek, where you going? Didn't you forget something?"

I stopped in my tracks. And I had to laugh. "I sure did, Harry," I said, and I handed him two hundred-dollar bills.

This was just another gun-to-head confrontation, but when a fellow is betting money like I did there are more subtle dangers involved. I was in Miami in 1948 for the Orange Bowl game between Georgia Tech and Kansas. By then I had a lot of followers around the country. People were waiting to find out who the Greek was betting on, including some people who would make my Ohio River rollers look like choirboys.

This time I liked Tech, a seven-point favorite. I thought they should be up by thirteen. Maybe that was because I admired Bobby Dodd, the coach. From the time I started gathering the out-of-town papers through my railroad porters in Steubenville, I learned that Dodd told it like it was. He said things like, "I'd rather be lucky than good." And, "I don't see why we shouldn't be favored over Georgia. We've got a better team." Dodd was noted for creating a razzle-dazzle offense, but when he had the material he forgot all about that and just stuck it to them. This year he had the material. I made a sizable wager on Tech and gave the points. When pressed, I confided the opinion to a few select inquisitors.

The line started going up, to eight and twelve and finally thirteen. As New Year's got closer, somebody mentioned the game had dropped to eight. I couldn't understand it. Tech hadn't come up with any injuries in practice.

That's when one of my special friends came to see me, and I discovered I was the man in the middle. "The word out of Chicago," he said, "is that you talked Tech down here and bet Kansas up there."

"My bet's on Tech," I said. "I never touched Kansas."

He said, "I hope so, Greek."

The next day I had a follow-up contact from some of my friend's soldiers, but I didn't convince them either. I knew I had to straighten this out or I'd really be in trouble. I found that the big bet in Chicago had been placed in Mel Clark's office by a gambler out of St. Louis who was trying to build himself up as Jimmy the Greek, too. His name was Jimmy Karras.

I called Mel. "I didn't bet you on the Orange Bowl," I reminded him. "I'm getting a bad rap from the other kid's bet. I'm going to have some people call you. Do me a favor and tell them what happened."

Mel did, and it straightened it out before game time. Georgia Tech won by thirteen. I won my bet, of course, but if Tech had lost, and certain people thought I had a wad on Kansas, I could have lost my hide.

I won't deny there were occasions when my contacts with the wrong side of life paid dividends. This happened in Miami, too, when I was on vacation at the Cadillac Hotel. I was going to the track every day. When I returned to the hotel I liked to take a nap, then shower and go out for dinner late, around nine. I'd always leave the light on in my room. One night when I came back from dinner, the room was dark. Next there was a gun in my ribs and the door was closed. The lights came on. There were two of them. I thought robbers come like martinis—one's not enough, two's just right, and three's too many.

"Your money, your watch, your ring," one said.

"You got it," I said, as softly as I could. "Don't worry. I'm not going to say anything."

"You got the right attitude, Jack."

One of them took a sheet off the bed, tied me up with it, and stuck me in the closet. It wasn't too tight, and after a few minutes I was free. As far as I was concerned, that was it. They got about three thousand dollars, plus a nice gold watch and my diamond ring. But I wasn't going to the cops about it.

The next day, looking for a loan, I went to Twenty-third Street, where all the gamblers loafed, and some of the tough guys, too. A godfather type, named Mikey, and a few fellows of vague reputation, used to call me to find out which teams I liked. I never tipped too many people, but I did Mikey. We had a cup of coffee together. "I got a story for you," I said, and told him what happened.

"What'd they look like?" he said.

"Forget it. I'm not looking to get even. It's over."

"Jimmy, what'd they look like?"

The way he said it, I knew I had to tell him now, so I described the two heisters as well as I could. Two days later, my phone rang. It was Mikey. "Stop down by the Hickory House before you go the racetrack," he said. "I got something for you."

What he had for me was my watch, my ring, and twenty-five hundred dollars. "They were broke," he said. "I let 'em keep five hundred dollars."

"Hell, here's five hundred dollars more to give 'em. On me."

Moving around in Miami and New York in gambling clubs and certain restaurants, occasionally you would see people from that other world. I avoided them. A friend of mine would say, "You see that gray-haired guy over there, with the black-rim glasses? He's in the mob. He's—"

"Don't tell me," I'd say. "I don't want to know." I didn't want to know anything more than was in the newspapers, and not all of that. I knew a few gamblers who thought they were getting into easy money, handling betting operations for the wrong people. It turned out to be the hardest money they ever saw. They could never shake loose. I was propositioned ten times to work as a handicapper, and I was always careful in the way I begged off. I came up with sound excuses why I couldn't and kept everything friendly. And they knew they could call me any time and I would give them an opinion on a game they liked. After *I* bet, of course.

The one time I did get involved was no fault of mine. I still don't know what I could have done differently. I had gotten into a slow-pay situation with two bookmakers in Ohio—they didn't have the money, and yet I had to square other bets I had lost. I called a friend in New York, a gambler, and tracked him down at Gallagher's restaurant on Fifty-second Street. I told him I needed forty thousand dollars for a couple of weeks. He didn't have it, but he said he would see what he could do the next morning. Sure enough, the next morning a guy I'd never seen before drove down from Pittsburgh and handed me an envelope with the money. I paid off my bets, then called the guy in New York to thank him. And got the shock of my life. He hadn't sent any money, but it took us only a few minutes to figure it out.

He said, "Jimmy, you know————?"

"I don't *know* him," I said, "but he calls me now and then about the teams I bet on."

"Well, he was in the place last night when you called. I was having an after-dinner drink. I mean he asks me to the table, you know?"

"Go on."

"When I get back from talking to you, I mention I feel bad because I don't have the forty thousand dollars, after all the times you—"

"Never mind. What else?"

"Nothing else. All he said was, 'I hate to hear that. The Greek is good people.' And I finished my drink and left."

"Oh, Christ."

"Maybe it wasn't him that sent the money."

"Who the hell you think it was?" I said. "The tooth fairy?"

A couple of days later my friend in New York finds out it was that man, all right, and says they gave him the word on relaying the payment. In a week I had that forty thousand dollars back. Then I held my breath.

Years went by. I had pushed the incident to the back of my mind. Then one fall I was in New York, busted again. Joannie was with me and she was pregnant. I was in the Hickory House when my long-ago benefactor walked over to me. "Greek," he said, "I need a favor."

"What do you need?" I said. What else could I say?

"We've got a big joint up in Montreal, but we need a little help on the sports. Can you go up and straighten out the sports for us? If everything works out, we'll take care of you."

In this man's language, "take care of you" was a weighty promise, like six figures preceded by a dollar sign. I had to do it. I *owed* him is the way I knew he figured. Well, at least I'd be compensated. "I'll fly up there tomorrow," I said.

At the time, some of the big bookmakers had left the United States following the Kefauver hearings and gone to Montreal to operate. Gil Beckley was the big man in the Montreal operation. He had been a horse bookmaker in Cincinnati, and he needed someone who knew sports. I knew I couldn't go up there with all those bookmakers and not have any money to play, so I borrowed two thousand dollars from Pops Popkin and three thousand dollars from Oscar Chason, a furrier. I left four hundred dollars with Joannie and got a plane the next day.

Three hours after I walked into Gil's joint up there, I realized what had gone wrong. There's a difference in bookmaking that even some people in the business don't realize. If Joe Blow bets you ten thousand dollars on a football game, you don't change the price. Joe Blow is Joe Blow, and his opinion doesn't mean a thing. But if a professional bets you fifteen hundred dollars, a guy with a helluva track record, you change it fast. In Montreal, Gil had been changing the price no matter who bet.

In a few weeks I had set all of this right, and in the meanwhile had run my forty-six hundred dollars up to thirty-three thousand dollars betting on college football. I didn't have the bankroll in my hand. It was in the book, on paper. Now the bowl games were coming up, with Mississippi–Navy in the Sugar Bowl, the big one, because Navy was the Lambert Trophy team, champions of the East; and the East was where we got our biggest play. My price on the game was Mississippi favored, but everybody else in the joint wanted to make Navy the favorite by three or four points.

"I'm not talking about which team is better," I said. "The price that'll get the most action is pick 'em, not Navy by three or four."

But by now Gil Beckley was going good. Where he had been a million loser, he was a million winner. He figured he didn't need Jimmy the Greek any more to tell him about sports.

"I'm opening it Navy by four," Gil said.

"I'll tell you what," I said. "Bet my thirty-three on Mississippi plus four."

"You're on," he said.

Right away, he cut the number to three, and then he dropped it to two. A few days before the game it was pick 'em, and then it was Mississippi by one. The only reason I had played the game was to get points with Mississippi and then, when the price dropped, to turn around and bet Navy to catch it both ways. I would be laying eleven-to-ten, or thirty-three thousand dollars to thirty thousand on both sides, with a spread of five points. So I was actually putting up three thousand dollars and could win sixty thousand if the result came inside the spread.

The night before the game it was Ole Miss by one and a half. "Take me off," I told Gil. "I want to bet thirty-three on the Navy."

"All right," he said. "I'll get you off tomorrow. Don't worry about it. We'll move it back to Ole Miss by one, but you won't have to pay the juice." That meant I wouldn't have to lay eleven-to-ten on my Navy bet, saving me three thousand dollars. I said okay.

The next morning, New Year's Day, the phone rang in my room at the Mount Royal Hotel. I never loafed around at night with the guys at the joint. I liked them, but I didn't socialize with them. I preferred to be a loner.

It was Gil on the phone. "Greek," he said, very softly.

"What's the matter?" I said.

"The boys raided the place last night."

"What boys?"

"The Canadian Mounted Police. The fucking Royal Mounted Police. They got everything."

"They can't do that," I yelled, meaning they can't just leave me with thirty-three thousand dollars on Ole Miss.

"The hell they can't. They did." They had impounded the books and some of the money, but not all of it. Some was stashed in other places. But that didn't help me. I didn't have a dime on Navy as far as the book was concerned.

Navy kicked hell out of them, 21–0, and there I was in Montreal with seven dollars in my pocket. I called Joannie. "Anything in the bank?" I said.

"About two hundred and sixty dollars," she said, "but I haven't paid the rent yet."

"I just want to write a check."

"What happened? What's the matter?"

"Nothing. Everything's great." That was always one of my rules, never to tell Joannie when things were bad. There was no reason for both of us to worry about it.

Being broke wasn't all that bad, comparatively. At *last* I was off the hook for that forty-thousand-dollar loan.

CHAPTER
6

A Little Help from My Friends

It wasn't only tough guys with guns who could rob you blind. I once got ripped off by my own pocket watch—with the help of my friends. This was 1946, after I had gone to Philadelphia to pick up seventy thousand dollars I'd won on a series of baseball bets. I came over to Atlantic City and took a suite in the Ambassador Hotel to kill a few days before the College All-Star game in Chicago.

My suite became a gathering place for all the top gamblers in town, and there happened to be a bunch—Harry Rosen was one of the country's top bookmakers; Kingie Schwartz, the Canadian who could read the pool numbers on a tote board and give you the odds for place and show instantly, was one of the highest players in horse racing history; New York Nate Linnett; and Cheesecake Ike Berger, somebody's guest since the day he put on long pants. Plus a few others I can't remember.

We would sit around all afternoon betting horses with each other. I kept a pocket watch in those days, one my father had given me, and I had it propped on the desk. Along about three o'clock I had a phone call I had to take in my bedroom. I came back in time for the next race, which was a mile-and-a-half race for jumpers. I was ahead on the day, and now everybody wanted to bet me on one horse, a long shot aptly named Long John II. I took five hundred dollars here and a thousand there. Long John II came in at eleven-to-one. I finished up loser for the afternoon by more than $137,000.

That night I was walking on the boardwalk, feeling snakebit, when I ran into Slim Silverheart, the Pittsburgh bookmaker who had been my friend—my "Uncle Joe"—for so many years. He walked along with me, and after a while he said, "Greek, what time you got?"

I took out my watch and said, "Quarter after ten."

"That's funny," he said. "I got twenty-five after. Your watch must be wrong, Greek."

Then it hit me. The boys had past-posted me on the race. They knew the result before they put their money up. I had a hunch it was more of an accident than a plot. One of them might have called for a baseball score and found out the result of the race, too. Maybe my watch was already slow, or maybe one of them set it back while I was in the next room. Either way, once they knew, they couldn't resist betting me. Slim had let me know what happened without really telling me.

I didn't say anything to him, either. I didn't say anything to anybody. I let on as if I didn't know it had happened. But I started scheming how I could get back at those guys.

I hadn't made a bet on the College All-Star game yet. The Los Angeles Rams had been sent out as an eight-point favorite, and in my mind that was a wrong number. The All Stars had guys like Pat Harder and Elroy Hirsch and they were loaded. I believed the game was a toss-up.

The next afternoon everybody was back in my suite again, and I picked up the phone right there and called Mel Clark's in Chicago. "I'll take the Rams," I said, "and give the eight for fifty thousand dollars." I hadn't raised my voice, but I spoke very clearly so all the boys could hear me.

"You like the Rams minus eight?" Cheesecake Ike said.

"I'm just monkeying around with it," I said. I could see that the others were all ears, too. Remember, those guys were mainly horseplayers, and none of them had the time or the interest to keep up with sports the way I did. They respected my opinion on a football game because they knew damned well I knew what I was doing.

I left the next day, a Thursday, and went to Chicago. The first thing I did was go up to Clark's place.

"What's the game?" I said.

"It's up to twelve," Mel said.

"Yeah? Where is all the money from?"

"We got a lot of money from the East on it. Most of it came in yesterday."

The day of the game I went back to Clark's, and now the Rams were favored by thirteen. "How about a straight price?" I said.

"You're entitled to three and a half to one," Mel said.

"I'll take it for twenty thousand dollars, and from now on, whatever you take at thirteen, I'll pay you two percent for it." This was a strong offer. Clark would customarily give bets away in return for one percent of the winning side.

"You got it," he said.

Now I was off my original bet on the Rams and playing the game in the middle. They didn't think anything of it. If a bookmaker gave eight and it came thirteen, it's a natural move. But I also had the All Stars with the odds, in addition to the points.

On the way to the game, I was in the elevator at the Blackstone Hotel when Nate Linnett got on at another floor. "Say, Nate," I said, "who'd you bet on?"

"Because you bet on the Rams," he said, "I made a big bet on the Rams, too."

"I didn't tell you to bet on the Rams."

"I heard you on the phone. You bet fifty thousand dollars."

"I'm playing the game even," I said.

"But I *heard* you bet the Rams," Nate said.

"I'm not kidding. I played the game out."

Nate shrugged. "I gave nine. I'll stick with it."

Hirsch and his boys beat Bob Waterfield and the Rams, 16–0. I got seventy thousand dollars for my straight bet and came sixty thousand dollars ahead on the points. It made me about even for the week, including Long John II, and it gave me the personal satisfaction of squaring those guys who had past-posted me. The next winter in Florida, when Nate and the rest were passing the story around, I had an answer for them. "That's right," I'd say, "but how much did you bet on the Rams?"

The College All-Star game in the 1940s was our Super Bowl. Gamblers would come into Chicago from all over the country. We'd be at the Blackstone and the Sherman and the bets would fly. Tommy McDonald's was another popular gambling joint. Both McDonald's and Clark's were right off Clark Street in the Loop. They had cigar stores in front, but the layout was wide open and, for that matter, so was the whole town.

Every summer I'd stay after the game and spend two or three weeks in the room at Clark's, matching wits with one of the great handicappers of all time, Professor Charles McNeil. McNeil had been a college professor at the University of Illinois in Champagne-Urbana, not far south of Chicago. He never wore a tie, but he always wore a white shirt and somehow he *looked* like a professor. He started coming up to Clark's and making little bets, fifty cents and a dollar. After a while he began betting two dollars. Then he was putting down five dollars and twenty dollars. Before long he was betting one hundred dollars and two hundred dollars, and finally Mel saw what he was and Jakie Summerfield saw what he was and they said, "Hey, come in with us."

McNeil was reluctant.

Jakie said, "You can make more here than you can teaching arithmetic."

"Calculus," McNeil said.

"Whatever it is, this has got to be more fun." And McNeil had to agree with that.

The professor was the first to put up teasers, where the bettor could move the line seven points up or down, but he had to make a two-team parlay and lay eleven-to-ten. It works out that a 6½-point teaser is even money. Nowadays, bookies shade it so you have to lay eleven-to-ten with six points, and with 6½ they want six-to-five or thirteen-to-ten and five-to-four. One day I said, "Mac, let's make a twelve-point teaser, with three teams." He did and got a lot of play, though the bettors were actually getting a one-team bet at six-to-five.

During the winter, Mac and I would match wits on basketball especially. One year he said, "I'm always giving you the numbers. Why don't you give them to me, the night before, and I promise to bet you three or four games." He meant he'd take either side of my line and lay me eleven-to-ten. He would bet eleven hundred dollars a game. He told me to call him every night about seven o'clock.

After a couple of weeks, I wasn't doing very well at all. He would win fifteen and lose ten, and seldom would it come my way, even with the eleven-to-ten in my favor. One afternoon I phoned Clark's and I was talking to Jakie about it.

Jakie said, "I'll give you a tip. Instead of giving him the line at seven o'clock, give it to him at nine."

I said, "Why?"

Jakie said, "Do what I tell you."

So that night when I called at seven I told Mac something had come up at the office and I couldn't get back to him for a couple of hours. He said okay, and I called back at nine-fifteen. I said, "Are you ready?"

He said, "Yep, yep. Any time, old Greek." This didn't sound like the professor, who was usually elaborate and formal at all times. I read off the numbers and he started at the top and bet *every* game.

What I had never known until now was that McNeil had a nightly custom. He stopped working at seven, and he spent the next two hours downing a quart of Scotch. Sober, he would bet only the three-point games. But when he was drinking he would bet even the one-pointers. Those were practically toss-ups, and that was the difference in the whole advantage. Now I was winning twenty and losing seventeen, and the eleven-to-ten edge started to mount up. I took a lot of McNeil's money that season calling at nine o'clock.

I didn't always have something extra going for me when I made a bet, but those are the bets that stick in my memory. I had a subsidy working through one entire basketball season because I knew the trainer at a college in West Virginia. He was on my payroll in a small way. This was a high-scoring team and played a major schedule. Its star player had a bad knee, and the trainer had to work on it just before every game. This kid was one of the nation's highest scorers, but when the knee was stiff his scoring slacked off. An hour before game time the trainer would call me. If the knee was okay, the trainer would bet on his team. If it wasn't, he'd say he wasn't going to bet on the game that night.

Of course, I bet every game, one way or the other. I won eighteen out of nineteen bets on the trainer's team that season.

There was nothing "wrong" there, because the key to the team's performance was the *physical* condition of its best player. It was only one step from that, however, to the *mental* condition of a key player. All of us had always known that basketball was the most susceptible of all the team sports to outside manipulation. There are five players, instead of nine or eleven. On the average team there are only two players, at the most three, who are vital to the team's success.

Since Paddy Ryan was knocked out by John L. Sullivan in 1882, the lore of betting in the United States has been rife with tales of tigers who went into the tank. That's easy enough, one on one, man against man. When I was a kid in Kios, Primo Carnera was knocking out guys named Farmer Lodge and Sam Baker and Bearcat Wright, and a couple of years later he knocked out Jack Sharkey for the heavyweight championship—after Sharkey had beat him in fifteen rounds when Sharkey didn't have the title. Larceny was a very convenient arrangement inside the squared circle. It was only a quantum leap from one to five, when basketball took the count.

One day in Steubenville I got a call from a bookie I knew in New York. He asked for a price on NYU against Buffalo in the Garden. I told him to call back in twenty-five minutes. I had files on all the basketball teams in the country in the late forties. I put a pencil to it, and it looked as though NYU would be playing reserves in the fourth quarter. When he called back I told him the game was fifteen. He said, "I got a guy here wants to take thirteen for five thousand dollars. You want any part of it?" I said hell yes. He said, "You got it, for two thousand dollars." A little while later he called back and said, "This guy wants to go another five thousand dollars at twelve. You want some?" I told him if I'd take money at thirteen, I sure would take more at twelve.

It was my habit in basketball season to call around the country and see who was betting what. I called Minneapolis and got Lou Walker, who later came to work for me. I asked him, among other things, what he had on NYU and Buffalo. He said seventeen. Then I asked him who was betting on the game. He said, "Jimmy, you know I can't tell you that."

I asked him if Billy Hecht, the boss, was there. Billy said the betting was out of New York. I didn't like it. Nobody is going to bet me and take twelve and thirteen and then give fifteen and sixteen in Minnesota. I asked Billy who in New York was betting. He didn't want to say. I said, "Billy, this is basketball season, but football is coming, too." Billy would lean on me for my opinions on football. He said, "Well, between you and me . . ." And he named the guy in New York who had been calling me for thirteen and twelve.

I said, "Uh oh, this is wrong. Why would the guy do this?" A half hour later I called Minneapolis back and it was sixteen, another little bit and it's fifteen, dropping to fourteen. I told the kids in my office in Steubenville, "Okay, let's go. We got to get off and get well. Call every small book in our neck of the woods." I came out ahead on the night, when NYU won by nine, but from then on I was determined it would never happen to me again.

I had gained a certain reputation by that time, and International News Service—which would later merge with United Press to become UPI—would call me from New York to get the point spread on the games in Madison Square Garden. After this Buffalo game, when INS called, I told them I didn't have a line. "I can't give you the numbers," I said, "because I don't know how to handicap games in the Garden."

A few years later, in 1952, New York district attorney Frank Hogan broke open the basketball scandals—but in the meantime there was a lot of paranoia. During this time I got a call from a New York friend, Butch Tauris, who used to be a song-and-dance man and now had fallen on predictably hard times. He wanted to know something to bet. I gave him Denison plus six over Ohio U., because I had just made a small bet on the game.

Later when I called Billy Hecht I found he had dropped the price to two. "And in New York," Billy said, "it is off the board," meaning no New York books would take action on the game.

My song-and-dance man had called every friend in town and told them Jimmy the Greek was betting Denison, therefore I must have the game in the bag. Denison won, and the next day the whole Ohio Conference was barred by every bookmaker in the country.

Big betting scandals have followed both world wars, because there was so much black-market money around, money that they couldn't put anywhere except in gambling. These were profits from dealing in whiskey and cigarettes. After World War I came the Black Sox sellout of 1919. The basketball fixes of 1950–51 stemmed from a lot of guys trying to be bookmakers who didn't know enough about it, and they were losing. A lot of people like Charley McNeil, Jimmy the Greek, Jakie Summerfield, Jerry Zarowitz, Bobby Berendt, and Eddie Kurd were beating them with superior handicapping.

In 1946 I won the biggest basketball bet of my life. I was in Florida, as usual, for the winter. I rarely came back from Florida with any money, because whatever I would win at basketball I would dutifully contribute the next day at the racetrack. This time I won so much money on basketball, near the end of my stay, that I didn't have a chance to lose it back on the horses. I had nothing but winners through the first rounds of the National Invitational Tournament at the Garden. I was betting at a little cigar store in Miami Beach across from the Roney Plaza. Slim Silverheart introduced me with the magic words, "Whatever this guy wants . . ." There was a high-stakes poker game going right upstairs. It was a fine place to bet because it was run by a guy from Chicago, and any bets that were made were sure to be paid. If somebody reneged, he was in serious trouble.

For the final game, between DePaul and Rhode Island, I knew I had to come up with a gimmick that would get all the other guys to bet me. Rhode Island was a high-scoring team, but it had a loose defense. I had DePaul the winner, but that wasn't enough. Finally, I thought I had an idea that would make them think I was wrong. "Fellas," I announced, "I have a proposition. I'll take six to five that DePaul sets the NIT scoring record tonight." Remember, this was the team that had George Mikan, the greatest pivot man in basketball to that time. Well, they lined up single file to bet me, covering fifty-two thousand dollars—until there was only one man left, a little fellow who seemed shy. I said, "What are you going to do, Dad?"

And he said, "Would you give me a hundred dollars of your side?" DePaul and Mikan broke the scoring record by eight points, as I remember.

That spring in Florida I came up with another gimmick bet that attracted even more play, this time on baseball. All the gamblers were talking about the coming season and Joe DiMaggio's return to the Yankees after three years in the Army. One night on Twenty-third Street in Miami Beach, where all the gamblers used to hang out, a guy said, "He'll have a great year. He'll hit three-fifty because he's the one guy who can pick up right where he left off."

I didn't think so. I had been reading about DiMaggio's domestic troubles. He was breaking up with his wife and there was a little son involved. I knew that made it worse for him, because I had been going through torture over my little daughter for the same reason. DiMaggio being Italian had something to do with it, too. I think there is some similarity between Greeks and Italians when it comes to children. Other people love their children, but it seems like we *live* for our children.

But for me to bet against DiMaggio, I had to come up with somebody I thought would hit higher, who wasn't an *obvious* choice. I knew nobody would give me Ted Williams—it had to be somebody out of left field, so to speak. Because I was living in Ohio, the Cleveland Indians were a thing with me, and one player in particular, shortstop Lou Boudreau. I lived vicariously with every play he made, every hit he got. If I could have changed places with anybody in those years, it would have been Boudreau. He had hit .306 the previous season and .327 the year before that. He figured to hit a solid .310.

So on Twenty-third Street I started announcing I liked Boudreau to outhit DiMaggio. "You're crazy, Greek," a guy said. "Boudreau isn't in DiMaggio's class."

I said, "I'll take six to five that Boudreau hits for a higher average than DiMaggio does." He gave it to me, and then they all started jumping on. I made them lay me seven-to-five, eight-to-five, and then nine-to-five because they were so anxious to back DiMaggio. Adding it up, I had something over one hundred thousand dollars riding on it.

Going into the last day of the 1946 season, Boudreau was at .293 and DiMaggio was just a couple of base hits behind him at .292. Boudreau had pulled himself from the lineup most of the last month because of a bad ankle. DiMaggio was in Philadelphia for a doubleheader. I had a spotter in Shibe Park phone me every time he came to bat. DiMaggio went one-for-seven and finished at .290—the lowest average of his career until the season he retired.

CHAPTER
7

H.L. Likes the Southwest

One of the turning points in my life came the week after Christmas in 1947 when my little daughter beat me to the telephone. Vicki picked it up and said, "Hello? My Daddy likes Texas."

For some reason—hell, for several reasons—that little incident sent a chill through me. I decided that was it. I closed down my Steubenville office and moved to Florida.

I had custody of Vicki, but I had heard of too many wives who had signed over their kids, changed their minds after six months, and then went to court to get them back. And you never knew what a judge was going to do, especially a judge who might think a gambler was somebody who lived under a rock.

For the next several years I kept a low profile as a bettor, getting money down through a partner if at all. Indeed, I did have a big bet on Texas that year because the Longhorns had Bobby Layne and were playing Alabama in the Sugar Bowl. I had the bet half and half with Ray Ryan, a total of $220,000 between us.

Now, I have known a lot of guys who bet money in my time. That was my life. But I have never—*ever*—known of a higher roller than Ryan. He was, and remains, an unforgettable character in my experience.

He was in the oil business and eventually got me into the same line—where I discovered that drilling for oil was an elevated form of roulette. A higher degree of gambling.

I first met Ryan at Marty Gilfoyle's gambling joint in Miami. He was a tall, handsome guy with an upbeat personality. Everything was always happy with Ryan, whether he was flush or busted. He looked like a movie star, with straight brown hair brushed back flat on his head—something like a latter-day Richard Arlen. He liked my style and I liked his. My onetime Miami partner and dear friend Harold Salvey didn't like Ryan, for reasons I never knew. "Stay away from this guy," Salvey used to warn me. "He'll screw you sooner or later." Salvey has been right about so many things, but his opinion on Ryan was never confirmed.

Ryan had bounced around as a teen-ager on his own, much the way I had, though I had stayed within the confines of Steubenville.

In a sense, Ryan's losses betting on the horses or sports made me feel like a piker—because for him oil and gambling mixed like oil and water. Where I would plunge for a hundred and fifty thousand dollars on one game, Ryan would do it on five or six. Ryan told me once: "I had bought two eighty-acre fields outside of Centralia, Illinois, on a tip. If you're well liked in the oil business, you get information—a truck driver, a worker you lent ten dollars six months ago, anybody can tip you to promising leases. Well, I had these two fields and I owed a man in Chicago nineteen thousand dollars from betting horses. I went to the Texas Company offices in Centralia and told them I would sell one of the fields for nineteen thousand dollars.

"I knew the man well, and he knew me. He said, 'The field is worth it, and probably more, but why nineteen thousand dollars?' I said I wanted the money by ten A.M. He said that was impossible. The company would want the title proved, and other technicalities. I said tomorrow the deal would be off. He said how about both sides for thirty-eight thousand dollars? I said no. One was all I would sell.

"I went back to my hotel. On my way upstairs I noticed the

gambling layout on the second floor. Race results. Dice. I think
roulette, too. An hour later the Texaco man called my room and said
come over and get the check.

"It was made out for thirty-eight thousand dollars. The company
said both fields or none, because it wouldn't run as much of a title
risk that way. Finally, I said okay, and I went down to the Western
Union and wired the nineteen thousand dollars to Chicago.

"I knew I had just sold away a fortune. I was disgusted with
myself. I went back to the hotel. That evening at six o'clock I got in
my car and took off for a vacation in Florida. I'd spent the afternoon
losing the other nineteen thousand dollars playing the horses. Both
fields came in. They have since produced over five million barrels of
oil apiece."

At three dollars a barrel, the rates at that time, in one afternoon
Ryan had pissed away fifteen million dollars betting horses that ran
second.

Ryan was known as a high roller about the same time I was.
Damon Runyon put the label on him. Runyon wrote in a column:
"Every generation seems to produce its own fabulous figure in lofty
gambling. As Nick the Greek has been used to connote high rolling
for years and before him Pittsburgh Phil Smith, now it is Ray Ryan.
He plays the highest gin rummy of any man since the game was
invented."

This publicity attracted another high-rolling gambler, oilman H. L.
Hunt, who was to fill a significant chapter in my life because he knew
Ryan well. Hunt fancied himself the greatest card player in the
world—second only to his talents at checkers, where he claimed
absolute superiority through all history.

Hunt started calling Ryan trying to get him to set up a gin game.
Both were busy men. Finally, Hunt learned that Ryan had booked
passage to Europe on a luxury liner, and he bought a ticket on the
same ship. Their ocean crossing was one high-stakes gin game—at
ten dollars a point, where thirty thousand dollars can change hands
within the space of twenty minutes—and Ryan stepped ashore in
England with $243,000 of Hunt's money.

Ryan liked to hobnob with actors, possibly because he had the
looks and personality to be in show business himself. In later years he

and William Holden went into partnership to create the Mount Kenya Safari Club in Africa. Ryan was a regular in Las Vegas before I ever went there. One day he was going into the hotel dining room out there when he was stopped by Johnny Myers, the Howard Hughes publicity man. "Ray, let me have five thousand dollars," Myers said. "I've got a real pigeon for a gin game." Ryan gave him the money.

Later, Ryan's meal was interrupted when actor Bruce Cabot rushed up to the table. Cabot needed some cash. "I've got a sucker tied up for gin," he said. "It's like finding money." Ryan backed him.

The baked Alaska and a faint suspicion arrived at Ryan's table in a dead heat. Ryan hurried to the card room, and there were Myers and Cabot, playing head to head.

Ryan was a restless guy. Any time he had a deal on, he would concentrate totally, then when it was settled he would want something else. He loved to bet on anything, and he loved to bet big. Once we were in the Warwick Hotel in New York with some friends, and Ryan got it into his head he wanted to bet on gin rummy. But he didn't want to *play* gin rummy. A waiter had just arrived with some drinks and sandwiches.

"Young man," Ray said, "do you know how to play gin?"

"Yes, sir," the kid said. "I play all the time."

"Good. I'll tell you what we're going to do. You play my hand, and if you win, you keep half the money. If you lose, I'll cover you. Fair enough?"

The kid thought he was either nuts or drunk, but New York waiters are inured to anything. "Yes, sir!" he said.

In the next two hours the phone rang a few times. It was room service wanting to know if our food had arrived, because the waiter never came back. I wasn't in the game, so I answered and told them the kid had delivered the order and left.

The kid was winning, but he didn't have any idea how much because he didn't know how much the stakes were. "We're going to dinner now, young man," Ray said finally. "Here's your money." Ray took out his money clip and peeled off five thousand dollars. I thought the kid was going to faint.

"Take it," Ray said. "You play gin very well, young man."

The next day, Ray thought that had been so much fun he would do it again. He called room service and asked for the same waiter. Eddie, the kid's name was.

"I'm sorry, sir," the voice at room service told him. "Eddie quit working here last night."

During the two years I had known Ryan he was always after me to come in with him on a proposition betting football games. He thought I was the best handicapper on college football, and I *was* the best. "I'll put up all the money, Greek," he said, "and you've got a third of it. You just give me the teams to bet."

Until now, when I decided I wanted to keep a low profile in betting for Vicki's sake, I had never taken him up on it. I told him I'd accept the deal on one condition. I'd cover my third, but I wanted to stay in the background. "I don't want anyone to know where the bets came from," I said. "I don't want to talk to anybody or make bets with anybody on anything."

The first week of the football season that year we happened to be back in New York, this time at the Savoy Plaza. I had him bet the Arkansas–Oklahoma A and M game. We had some other bets going, but this was the big one, a triple bet. And it turned out to be a triple loser, a hundred thousand dollars' worth. I was sick. This was my top bet, and we'd blown it. That night, when Ray came back to the hotel room, he knew the result. "Now, look," he said, "I know how you feel about it, but don't worry. I got plenty of money. I can carry you if you need it. But most of all, I believe in you." Knute Rockne or Vince Lombardi never gave a better pep talk as far as I'm concerned. The next week I had a big winner, and the rest of the season it kept on like that, collecting all the way.

Then Ryan introduced me over the phone to H.L. Hunt in Dallas.

The old fellow was already a legend. When *Life* magazine finally got a photo of him, using a telescopic lens as he was crossing a downtown street, it was so impressed with itself it ran the thing full page. When J. Paul Getty was asked if he or Howard Hughes was the richest individual in the world, Getty said, "In terms of personal wealth, there is only one—H.L. Hunt in Texas."

The stories about him soon became clichés—how he always brought his lunch to the office in a brown paper sack, that he drove an old Ford which he parked blocks away to save the parking fee. All true, but clichés nevertheless. I would call H.L. once a week, on Saturday mornings, and after a few weeks we talked of other things besides football. He told me that he had won his first big stake in the oil business playing poker, taking a man's lease with three queens over two pair. He said he had quit smoking when he worked it out that just taking the wrappers off cigars had cost him $380,000 over the years—that's how valuable his time was.

H.L. loved to bet on games in the Southwest Conference, and my expertise was concentrated on the Southeastern Conference. We would bet fifty thousand dollars a game, head to head, with no eleven-to-ten either way. His accountants would settle up, sending a check to Ryan's office as if it were another expense of the oil business. Or Ryan would send a check to him, which was seldom. H.L. would call Bookie Shaeffer's joint in Chicago and get the line on the games. He would pick three games against the line, giving or taking points, and I would take three the same way.

One Saturday well into the first season, H.L. said, "Young man, I think we should delete the Southeastern Conference."

"Well, sir," I said, "that's your prerogative, but if we delete the Southeastern Conference, I think we should delete another conference of my choice."

"That would be fair," he said.

"All right, then we'll delete the Southwest Conference."

There was a bit of a pause, while H.L. realized he would never be able to bet on SMU again, and he said, "No, we'll let it go as it is."

As usual, Ryan and I tried to use any edge we could get. Ryan gave me the name of a secretary in Hunt's office to call late in the week. The old man had a habit of jotting down his favorite team on a note pad at his desk, and by his top choice he would put a star or two. The secretary could tell me who he liked as a best bet. I would have Ray bet twenty thousand dollars on the team with Bookie Shaeffer, so when Hunt got the line on Saturday, his top choices would be a half point less (or more). At other times, when H.L. picked a team I thought was right, I would get Ray to lay off the whole fifty thousand dollars.

After two seasons we had hit him for six hundred thousand dollars, of which two hundred thousand was mine, per my agreement with Ryan. By then I had other interests, and H.L. didn't seem reluctant to call the arrangement off.

For one thing, that wasn't a good year, 1951, to be using the telephone, as the Kefauver hearings would soon establish. But I didn't forget my old friend, H.L. Hunt, or his unlisted number. Our next contact was in 1957, after I had tapped out in oil and gone to the holy land, Las Vegas, to repent.

I became close friends with Bernie Einstosh, who owned the Horseshoe Club in Reno, and together we got it back on with the old man. That was to be the last year Hunt would ever gamble, and he would quit while owing Einstosh and me $140,000, half of it mine. He never paid it.

But there was a reason, very much in character for this hard-bargaining old mule-skinner. Hunt told anyone he owed to go to Johnny Drew and collect it. Drew was a colorful guy, a bookmaker who moved between Vegas and Chicago, said to be chummy with some of the Capone mob. He was fined once for running a crooked dice game at an Elks convention.

H.L. had lost a lot of money to Drew and paid him. But, then, all of a sudden, Hunt went on a hot streak and won, I heard, close to a million. And Drew stiffed him. So when he told Bernie and me and others to see Johnny, it was his way of putting on the pressure in hope of collecting what was due him.

I wanted no part of that. But I only called back once, in 1962, when the Justice Department cleaned me out and Tina, my daughter, was deathly ill. I asked H.L. to pay the 70 grand he owed me.

"I hear Johnny Drew is still alive," he said, "why don't you get it off him?"

I said, "H.L., you know Johnny isn't going to pay me."

"Well, Jimmy, you know I've always fulfilled my obligations. But I got screwed by Drew and I'm just not going to pay."

"In a way," I said, "I can't blame you. But it really isn't fair to put your problems on me. If someone didn't pay me, and I laid off some of your bets, I'd still be responsible to you."

"I'll think about it."

"I wouldn't call you," I said, "if I didn't need it."

"Yes, I realize that."

The conversation ended pleasantly, but I never collected and I never brought it up again. Hunt quit cold. When Drew welched on him he never gambled again, with anyone, on anything. And H.L. *loved* to bet. That was his weakness, sports and politics. Sometimes we'd talk half an hour on the phone, five minutes about the teams we were betting and the rest on politics.

He was a man of unshakeable convictions, but they were not always consistent. He tried to persuade General Douglas MacArthur to accept the Republican nomination in 1952, though he considered himself a Democrat. He didn't like Ike, contributed a ton of money to the cause of Senator Joseph McCarthy, loved Barry Goldwater, but voted for John Kennedy against Nixon in 1960. "Nobody," he said, "can convince me that old Joe Kennedy's boy is a liberal."

I no longer remember the name of the hotel, or even which city it was, but I once saw him in the hallway, on his knees, slipping right-wing literature under the doors of the guest rooms.

Johnny Drew and H.L. Hunt both died in 1974, about six months apart, Drew first of a heart attack. Hunt was 85. I surely could have used that money, but I understood how he felt, and my memories of him are friendly.

The last time I saw H.L. was years after he stopped gambling. In 1970, a nutty outfit called the Bonehead Club in Dallas gave his son, Lamar, an award for his role in the pro football merger. The terms of the merger had included an eighteen-million-dollar indemnity by the AFL, a payoff that seemed even more ironic after Lamar's Kansas City Chiefs won the Super Bowl that year, the last one between the disunited leagues. As the previous winner of the Bonehead award— for making the Colts a seventeen-point favorite over the Jets the year before—I had the honor of introducing my successor.

Lamar and his father were both seated at the head table. H.L. was over eighty, a tall, disheveled figure in a suit two sizes too big for him, a wisp of white hair circling his head like a halo. Lamar said, "Dad, you remember Jimmy the Greek, don't you?"

The old man studied me. "Jimmy the Greek," he repeated. "Yes, I know you. You were strong on the Southeastern Conference."

I had started courting Joannie in 1949, making trips to see her at school in Terre Haute, and meanwhile spending a lot of time with Ryan at his home office just a few miles south in Evansville, Indiana. I had accumulated nearly eight hundred thousand dollars over the years, and I wanted to get away from betting altogether—both for Joannie's sake, and for the practical fact that I didn't think her family would approve of the marriage unless I was in a legitimate business.

It was an oddity that my first oil deal had nothing to do with Ryan. Through him I had met a pair of drillers, Bob Tulley and Truman Carter, and they got me to take five-eighths of a well they were sinking on the Otto Chase farm across the river from Evansville, outside Henderson, Kentucky. It hit, too, for a thousand barrels a day, and I thought, "This business is a cinch." Then I learned that it was a "lime" well and the flow dies down quickly. Ryan got all excited when we hit, and he had offered me a flat seven hundred and fifty thousand for my share. I laughed at him, and that was my first mistake in the oil business, certainly not my last.

But then I had to suffer a national embarrassment, along with a lot of other people, because a senator from Tennessee, a fellow famous later on for his coonskin cap, was determined to rid the United States of the evils of gambling.

One afternoon in March 1951, I came home from the racetrack to the big house I had in Miami at 995 Venetian Way. I was doing real good and could afford to have a couple live in and run the house for Vicki and me. Their names were Walters and Katie. This day, when I got out of the car, Walters was outside waiting for me.

"Mr. Snyder," he said, "I heard your name on the radio."

"What about?"

"That thing up in Washington, the hearings."

I realized what he meant. The Kefauver Committee was conducting hearings in an investigation of organized crime in interstate commerce. "They even mentioned the house number," Walters said. He was wide-eyed.

"Don't worry about it," I said. No, let me worry. And I did, plenty. I was having a ball, had plenty of money, a steady income from my coal-stripping company, and I didn't want anything to spoil it. There was always the basic worry about Vicki, that notoriety would endanger my custody of her. Sure enough, the next morning in the Miami *Herald* there was a front-page story, labeled "KEFAUVER HEARINGS—JIMMY THE GREEK CONSULTED COACHES BEFORE MAKING BETS."

What had happened was that several years earlier, before I closed my Steubenville office, I had bet with a guy in Milwaukee named Sydney Brodson. (It wasn't until the Kefauver hearings that I knew his first name was Sydney. Everyone knew him as "Shoebox" Brodson—because he had once shown up at a bookmaker's carrying his figures in a shoebox.) I hadn't talked to him since then, until the previous football season, when he called me at home one night.

"How'd you get my number?" was the first thing I wanted to know. It turned out a guy from Miami ran into Shoebox at the Chicago Airport and they had nothing better to do than exchange the Greek's home phone number. At the time I had no contact with gamblers. Even before, when I was doing business with them, my social life was kept separate. When I entertained, one night I would have gamblers, another night all the young crowd. The third time I would have politicians and older people. I was part of all three groups, but I never mixed them socially.

Shoebox was calling because he wanted to know how the weather was. Miami was opening its schedule against Georgetown. "It's sprinkling," I said.

"I thought you might be doing something on the game," he said. "There's a lot of talk up here that it's pouring down rain down there. Miami's the big favorite and everyone's taking the points."

"I don't like anybody," I said. I just wasn't interested in the game at all. My interest now was the oil business.

They must have checked Shoebox's telephone calls, because here he was before the Kefauver Committee telling the world about Jimmy Snyder. As follows:

MR. DOWNEY RICE, associate counsel for the committee: Directing your attention to a man by the name of Snyder down in Miami, will you tell us how you met him and who he is; James Snyder?
BRODSON: Yes. I first knew Mr. Snyder, in the form of an O.K.
RICE: You got an O.K. on him?

BRODSON: Yes, and I assume he must've gotten an O.K. on me or he
would not have done business with me.

RICE: You did not meet him formally?

BRODSON: I did not. In fact, I never met him for a period of— I was
doing business with him over a period of four or five years, and
never had occasion to meet him until last year.

RICE: And you met him down in Miami when you were there?

BRODSON: Yes, when I was there for a vacation.

RICE: Now, sir; is Snyder from Steubenville, Ohio?

BRODSON: I believe so.

RICE: What type of business do you do with him; the same thing?

BRODSON: No. Snyder is no longer in business.

RICE: He is no longer in business?

BRODSON: No.

RICE: Well, when you were doing business with him, was it the same
type of business?

BRODSON: Yes.

RICE: Football?

BRODSON: Basketball.

RICE: Football and basketball?

BRODSON: Primarily.

RICE: And you bet back and forth with Snyder?

BRODSON: Yes.

RICE: Did you do anything else with him? Was he an information
getter or anything like that?

BRODSON: Yes.

RICE: Tell us about that.

BRODSON: Well, Jimmy had an opinion which was very, very well
respected.

RICE: On what?

BRODSON: On basketball and football games.

RICE: Yes.

BRODSON: And when you say you respect a man, the man comes
up with many more winners than he does losers, and that is
what makes him good. In this business if you come up with winners you are a hero, and if you come up with losers you are
a bum; and that is the sole distinction. Jimmy was known to

have—to come up with more winners than losers, and consequently—

RICE: Did it come to your attention that possibly the reason he came
up with more winners was because he knew a few coaches?

BRODSON: No, it didn't come to my attention.

RICE: Do you know that?

BRODSON: I don't know why Jimmy came up with more winners than
losers. He had his sources of information which I never inquired
into.

RICE: Did you call him from time to time and discuss the situation
with respect to certain teams before making a bet for purposes
of research, shall we say?

BRODSON: Yes.

RICE: And you considered him an expert along those lines, and had a
good source of information to tell you the condition of the
teams, the players and the chances?

BRODSON: Jimmy might— I don't know what his sources of
information might be. He might have known coaches whom he
spoke with.

RICE: As a matter of fact, he told you sometimes he was in touch
with some coaches, did he not?

BRODSON: Yes, but lots of people tell you they are in touch with
coaches, who are not actually in touch with them.

RICE: I did not hear your answer.

BRODSON: I say a lot of people tell you, and they are not.

RICE: Did he tell you that?

BRODSON: I believe he may have mentioned that; yes, sir.

RICE: All right, sir.

BRODSON: I don't believe— Jimmy may have conceivably known
coaches on a social basis; I don't think there was ever any
question that coaches or anybody else were making the results
go in conformity with Jimmy's desires.

RICE: We understand that.

BRODSON: He might have conceivably known a coach who might
have told him that his team was not in good shape; that it had
looked bad in practice all week.

RICE: More or less through inadvertence, not knowing that Jimmy—

BRODSON: Not knowing that Jimmy was using it for gambling. He might have told him strictly on a friendly basis.

RICE: Yes.

ESTES KEFAUVER: Mr. Rice, in that connection, I think I feel that some improper inference might go out—what you are talking about is not with respect to any coaches.

BRODSON: I am not talking about the veracity of any coaches.

KEFAUVER: Just a minute. That any coaches would be selling out to him, but he would worm his way in and try to find out information about how the coaches felt, how the players felt, whether they had any casualties, or that some players were laid up.

BRODSON: Yes.

KEFAUVER: And whether they thought they had a good chance of winning.

BRODSON: Which, so far as I know, is a perfectly bona fide and legitimate inquiry.

KEFAUVER: And in the case of this fellow, Snyder, he was posing as being an oilman of some sort.

BRODSON: That I don't know.

RICE: You say he got out of the business. What happened to him?

BRODSON: Pardon me?

RICE: You say he got out of business. What happened to him?

BRODSON: What happened to him? Well, Jimmy, I believe, had been very successful and had accumulated a relatively large sum of money as a result of his endeavors, and that I know only by hearsay.

RICE: Yes.

BRODSON: I believe he had some marital trouble, and there was a question arose as to the custody of the child, and I believe when the question about the custody of the child arose, it was—

RICE: Let us not go into that. He is out of business?

BRODSON: Yes.

RICE: How long would you say he has been out of business?

BRODSON: About three years, I would estimate.

SENATOR ALEXANDER WILEY (WISCONSIN): Mr. Chairman, I do not want to divert from that, but I do think that the particular idea that you brought out in your question might be well amplified in view of this man's large experience. Do you want to give it, as your judgment that, by and large, the basketball coaches and the players of this country are not selling out; that [there is] only the occasional sellout?

BRODSON: I would say to the best of my knowledge no coach has ever sold out. I have never even heard of it in the grapevine that a coach has sold out. I heard in the grapevine that a coach might occasionally be conceivably betting on his own team to win. I have never heard of a coach betting against his own team.

SENATOR WILEY: That is the grapevine. But let us get it straight so that everyone else doesn't get the idea that all colleges and all the players of this country have gone to hell.

BRODSON: They haven't; believe me, they haven't.

SENATOR WILEY: No.

BRODSON: They are in the very small minority.

RICE: Getting back to Miami, with respect to telephone Nos. 82-5543 and 82-5544, listed to James Snyder, 995 North Venetian Way Drive, Miami, Florida, did you ever discuss with him conversations that he might have had with professional football players?

BRODSON: You go back to James Snyder? I missed the beginning of your question.

RICE: Incidentally, do you bet professional football games?

BRODSON: Occasionally; yes.

RICE: Did you ever discuss with him conversations with professional football players he might have had?

BRODSON: No; he did not discuss any conversations he had. He had convictions on certain professional football games, but I can't say he got them on the basis—

RICE: Did he indicate to you that he was in touch with certain professional football players?

BRODSON: I don't think he did.

RICE: Would you say that he did not?

BRODSON: What I mean by that is I can't remember any particular players that he may or may not have been in touch with. He might have intimated that he got his information from somebody, but as for mentioning any specific player or any specific team, I can't say that he did.

RICE: It would not surprise you then if he was in touch with certain professional football players; is that not right?

BRODSON: I can't say it would surprise me; no.

RICE: Did he ever tell you—

BRODSON: But, on the other hand, numbers of people are.

RICE: Did he ever tell you he was from Steubenville?

BRODSON: Yes; that is right.

RICE: Who put an O.K. on Snyder down there in Miami?

BRODSON: Who put an O.K. on Snyder in Miami?

RICE: Yes.

BRODSON: Well, my first contact with Mr. Snyder was in Steubenville.

RICE: You started doing business with him when he was in Steubenville?

BRODSON: Yes.

RICE: He was O.K.'d by whom in Steubenville?

BRODSON: Nobody actually O.K.'d him. What happened was when I first got started in this business, I didn't have an office, and I used to go down to Chicago, and I knew he did business with a couple of reputable houses in Chicago, and was found to be of good reputation, and they were satisfied, and I was satisfied that if they were satisfied I would be satisfied.

RICE: Who were these reputable houses in Chicago?

BRODSON: Well, there are several recognized houses in Chicago.

RICE: For instance?

BRODSON: I would have to say—you mentioned the name Clark.

All of this came out only a few weeks after the disclosure by the New York district attorney's office of fixed games in college basketball. Brodson's testimony that I was friendly with many college football coaches made it appear I might be a master fixer. I learned later that the Kefauver Committee had a list of my phone calls a few months earlier when I was talking to more than a dozen coaches and a few players around the time of the Clemson–Miami Orange Bowl game and the North–South game.

Senator Charles Tobey of New Hampshire wanted to subpoena me, but Estes Kefauver talked him out of it. Kefauver had had me checked and found no arrests. The way I understand it, Kefauver told Wiley, "If Snyder had talked to one coach, well . . . but he talked to a dozen, all of them famous men. Nobody would believe all these men were involved in anything wrong."

The coaches I had talked to during that period were Bud Wilkinson, Paul Bryant, Ray Graves, Wally Butts, Andy Gustafson, Jim Tatum, General Bob Neyland, and Red Sanders. I had invited them to the party I gave each year the week of the game, which fell on Christmas night. But, casually, out of the usual cocktail conversation that develops at such socials, came a 150,000-dollar bet on Kentucky against Oklahoma in the Sugar Bowl. Kentucky was the underdog, but Bob Gain was on that team and I liked them, 50,000 dollars' worth. Some comment by Wilkinson—something beyond the usual expression of coaching gloom—prompted me to press my bet for another 100,000 dollars. Kentucky won the game, 13–7. I figured Bear Bryant owed me that one—I had lost 250,000 dollars betting on his team against Santa Clara in the Orange Bowl the year before.

But, the point is, none of these coaches knew I gambled. And the end or even the middle of a season was never the best time to talk with them. The time to get what I considered *hard* information was before the coach opened the season. I liked to gauge his own mental attitude—what coach he was mad at, what team he wanted to beat most—because he would instill this in his players.

Several months after the long Kefauver hearings had come to an end, I was staying in a penthouse apartment in New York, two doors from the Gotham Hotel, where I would go to buy newspapers. One evening I strolled over there in my slippers to get the early editions when this Lincolnesque man approached me. "How do you do?" he said. "I'm Estes Kefauver. I'm running for the vice-presidency."

"I'm Jimmy the Greek Snyder," I said. "You mentioned me in your hearings last year."

"I remember the name," he said. "You were the gambler. What are you doing now?"

"Same as I was doing then. I'm in the oil business."

"You were the fellow who knew all the coaches. Did you really know them?"

"Yes, sir. I knew them as casual acquaintances."

"That really impressed me," Kefauver said, "that anybody could know so many coaches and great players."

"That was my business," I said. "And when I quit gambling, we remained friends."

I would soon need all the friends I could get. I was taking a piece of Ray Ryan's oil action here and there, never anything more than a fraction, but I was doing a lot else on my own—like drilling twenty-one straight dry wells. The twenty-second try was a lulu—I hit oil!

This was in the Denver-Julesberg basin in Colorado near Fort Collins, where I had 160 acres. Earlier I had almost gotten into a deal with Bud Robineau of Frontier Oil on a refinery in Florida. It fell through. Now Robineau called me about the Colorado strike.

"Jimmy," he said, "let's make a deal."

"What kind of deal?"

"You can't lose. We'll give you everything you've invested in the well so far, plus a twenty-five-thousand-dollar profit. Then we'll take it over, drill it, and you'll get twenty-five percent of it."

"No, sirree," I said, "this baby is all mine. This time Jimmy the Greek is getting on a pipeline."

I had smelled the oil that saturated the coring. I had rubbed my fingers in it. The gas pressure was high. This *had* to be a winner or why would Robineau have offered me anything? Now I had to raise the drilling money myself.

Joannie was out in Colorado with me. One morning I got up early and took her big diamond engagement ring and a diamond bracelet out of her jewel box. I borrowed short on them. I called Steubenville and got George to mortgage his house for me—that good old house I had broken Slim Neal to get. That meant ten thousand dollars more. I got the rest off my Uncle Anthony in Baltimore.

It reminded me of the time Ryan told me about a deal of his: "We went to Louisiana, got some money, and bought some leases—"

And I said, "Wait a minute. Where did you get the money to buy the leases?"

Ryan gave me a puzzled look. "Where?"

"Yeah, where did you get the money? Did you win it, have it, or borrow it?"

"Listen," Ryan said, "for an oil deal you get money wherever you can. Your mother, your brother, your maiden aunt. Your friends, your enemies. But you get the money."

Now I knew what he meant.

In a few days I had raised thirty-seven thousand dollars, enough to drill the well. We found oil, all right, but we had drilled into what is known as "a low." There was oil there, but there was also enough water to make it worthless. It kept coming up that way, oil diluted with water, at a thousand dollars a day for equipment and manpower.

"What can we do about it?" I asked my foreman.

"There's nothing we can do," he said. "We can't shut the water out of it."

"Then plug the goddamn thing!" I said.

That was it. My eight hundred thousand dollars was gone. I decided I had been gambling the past few years at another man's game. Now I could only go back to mine. You couldn't make odds on Mother Nature.

CHAPTER
8

The Dance Is Over

In 1956, at age thirty-seven, I added up my assets. There was no bank account, except for a little walking-around money. I decided the only real bankable commodity I had was my lifelong knowledge of sports and the manipulation of odds and point spreads. Federal laws and the intense publicity pressure resulting from the Kefauver hearings had made gambling a bad risk throughout the country— except the one place where it was legal, the state of Nevada. I would take my assets and go there.

"I have to go back to gambling," I told Joannie.

"Why do you *have* to?" she said.

"Well, you want to eat, don't you?" She said she didn't know if she could live with the uncertainty of that kind of life. I asked her to give me "a couple of years," and I'd send for her. That's what we finally agreed, though by a "couple" I had in mind four or five.

Vegas in the fifties was a small town, maybe 40,000 people. The Desert Inn was then the glamour spot, the big hotel. The Stardust, Caesar's Palace, the Frontier had yet to be built, but the place already had all the glitter and excitement of a fantasy land. That's

the key word for Vegas. Excitement. Then and now. Flashing neon in
the middle of a sandpile. A flame in the desert that drew moths. And
Vegas has always had the appeal of a faraway place. You have to
drive a long way through a lot of nothing to get there. Or else you
drop in out of the sky, out of an Arabian night. When a gambler gets
to Vegas he says to himself, "King's X, they can't get me now. I'm
going to bet my money *legal.*"

I understood the appeal of the place, but it never touched me
quite that way. The longest I had ever stayed in Vegas was three
weeks, with Ray Ryan in 1948. What grabbed me then was what
grabbed me now. This was the one town where a dozen or so guys
had concentrated, guys who would match wits and money with you.
I had seen that green felt jungle all my life, the tables and the wheels
and the blackjack layouts, and by now I no longer saw it. They say
there is no cure for a dice bite. But any type of gambling where you
can take a piece of paper and figure the percentage *against* you, that
turned me cold.

A casino was just something I had to walk through to find the
action I wanted. They always built the damned things so you had to
go past the tables to reach the coffee shop or the bar, and that's
where my people would be sitting, hanging around. For seven years
this was almost a nightly ritual with me, a tour of the big casinos on
the Strip. In those days, before the corporate setups took over, every
hotel was owned by 10 or 15 or maybe 20 stockholders, and all of
them were players. They *gambled.*

There is a feeling you get, once inside a Vegas casino going at full
blast, that is guaranteed to make your adrenalin pump. I could stand
at the top of the stairs and hear the jungle sounds rising, the chirp of
the croupiers, the clicking of chips in nervous hands, the jingle and
cough and clatter of coins spilling from the one-armed bandits, even
as I checked out the room. But the tables? They were laid out like a
minefield, and I walked right around them.

I have seen people transformed by that music, as though they had
walked through a veil. It is contagious. In their hearts, everyone is a
high roller. The bellmen bet on which way an elevator is going. A
housewife who once could have been pacified with a book of trading
stamps will break your arm if you so much as approach the nickel slot

machine she is saving, after she finishes this one. A Las Vegas judge, Myron Leavitt, once performed a wedding ceremony in front of the keno booth at the Horseshoe, because the happy couple was in a lucky streak and didn't want to leave. Most of the players on the floor paid no attention.

Vegas has always gloried in its reputation as a city of sin, gin and din. But the late fifties were a kind of heyday, at least in my book. From Monday to Thursday the town belonged to us, the professionals. The public, riding the free junkets, came in on the weekends. Almost any big bettor who blew in from anywhere in the country, the floor men and the pit bosses knew seventy-five percent of them by name. Until about 1961 it was a world of its own.

Then the computers and the business people began taking over, and it got bigger and bigger. The casino hotels became attuned to the masses, instead of the elite, and for me the place lost something. Some romance, some intimacy, some excitement. The high player stopped coming, and the slot machines were lined row on row. At first, in the times I liked best, the bigger casino hotels wouldn't deign to have slots because they felt it detracted from the atmosphere. They were right.

Today most of the major hotels are owned by public companies: Del Webb, Hilton, Caesar's World, Howard Johnson, MGM. You can buy their stock in the market. Yet I am still asked, will always be asked, I guess, if organized crime controls Las Vegas. All I know is that Howard Hughes bought out a lot of people who had been around for years. I can't say if they had mob connections or not. Some were reputed to have.

But the gamblers who helped build Las Vegas are gone. Some died off, some got rich and semi-respectable, others grew old and complacent and sold out. The newspapers and magazines kept alive the mob image. In an ironic way it was good for business. When I was handling PR for Caesar's, whenever reservations slowed down we'd send out another note or news release denying the Mafia rumors, and the hotel would fill up in three days.

There are more myths about Las Vegas than there are about the Bermuda Triangle. One has to do with a thousand-dollar-a-night hooker known as The Princess. Let me tell you how that one started.

As a PR gimmick at Caesar's, I instituted a code name for the cigarette girls, and whenever one was paged it was always as Princess Fatima. *"Telephone call for Princess Fatima."* You can't believe how the stories spread. I have heard sober, intelligent, Midwestern American businessmen, or their wives, describe how they happened to walk past her suite, and saw her sitting there in all her bejeweled splendor, entertaining her suitors. They still page Princess Fatima when they want the cigarette girl. And that's good for business, too. The Princess *always* stays at Caesar's.

Hookers are part of the mystique of Las Vegas, but it isn't the industry some people seem to think. The most beautiful girls in the world come there, are taken for hookers and, in many cases, do enjoy a kind of temporary visa. Any schoolteacher, secretary, airline hostess or model who wants to supplement her income can come to Vegas for a weekend and score. And they do come, from throughout the U.S., straight chicks and housewives who turn pro from Friday to Sunday.

They can't miss, these fresh young things from Utah, Texas, Nebraska and thereabouts. They may earn five hundred dollars, a thousand or fifteen hundred, depending on how pretty or cute they are, who they run into and how his luck runs at the tables. A few have scored big, up to ten or fifteen grand, because the guy they were with got hot at the crap table and shared the winnings with his lucky piece, no pun intended. It has happened at Caesar's and the Dunes. Any pit boss in town can give you a story like it.

And isn't that supposed to be one of the great female fantasies? To be a whore for a weekend, or a day, or an hour?

In Vegas even the hookers tend to look like ingenues. They are in demand, because gambling is a very sensual sport, and a fellow can grow very attached to his lady of the night. A friend of mine from Salt Lake City used to come down every year; he loved to play, and the price was twenty-five dollars the first time he lined up Yvette. The next trip to town the price was fifty dollars, and a year later it was seventy-five dollars. Two years passed before he happened to call again, and this time she told him her rate had gone to one hundred and fifty dollars. "Goddamn," he bellowed, "you just priced me out. Inflation got to you, too, huh?"

As I say, all of this happened later, but Vegas in the fifties was my kind of town. Maybe I would walk through the Riviera to the restaurant and find one of the owners, Gus Greenbaum, a guy who had to challenge you. He would like Johnny Saxton over Basilio in a title fight, and I would like Basilio. Or the Dodgers over the Giants. Whatever it was, Gus wanted to get something going.

When I first settled in Vegas I was offered a piece of the action by certain casinos to go with them. I already had that kind of reputation, enough of a "name" within the business. But I wouldn't go with anyone because, for one thing, I didn't want them to know I needed a job. Whenever I was broke I made it a point not to let it show. A friend from my Ohio days owned a big restaurant in town, Luigi's, and I borrowed seven thousand five hundred dollars from him. For the first few weeks I did all my betting downtown, along the Gulch, because Niggy Devine had a place down there and I could get credit. Niggy had owned a gambling spot in Cincinnati when I was operating out of Steubenville. But from the start, I moved into a place right on the Strip, the El Rancho, and lived there for the next two years.

One of the first fellows I ran into in Vegas was the owner of a small gambling club who knew my reputation for setting up betting propositions that would attract business. He was a big, heavyset guy with a dynamic personality, and he was quite a ladies' man. One of the Gabor sisters said, "I never knew what it was to be a woman until I spent a night in his arms." Even considering the talents for exaggeration in the Gabor family, this was a high rating. I'll call him Frank Crandall. I don't want to use his name—because he turned out to be a crummy, lying, crooked, dangerous shit-heel, the grand champion of all the bad numbers I'd ever known. That is, he stole my money and then tried to get me maimed when I complained about it.

But in my first days in Vegas I needed a place to drop anchor, and Crandall kept begging me to "come in" with him. "Make book out of my club, Greek," he said. "I'll back your play and whatever you win we'll split even."

This happened to be the week of the Tournament of Champions at the Desert Inn, and all anybody could talk about was golf. I didn't know a damn thing about the pro golf tour, but I wondered if there wasn't some new way to bet on it. I spent a day or two looking at it from every angle; then I came up with a fresh one. I grouped the players according to their Vardon Trophy scores, their strokes per round through the season, and I made it six-to-five so you could back one guy against any other guy in that group. I put Billy Casper, Gary Player, and Arnold Palmer in one group, for instance. They were all shooting 70.8, so it was even money whoever you took.

I agreed to book these bets out of Crandall's club. It was a big success, and it went like I figured. I made 26,000 dollars, which is just what I should have made, because I handled about 220,000 dollars all together.

I went over to Crandall and said, "You got thirteen and I got thirteen."

He said, "Keep it. Stick around, move in. *We* can keep it going."

So I did, and, picking my propositions carefully over the next six months, I built up 480,000 dollars, which I left in the cashier's cage at Crandall's club. Any time I needed money for a bet, I went to the cage and got what I wanted.

That summer in 1957, Sugar Ray Robinson was coming up to a rematch with Gene Fullmer in Chicago for the middleweight title. Fullmer had won a fifteen-round decision in January and now he was a five-to-two favorite, but I really liked Robinson to win and I bet ten thousand dollars that way. I was out of town for a few days before and after the fight, which Robinson won with a perfect left hook in the fifth round.

When I came back to Vegas I picked up the twenty-five thousand dollars from my bet and took it to the cage. I noted that my "draw" was down to four hundred thousand dollars. When I asked about it, the guy in the cage said, "Crandall drew eighty thousand dollars."

I went over and asked Crandall what that was all about. He just waved a hand at me. "Aw, Jimmy," he said, "after you left I got a call from Gil Beckley in Chicago. He was there for the fight and he said he had good information on Fullmer. So I bet the eighty thousand dollars for us."

"But you knew I liked the black," I said.

"Yeah," he said, "I know, but Gil was so sure he had the straight information, I figured I would cover for you."

"Where'd you place the bet?"

"Oh, Gil placed it."

"Oh."

In the next few months the money in the cage went down to 126,000 dollars, which means my half was 63,000 dollars. When I wanted to make a good bet on TCU, the cashier told me there was no draw left.

Crandall was sitting at his usual table near the bar. I said, "Frank, there is a misunderstanding in the cage. I want to draw sixty thousand dollars to make a bet."

"Don't bother me with that penny-ante crap," he said. "I've got troubles. I've got to pay a guy two hundred thousand dollars."

"What's that got to do with me?" I said. "There's sixty-three thousand dollars of my money in that cage." The Greek's temper started to go, and I said a few other things, too.

Crandall said, "Greek, you got sixty seconds to get out of here, or I'll have you thrown out." Then he looked over his shoulder and for the first time noticed an empty wall. "Ralph," he shouted. "Where the hell is Ralph?"

Ralph Lamb, and the rest of his "security" people had conveniently disappeared. Lamb knew I was getting screwed and wanted no part of it. He was later elected sheriff, an office he still holds.

I said, "You know something, Frank? You'd make a maggot gag." I left.

The rhubarb with Crandall was all over town in a few hours, which is the way stories fly in Vegas. Then it got back to me that Crandall was saying *I* was the one who had blown the money. This figured, too, along the line that the best defense is a good offense. But even his credit manager, Johnny Dunn, knew better.

A year after all this went on, I was in the Horseshoe Club downtown and ran into an old hustler I knew named Natie. He was an old second-story man gone straight. I trusted him, on the theory that there was no one more reliable than a reformed thief. I used him as a courier on out-of-town bets. From time to time, friends of his would be in jail, and I would lend him the money to bail them out. This night he was at the bar with two other people.

"Greek," he said, "I want you to meet a couple of friends of mine from L.A."

I shook hands all around. Natie had the dignified look of a banker. The two strangers looked like longshoremen.

"They made the trip especially to meet you," he said.

"What for?"

"They came to town," Natie said, *"to break your legs."* The two guys laughed, but Natie wasn't laughing. "Your old partner sent for them, but when they got in they called me, wanting to know who is Jimmy the Greek? I told them who Jimmy the Greek is, and what I want them to do is go break the legs of the guy that sent for them."

"What?"

"That is, if it's okay with you."

The two guys were looking at me, expectantly. I felt like I had them on a leash and all I had to do was let go. "No, no," I said, "forget it. I couldn't live with that. But thanks anyway. It's only money."

Nobody ever did anything to Crandall, and in his heyday he stiffed guys you would be afraid to be in the same room with. Vegas was his sanctuary. Nobody wanted to make any violent trouble in Vegas.

In fact, it is everyone's sanctuary. It remains a matter of record that people connected with gambling do not meet violent deaths in Las Vegas. They might meet them down the road a ways, such as in Phoenix, where poor Gus Greenbaum and his wife were found with their throats cut, ear to ear, or in Los Angeles, where Bugsy Siegel was gunned down.

But not in Las Vegas. No gambler, no mobster, no so-called *bad guy* has ever gotten himself killed or dismembered there. It is a kind of unwritten law. This is the last place, the last haven, a modern equivalent of Butch Cassidy's Hole-in-the-Wall, and no one wants to risk ruining it. If they blew Las Vegas, what's left? Gamblers have been chased out of England and Puerto Rico. Where can they go? Mexico?

Besides, there were more subtle ways of putting someone out of circulation. I had my own experience with that.

My place at El Rancho Vegas was a private cottage on the

grounds. One night, in the small hours, the screen door on my porch went bang, followed by a knock, and I heard a girl's voice call, "Jimmy?" I opened the door only a crack, and a broad I had never seen before was standing there.

Before I could ask what she wanted—I thought I knew—she started screaming, then she ran off the porch, tearing at her clothes. I just stood there for a minute or two, stunned. Then I sat on the bed and puffed a cigarette. Half an hour later the phone rang. The police. It seems they have a girl at the station who claims I raped her, and she is prepared to sign a warrant for my arrest.

I dressed and went downtown, crowding the speed limit. I knew both of the cops handling the complaint. The broad was in the next room. "This is a lot of bullshit," I roared.

"Yeah, Jimmy, we know," one of them said, "but what can we do? We have to take the warrant."

This was one of the times in my life that I let my pure Greek temper all hang out. I started yelling that I was going to sue everybody in sight for false arrest. And then I said they could damned well make her submit to a medical exam. I demanded it. I screamed it. It was the only thing I could think of.

I was in luck. In what was surely one of the rare occasions in this chippie's adult life, she came up clean. There were no traces of recent sexual intercourse. She was irate and insulted—she thought they were testing her for the clap.

So the case was dropped, and I went back to the El Rancho to get what sleep I could. The whole thing, the question of who tried to set me up, was no mystery. I thought at the time I didn't have an enemy in the world. But I sure had one helluva ex-partner.

Eventually, I was able to get into business for myself, with the Vegas Turf and Sports Club. Joannie's brother, George Specht, came in as a fifteen percent partner and licensee. The club was downtown, a couple of miles from the hotels on the Strip, and before long we were doing eighty-five percent of the bookmaking business on sports and horses.

We were selling my odds nationally to people at twenty-five dollars a week, and we would make a one-dollar service charge for every follow-up phone call they made. In the first few weeks we had 161 people buying the odds and phoning the office.

Then the federal law was enacted forbidding interstate transmission of gambling information for purposes of betting. It didn't stop us. For one thing, we didn't know if it was being enforced anywhere. For another, thought that because we were home-based in a state where gambling was legal it might not apply. That was naïve—even dumb—but when you have been doing something routinely for almost thirty years, it's hard to get it in your head overnight that it's illegal.

At this time I was getting calls from a Salt Lake City mortgage banker named Jimmy Dunn, who liked to play. "Utah goes against Utah State tomorrow," he said one night. "What price do you think it will be?"

"Utah is the home team," I said. "It should be about four, Utah. That's how it looks to me."

A month later there was a grand jury investigation in Salt Lake City about gambling. They had subpoenaed some of the businessmen there to find out what was going on. Somehow the question came up about how they got their odds and Dunn answered very innocently that everybody got the odds from Jimmy the Greek in Las Vegas. Like, who else would they get them from?

Suddenly, the whole grand jury investigation was forgotten. The target now was Jimmy the Greek, as I discovered that Friday night when I was home and the phone rang.

"Jimmy," one of my men at the Vegas Turf and Sports Club said, "you better get down here. The FBI is here."

I didn't bother to finish dinner. Two agents were waiting for me. "We want to see your books," one of them said.

"Be my guest," I said. "I've got nothing to hide. I'm paying ten thousand dollars a month in taxes to you people."

They were looking for the *black book*, the one with the names of the big bettors. They never found it.

In four months I was out of business. The money I had put aside—I soon discovered I needed it all and more for attorney fees. That's when I found out who my real friends were, guys like Eddie

Levinson and Paul Wyerman, two of the owners of the Fremont
Hotel, who came up with seventy-five thousand dollars in cash in the
middle of the night so I could post bond. There were others, like
Irving Devine, who owned the New York Meat Company, Sid
Wyman, and Milt Jaffe. Jaffe is one of the executives of the Stardust
Hotel, but thirty years ago I had known him around Pittsburgh when
he had part of the Bachelors Club and was managing Billy Conn, the
boxer. Wyman is one of the owners of the Dunes. They lent me
thousands of dollars without me even asking for it. No collateral, no
interest, and no time limit. "You must need it," I remember Jaffe
said. "Pay it back when you get it."

I was under federal indictment in Salt Lake City, and my attorney
was hoping for a change in venue. Salt Lake City is a Mormon town,
and the Mormons frown on gambling, among a lot of other things.
We requested the trial be moved, preferably to Nevada, but failing
that at least to any state that had a racetrack or some understanding
of gambling. The federal judge in Utah denied the motion. This was
at a time when Joe Valachi was telling the FBI about hidden mob
interests in Las Vegas, and I was in the headlines elsewhere on the
same front page. It made me look like I was one of the characters,
too. I heard later that the Justice Department had moved in on me
because they thought—with me handling so much money at my club,
two million a week—I had to have some Mafia connections.

Of course, I had about the same Mafia connections as the
Reverend Billy Graham. But you couldn't prove that in Utah. I also
had another powerful adversary in the case, U.S. Attorney General
Robert Kennedy. He had sent some of his task-force people to Salt
Lake City to make sure I faced trial there.

"I don't have a chance," I told my attorney.

"We can always appeal it," he said.

"Isn't there anything else we could do?"

"With the judge's permission," he said, "you can plead *nolo
contendere* in Vegas." That's a legal phrase, I discovered, which
admits your case is too weak to contest in court. In effect, a plea for
mercy.

The judge was reluctant to agree. He delayed his ruling on the request, and I suspected Kennedy's influence. Alfred Wright of *Sports Illustrated* wrote in the magazine:

> It's not that Jimmy Snyder could seriously be undermining the moral fibre of the nation, but the Attorney General of the U.S. has had agents by the hundreds sifting through every piece of paper in Las Vegas in his efforts to pin the donkey's tail on Jimmy Hoffa, who has been pouring teamster funds into the area. Snyder was just a minnow that happened to be boated during the Department of Justice's angling expedition.

In early September of 1962, President John F. Kennedy had met with the U.S. Attorneys at the White House to report on the drive against organized crime. In a speech later reported in the papers, he told them: "One Las Vegas gambler is supposed to have said he hoped we'd be as tough on Berlin as we've been on Las Vegas. Well, we intend to be."

The gambler was Jimmy the Greek, as the Justice Department by then already knew, and what I had actually said was: "They lost in Laos, they lost in Cuba, they lost in East Berlin, but they sure are giving the gamblers a beating."

For a fellow whose business taught him to chew his words with care, that may have been the most costly sentence I ever spoke. Most of my government troubles, I have always believed, could be traced to that statement. It appeared in another *Sports Illustrated* story, "The Bookies Close up Shop," by Bob Boyle, in the issue of September 3, 1962.

The guys at *S.I.* were damned near killing me with kindness. They had long been favorites of mine, had given me my first national exposure and quoted me, and my odds, on many major events. Few had heard of Jimmy the Greek until December, 1961, when Gil Rogin wrote a text piece on my career as the last of the oddsmakers, under the title, "The Greek Who Makes the Odds."

Almost from the day the magazine began as Henry Luce's legacy to sports, Bob Boyle had been after me to tell my story. I had resisted, not out of modesty, but on the theory that my life was going to get a lot more interesting in the next few years. It sure as hell did, but not exactly in the way I would have wished. My ambitions did not run to being arrested.

That foreign policy quote, I was told, led to some angry phone calls from the Justice Department to the executive offices at Time-Life. Bobby Kennedy did not have an enemies' list; he had a shit list, and it didn't do to get on it. I learned later, from my friends in the FBI office in Vegas, that Bobby was calling every few weeks, asking, "What's happening with Jimmy the Greek? Have we got anything?"

It wasn't exactly a vendetta. Let's just say that Bobby had a special distaste for me, based on his department's belief that I was a bigger fish, a shadowy guy who got his money from the mob or Hoffa, and his own belief that I had wrongly knocked the Kennedy Administration— And in the worst place, the pages of a sports magazine. If it had been the editorial page of *The New York Times*, no one would have remembered it.

Finally, the judge agreed to accept my plea and toss the minnow back. This was the first and only time in my life I had ever been arrested, much less charged or sentenced. Once again I was busted. I owed six hundred dollars a month on my fine. What was even more important, I felt a compulsion to change my image—and as quickly as possible. I needed some respectability.

I dropped in to see Hank Greenspun, the editor of the *Las Vegas Sun*. "I want to be a columnist for you," I said.

Greenspun acted puzzled. "What are you going to write about?" he said.

"Odds," I said. "Let me present the odds in my column—on football, baseball, the political elections. You name it and you'll have the odds in the *Sun*, in my column."

"You've got a job then," he said. "One column a week for twenty-five dollars."

The money was a joke, but the money wasn't the important thing. I'm still doing the column, and I'm getting much more than twenty-five dollars per column, though I usually do three a week now. The important thing was that it was extremely helpful to me at a pivotal point in my life. I remember Bryan Armstrong, the paper's managing editor, saying to me, "I don't know you, Jimmy, but this is without a doubt one of the smartest moves I've ever seen a man make."

It wasn't a bad move for the *Sun*, either, but it helped me more than it helped the paper. It made me an instant celebrity in Vegas again, a respected member of the community.

For one final and ultimate time, the saga of Jimmy the Greek, Gambler, was at an end.

The story of Jimmy the Greek, oddsmaker to the world, would now begin.

PART II

PEOPLE, POLITICS AND SPORTS

CHAPTER
9

Public Relations:
What Have You Got to Hide

After the Justice Department busted me in 1963, thereby making the country safe for decent folk, I sat down and did some heavy thinking. I began a planned and measured campaign to bury the image of Jimmy the Greek as rococo gambler.

It was a conscious act, one that disputed the habits of a lifetime. For years I had moved in quiet corners, had kept what people now call a low profile. A gambler has little use for exposure *outside* his circle.

I started by making myself available to the news media—my odds, my information, my hospitality. Understand, I was looking for acceptance, not publicity. No call, no request went unattended. In return I asked nothing. I just wanted them to know who, and what, Jimmy the Greek was. In my circumstances, broke again and on probation, I saw only one way to get respectable, and that I took. Making the odds had given me contacts all over the country. Now I would turn that into a new career in public relations.

It wouldn't hurt, I figured, to have the writers and TV people on my side. And I tell you without hesitation, they *made* The Greek.

In 1965 I formed my own PR firm, called Sports Unlimited. A few months before I picked up my first big account, Caesar's Palace, I developed one of my less inspired ideas: The Las Vegas Air Races. At the time it seemed a lively way to promote the city and attract new convention business.

Such races suggested a more romantic time, of barnstormers and scarves and goggles and Chester Morris going down in flames. Actually, most of the contestants were test pilots who flew their own propeller planes, World War II vintage. The show went off beautifully. It was only a financial disaster.

Wilbur Clark, my friend and political betting nemesis, then the owner of the Desert Inn, agreed to back me and posted fifty thousand dollars in prize money. The pylons were erected and the course was laid out over a private field at Boulder City. In late July, with the races less than a month away, Wilbur left for a business trip to Disneyland, where he was planning to build a hotel. I reminded him that I had just enough cash on hand to cover expenses and to meet our payroll through the third of August. "Don't worry," he said. "I'll be back by then."

He was. But in a coffin. The day before the money ran out, Wilbur Clark died of a heart attack in a San Diego hospital. The death of a close and devoted friend made the prospect of a business setback seem trifling. But the combination of the two was unspeakable. I wavered between grief and guilt.

Still, obligations had to be met. I borrowed all the money I could get my hands on. The races were held with all the appropriate pageantry, before grandstands so empty the planes could have landed in them. Great numbers of people had come to town to see the races, but we had overlooked one minor detail. We had forgotten to hire a detachment of armed guards to get them out of the casinos.

Private buses had been arranged to pick up the passengers at each hotel, where hundreds had signed up. But when it came time for the buses to depart, maybe six people got on from the Dunes and ten from Caesar's Palace, and it went that way all over town.

I wound up losing 130,000 dollars. I was busted and back in debt again. But I had made an important discovery. I had learned that you can't compete with that green cloth and the big marquees with all the lights.

In September of 1965 I landed the PR account for Caesar's Palace, one of those Las Vegas luxury hotels that seem to be built with King Farouk in mind. But this was only a month after it opened and the place was a mausoleum. Half the rooms were empty. My first move was to start bringing in the entertainment writers from around the country, relays of them, just letting them get a whiff of the scene.

At the same time, when anyone called for a reservation, the operators were instructed to tell them the hotel was full, but if we had a cancellation we'd call them back. We always did. In sixty days Caesar's had caught on, not because of the gimmicks, although they didn't hurt, but because of the greatness of it.

In many ways the hotel business is a self-contained world, with all the human complications. Caesar's had three partners; Jerry Zarowitz ran the casino, Nate Jacobson watched the money, and Jay Sarno was the promoter. When the hotel began to prosper, each one thought he had done it all by himself. If a story or a layout appeared on one, I could unfailingly expect complaints from the other two. Never were all three happy at the same time. *West* magazine once did a feature spread on Caesar's Palace, with Sarno on the cover, sprawled on a couch in a white toga with dishy slave girls feeding him grapes, the whole bit. Sure enough, the other two sulked and grumbled. But I wish I had a commission on every customer that cover brought in.

Even with the petty jealousies that exist in any partnership I have known, they gave me carte blanche. They never questioned whatever I spent. I was valuable to them because I had a job they didn't understand.

One day Fletcher Knebel, the *Look* magazine writer, flew into Vegas and phoned me. "Come over tonight for dinner," I told him. "Whatever you want here, you have an open door."

Now this was a brilliant reporter, later the author of a best-selling political novel, *Seven Days in May.* He was no ham-and-egger. But at Caesar's that night Jacobson was visibly disturbed. He came over to our table and called me aside.

"You know about this guy?" he whispered.

"I know he's a helluva writer," I said.

"He's here to do a butcher job on Vegas," he said. "I don't want him around here."

"If he's going to butcher us," I argued, "he's going to butcher us. We won't stop him with rudeness."

"Get him out of here," Nate said, his voice rising.

Before I could say anything, I noticed Fletcher getting up from the table. He apparently had heard Nate and he was walking out on his own. I had to give him points for that. I walked out right behind him. The next morning Nate called and asked me to stop by his office. He lectured me for ten minutes. When he finished it was my turn.

"What have you got to hide?" I said, coaxing. "You have a great hotel. Let him see it. Take him everywhere. Show him the books. Gambling is not illegal in Nevada. You're running a legitimate business, licensed by the state. Hell, maybe Fletcher will even praise us a little. What have you got to lose?"

Nate straightened in his chair. "You're right. Absolutely right. Tell him I'd like to apologize."

I called Fletcher at the Tropicana, where he had moved after the incident in the dining room.

"You want to interview Jacobson?" I said.

"You're kidding, of course. You've got to be kidding."

"No," I said. "Mr. Jacobson wants you to be his guest tonight at dinner."

That night at dinner in Nate's suite, I couldn't stop Nate from talking. He was, I thought, overcompensating for his discourtesy of the night before. Two months later, the story appeared. Only two hotels received any praise—Caesar's Palace and the Tropicana. All the pictures in the layout were taken at Caesar's.

"Turned out good," Jacobson told me.

That was all he said, but that was enough. It was part of the job, except that it wasn't my job for very much longer. Actor Telly Savalas, another Greek, was the innocent cause of my leave-taking. Caesar's had decided that instead of using an entertainer in the nightclub they would offer Broadway musicals. The management was negotiating to get *Fiddler on the Roof*.

© 1971 by NEA, Inc.

"FRANKLY, JOHN, I DON'T CARE ABOUT THE GALLUP POLL, OR THE HARRIS POLL —— WHAT DOES JIMMY THE GREEK SAY?"

By Jim Berry. Reprinted by permission of NEA.

'HELLO—JIMMY THE GREEK? I WANT TO GET SOME ODDS . . .'

By Pat Oliphant. Copyright © *The Washington Star*; reprinted with permission Los Angeles Times Syndicate.

Hometown boy makes good in Steubenville, Ohio.

Discussing the odds with Joe Garagiola and Frank Blair on "The Today Show." (Wagner International Photos, Inc.)

Giving equal time to Harry Reasoner and ABC.

Politicking with Senator Hubert Humphey as Tommy Smothers looks on.

Telling it "like it is" to Howard Cosell.

A rare moment of relaxation with Mama Cass.

Pondering the Joe Frazier–Muhammed Ali heavyweight fight.

June 14, 1952. The best decision I ever made.

An informal family portrait. Jimmy Jr., Anthony, Stephanie and Joan. The one who is camera shy is Napoleon. (By Stanley Tretick, People magazine)

My son, Anthony, helps me keep in shape. (By Stanley Tretick, People magazine)

One day I was in the health club, taking a steam, with Savalas.

"Jimmy," he said, "put in a word for me. I'd love to play Tevye." That was the part of the dairyman in *Fiddler*.

"You can't," I said, winking at him. "You're Greek. That's a Jewish part in a Jewish play."

"Listen," he said, with a laugh, "I can play a Jew better than any Jew can."

Jerry Zarowitz had told me that the negotiations to bring in the play had been completed. So the next day I wrote a publicity release, which went to every major paper in the country, that began: "Telly Savalas is a 2 to 1 favorite to play Tevye, the dairyman, in *Fiddler on the Roof* at Caesar's Palace. . . ."

The next voice I heard was Nate Jacobson's. "Greek," he screamed at me in his office the next morning, "do you realize what you've cost us with this release?" He had it in his hand, shaking it at me.

"What are you talking about?"

"I'm talking about half a million dollars," he roared. "That's what you cost us. We don't have *Fiddler* signed yet. They'll want another half million for it now. Why didn't you let me see this before it was sent out?"

"I've been sending out releases for nine months," I said, "and you never asked to see them."

"From now on I want to see every one."

"Cool off, Nate, I'll be back in half an hour."

I walked through the lobby and out to the grounds and let the sun hit me in the face. The more I walked the more I realized the account wasn't for me. I was being paid a fat salary, but I was working seven days a week. I'd be in the office in the morning, in the afternoon, and back at night. I seldom had time for my family. The condition of Tina, the baby, was growing worse. I decided to resign.

I turned around and went back to Nate's office. "You and I have got to be pretty good friends," I said. "I'd like to keep it that way."

He understood. I left with Nate's friendship and a check for seventy-five hundred dollars in severance pay. There had been talk of my eventually getting seven-tenths of a point in the Caesar's ownership, but now that was out. Too bad. It would soon have been worth four hundred thousand dollars. That ought to give you a clue to the value of a going Las Vegas health spa.

When I walked into my home that night and announced I had quit, my wife and kids gave me a standing ovation. I welcomed the chance to get reacquainted with my family. Soon I would have a new client named Howard Hughes, and once again my time would not be my own.

For the most part, I have been fortunate in the way of men who are able to earn a living doing what they would do for free. My worlds overlap. Often accounts have come to me through my interest in sports and politics. One example was John J. Hooker, the board chairman of STP Motor Oil (a client), whose path I first crossed in Tennessee, where he was a candidate for governor in 1968.

While other polls had him in the lead, mine projected him as the loser in a close race. John J. lost, a defeat that cut deep. He was one of those people born to be a politician, the son and grandson of Tennessee governors. His great-grandfather, a Union general, had won an even more enduring fame by lending his name—unintentionally, no doubt—to a certain category of professional ladies. It was General Hooker's custom to celebrate his military victories with a party, to which he invited those girls, camp followers, who for patriotic and economic reasons attached themselves to Army field units. They became known as Hooker's girls, a phrase shortened even more, in time, by popular usage.

You would automatically have to like a fellow with that kind of heritage. I was even more sold on John J. Hooker when I saw how he could handle adversity, a quality with which I was not unfamiliar. Hooker was one of the founders of a company called Minnie Pearl Fried Chicken. He once told a meeting of financial people about the rise and fall of his fortunes:

"The stock took off," he began. "My holdings were suddenly worth ten million dollars . . . twenty . . . thirty . . . forty . . . my god, fifty! But then the day came that it started going the other way . . . forty . . . thirty . . . twenty . . . ten . . . and, finally, minus two."

He paused. "Gentlemen, I want you to know one thing. When my holdings were plus fifty, that was great, but it was all on paper. The minus two was *real*. That was mine, and it was cash." It took John J. a year or two to pay off his debts, but to his credit he did, every dime. He's coming back strong with STP, but regardless of his success in business, my guess is that Hooker will in time run for the Senate. That's his destiny.

His story illustrated the vagaries of high finance, a world not too dissimilar, I found, from the one in which I had spent most of my life. The major difference was that on a bet you put up your money immediately.

We didn't meet until 1972, at a party I gave in New Orleans on the eve of the Miami–Dallas Super Bowl. John Y. Brown, who had made a fortune in chicken (Kentucky Fried) brought Hooker, who had lost a fortune. Even before Brown could introduce us, Hooker breezed into the room and said, "Greek, if you hadn't made me an underdog I believe I still could have won that race."

I laughed and said, "I'm sorry, John, but that's how it showed."

He clapped me on the back. "That's all right, Greek. You called it like it was. I'm not mad at you."

I have found that sports, politics, and business marry well. They did in the case of John Y. Brown, a power in the Democratic party who produced the telethons that paid off the party's huge debts left by the losses to Nixon. He was also a devout sports fan, whose wife, Ellie, became the first woman to own and operate a major-league franchise (the ABA Kentucky Colonels).

An exciting sports event is to business what a Sinatra ballad once was to the backseat of a car. It was after the Ali–Frazier fight in New York, in March of 1971, that John Y. offered me the national account for H. Salt Fish and Chips, a subsidiary of Kentucky Fried Chicken. I had been pitching it for a year, and in the process we had become friends. The Browns were my guests at the fight.

That night we toasted our future success as the kingpins of the fish-and-chip industry. The next day John Y. visited Wall Street, where talks began that led within weeks to his selling out of Kentucky Fried Chicken, including H. Salt. But it wasn't really a loss for the Greek. Brown soon acquired the Lum's fast-food chain, and I landed that one.

It was through Brown that I enjoyed one of my great moments of theater. He had brought in Colonel Sanders himself for the Democratic convention in 1972, and one night we were sitting together in John's box. NBC put a camera on us, and John Chancellor commented that there was a piece of Americana, Colonel Sanders, sitting with Jimmy the Greek.

The Colonel gave me some fatherly advice. "Greek," he said, "you do a helluva job. But it's only in the newspapers. People talk about you, *but they don't recognize you.* Let me tell you what you should do. Start wearing a white suit. Do it. You'd be a famous man."

I loved him for that, but I never took the Colonel's advice. A white suit wouldn't have looked right, somehow, with my blue, low-top tennis shoes.

If you are going to survive in the public relations business, you need more than a gimmick. You need a philosophy. Mine isn't finished yet, but I've been working on it real hard. My approach is a little different from that of the orthodox PR types. We believe in promoting the head of the company. See, to sell a product, to really expose it, has always been damned hard. It became harder after the payola scandals. Today magazines will rarely, if ever, lend space to stories about products. But they will give space to people, interesting, dynamic, authentic people. So we work on the head of the company, and identify him with the product. If the public recognizes *him,* they'll know what he's selling.

One of my rules is never to lie on behalf of a client. When he hires Jimmy the Greek, he buys my credibility, and I don't toy with that. Once, when I agreed to do a television commercial for Edge shaving cream, a New York ad agency sent me the storyboards, which called for me to say, ". . . for a smoother shave, it's Edge, three-to-one." They included the results of a poll from which the figures were taken. I checked them, and it came to five-to-two.

I told the account man that the commercial had to be changed. He was upset, as admen so often are. "What the hell's the difference?" he demanded.

"The difference," I said, "is that it's not three-to-one, it's five-to-two." And that's how we filmed it, "Edge . . . five-to-two."

I find it as practical to apply odds to a marketing effort as to a game or an election. Another of my clients was Aurora Products. I could walk through their toy fair with the president of the company, Chuck Diker, and look at the lines and give him odds on which would sell and which would not.

My PR business has taken me around the world. In 1973 the government of Greece—then the military junta of Colonel Georgios Papadapoulos—invited me back to my father's land to discuss my representing them. I researched that, too. The idea of a dictatorship is unacceptable to the American spirit, though, as a practical matter, we have tolerated several over the years, including Spain and Yugoslavia. I found that a sizable majority of the Greek people approved of the government. The economy was getting stronger. Greece was building schools and hospitals. I went there with an open mind, and I took my family with me, to visit Kios, to enjoy the sun and the sea, the fig trees and the fruit produced by the rich earth, to see it all as I had seen it as a small boy. But, of course, they couldn't.

I met with the premier and his cabinet. Papadapoulos said to me, "Jimmy, we have been so pro-American. We love America. The bases are here, the sailors are here, we want your country's friendship. Her enemies are our enemies. Why do the American people dislike our government?"

I answered him in Greek. "Mr. President," I said, "you have to understand what Greece means to us. It was the cradle of democracy. Americans think of that, the culture, the traditions. That was the Greece they knew. All you need do, somewhere down the line, is hold the elections. Put it to a vote."

He looked at me sharply. "We will have an election," he said, "in time. But when Greeks vote, brothers start killing each other. In the last one hundred and sixty-nine years, Greeks have had two hundred elections. What good has it done?"

I didn't get the account. In late 1974, the Papadapoulos government was thrown out and elections were held. His question waits to be answered. The idea of an election, I wish I had told him, was to give the people the right to make their own mistakes. It is a hard lesson for men of power to learn.

In a sense, I have been in public relations all my life and didn't know it—doing favors, making contacts, putting in touch people who could use each other, pressing the flesh in a hundred ways. I was slow to discover that you could get paid for it, sometimes. I have been trying to catch up ever since.

The wildest public relations experience of my career, and in a way the biggest coup, involved the celebrated tennis match between Bobby Riggs and Billie Jean King in August of 1973 on the floor of Houston's Astrodome. When the publicity for the show began to take off, when it became apparent that this was going to be not a sports event but a *happening*, Charley Diker, the president of a Nabisco subsidiary, wanted me to get involved.

Nabisco's candy division sold an all-day sucker called the Sugar Daddy, which seemed to fit right in with the male chauvinist angle Riggs had been pushing for months. All I wanted was for Bobby to present Billie Jean with a giant Sugar Daddy—we'd bill it as the *world's largest*—at midcourt, before the match, on national television. The company was prepared to pay them fifteen thousand dollars each.

I made the proposal first to Riggs and Jerry Perenchio, the promoter of that cosmic event. Jimmy Welch, the president of Nabisco candies, was with me. They almost laughed us out of the room. "Think it over," I said, looking at Perenchio but talking to Riggs. "After the match this may be all he has. He ought to get it while he can."

But the idea began to grow on Bobby, as did the fifteen grand I offered him, and a contract as the tennis host at the Tropicana for one hundred thousand dollars a year. In a few days Perenchio called and said it was set. Billie Jean had agreed to go along. My only concern now was that Riggs would carry it too far and get us all thrown out of the arena. But the night of the match turned out to be a press agent's dream. The ABC cameras covered the whole ceremony. (Billie Jean, who had refused during the weeks of the buildup before the match to lower herself to Riggs's level, maintained her dignity by entering the Astrodome on a litter borne by male galley slaves. Under one arm she carried a piglet, which she gave to Riggs after accepting the Sugar Daddy.)

Fifty million viewers looked on, with commentary by Howard Cosell. It was one of the last great moments of pure comedy the country will ever know. Bobby gave his all, even wearing a yellow warm-up jacket with *Sugar Daddy* emblazoned in blue across the back. He didn't discard it until after the fourth set, trailing early and headed for an inglorious, upset defeat.

What all this had to do with tennis has never really been made clear, but beyond any question it turned the whole country on. For months afterward people were still asking me if Riggs—I had made him a five-to-two favorite—had thrown the match.

The answer was no. He lost because he had worn himself out promoting it. He had worn himself out another way, too. It may have been billed as "the battle of the sexes," but I can tell you that Bobby was collaborating like hell with the enemy. I mean, he needed those four hundred-odd vitamins he was washing down daily. Over the ten-day period leading up to the match, Bobby had entertained a total of twenty-six ladies in his room, around the clock. That number is an educated guess. I may have missed one or two. But Bobby didn't.

The night before he was to meet Billie Jean, I told Riggs he was going to lose. "You've done a great job," I said, "but you forgot one thing. The tennis match." It was just a tired old man who lost to Ms. King the next evening, before an international crowd of thirty thousand, who dressed as though they were going to the opera.

Sugar Daddy was one of the night's big winners. We got a million dollars' worth of TV time for thirty thousand dollars. Sales for the first quarter after the match went up nearly thirty percent (although Jimmy Welch said sugar costs did, too).

For my money, Bobby Riggs established himself as one of the great PR men of all time, better than some of the acknowledged giants of the field: Joe Namath, Evel Knievel, even Muhammad Ali. I base this on what he had to work with, a fifty-five-year-old body and a face like Bugs Bunny.

But within months Riggs was virtually gone from the national scene, turning up at an occasional event to lend a little fringe color. And that is one of the weaknesses of public relations. When it is all over, and you've lost, the image you created is what you have left.

Few people would remember that Bobby Riggs had once played at Wimbledon. They would only remember that he had lost to a girl who wore glasses. The circus was over.

CHAPTER
10

Howard Hughes:
He Wasn't There

In February of 1970, at a time when the famine was upon the boxing game, I received a call from a promoter named Harold Conrad. "I'm here in Vegas," he said, "with Bob Arum. We'd like to see you."

Arum was an attorney for Muhammad Ali, at that moment unlicensed to box and still appealing his conviction as a draft resister. A fight between Ali and Joe Frazier, Ali's successor as the world heavyweight champion, was worth millions, but no state would take it.

It was a bad time for boxing. Promoters went right on, gamely selling second-rate fights at high prices, just as though their hearts were not breaking.

Conrad and Arum were shopping for a state that would license Ali to meet Frazier, in a dream match between unbeaten heavyweights in the prime of their years. I had known Conrad since 1963, when he promoted the second Liston–Patterson fight in Las Vegas. He had been back with Ali and Patterson in '65. Soon after the phone call that day they were in my office.

Conrad got right to the point. "Can you help us here?"

"I don't know," I said. "I'm sure the governor is opposed to it, but I know him well enough so that I can sit and talk to him."

"If you get it on," Conrad said, "you're in for three percent."

Such a deal is not unusual in boxing (or in Las Vegas), but this one represented a substantial amount—thirty thousand dollars out of every million. I wanted it clarified.

"Of the gross," I said, "not the net."

"The gross. Three percent of everything."

"The live gate, the TV, everything," I said. "The gross of the whole shebang. I don't want to hear about expenses."

"The whole shebang," Conrad said.

"I'll see what I can do," I said.

I arranged a meeting at which Conrad and Arum would make their pitch to the governor of Nevada, Paul Laxalt, and the members of the state boxing commission. The night before the meeting I had dinner at the Sands with the governor and Charles Barron, a retired Air Force general who had no sympathy for Ali. Laxalt had knocked out an Ali–Patterson bout in 1967, shortly before Ali refused induction into the Army, so I knew I was an underdog. But if I was honest with him, told him the whole story, I figured he at least would listen.

"Governor, this is a big score for me," I told him, emphasizing my three percent. "Please consider it."

He said that he would, but he didn't commit himself either way. The next morning, I was in the lobby of the El Morocco Hotel, five minutes before the meeting was to start. From behind the registration desk, the switchboard operator paged me for a phone call.

"Jimmy," said the voice on the phone, "Mr. Hughes doesn't want this fight."

Mr. Hughes was Howard Robards Hughes, Junior. I didn't say a word. I replaced the phone, gently, and walked over to Conrad and Arum. "I just found out," I told them, "that you don't have a chance. Don't even propose the fight. Before the meeting even starts, thank the governor and tell him that maybe you'll be back when the climate for the fight is better."

They understood. That was the end of whatever chance Las Vegas had for the fight and whatever shot I had at my three percent. To this day I don't know what Governor Laxalt would have recommended in that meeting. But I do know that if an Ali–Frazier fight in Vegas had grossed the twenty million dollars it grossed in New York a year later, Howard Hughes cost me about six hundred thousand dollars.

Not that I had much choice. At the time I worked as a public relations consultant for the Hughes Nevada Operations.

Before you ask—no, I never met Howard Hughes and, no, I never talked with him. I saw him once, from a distance, in a dining room, years before he settled in Las Vegas. Except for the moustache, he had the kind of face people can never describe to the cops.

I will say this about him: for someone you never saw, his presence was everywhere. To be involved with Hughes in any way was to feel like a character in the second act of a play.

My orders came from Bob Maheu, a bulky, balding ex-FBI agent who headed Hughes's Nevada holdings. He was the second most powerful man in the state, until the night of the long knives, Thanksgiving week of 1970. It was Maheu's son, Pete, who had called about the fight.

Bob Maheu had never met Hughes either, though he had worked for him since 1953, starting out in security jobs, which included keeping an eye on some of Howard's lady friends. He had moved to Las Vegas four years before to act as a surrogate for the boss. Bob spoke often to Hughes in his penthouse hideaway on the top floor of the Desert Inn, but he was even reticent about that.

"Those who do talk to him, don't say," Maheu told me, "and those who don't talk to him, may say."

The power of Howard Hughes radiated from that top floor, which had a mystique all its own. Except for his six personal aides—the "Mormon Mafia," chosen because they did not smoke, drink, chase women, or have liberal ideas—no one really knew what the inside of the penthouse looked like after Hughes had it remodeled. The story had become a Las Vegas legend, how Hughes had checked into a suite at the Desert Inn in 1966—again, on Thanksgiving Eve—and five months later was asked to move because other guests had reserved the rooms for the Tournament of Champions. Rather than move, he bought the hotel lease for 13.6 million dollars.

Now that he owned it, he took over the entire top floor. Indulging his passion for secrecy and confusion, Hughes let the story spread that he had imported a group of carpenters from Los Angeles to remodel one part of the space. After them a new shift of carpenters arrived from Houston and completed another section. Then a third group, from Dallas, finished the job. That way, there wasn't even a carpenter who could describe the entire suite. It was a clever story, except that it didn't happen. The suite was never touched.

From the privacy of the top floor—"Up There," I always called it, with reverence—Hughes ruled a business empire reputed to be worth four billion dollars. His tool company, aircraft company, Nevada operations, and airlines employed some sixty-five thousand people. His holdings were rivaled only by those of J. Paul Getty and H. L. Hunt, my old gambling buddy.

Hughes invested nearly half a billion dollars in Nevada real estate, though for reasons of his own the figure he allowed us to quote was never higher than two hundred million dollars. His holdings included five hotels—the Desert Inn, Sands, Frontier, Landmark, and Castaways—and two casinos—the Silver Slipper in Las Vegas and Harold's Club in Reno. It was out of the Silver Slipper, which was privately owned, not a corporation, that Hughes made his political donations, including the now-famous hundred thousand dollars to Nixon (and fifty thousand dollars to Humphrey). Always in cash.

The wealth of Howard Hughes, so freely used, gave Las Vegas a new image and a new vitality. You could sense it everywhere. A few years before, Vegas had been thought of as a haven for mobsters and outlaws. Bugsy Siegel opened the Flamingo Hotel, the first of the fabulous hotels on the Strip, before he died one night of hyperventilation, caused by several large bullet holes in his chest. The town was corrupt.

Later on, Las Vegas meant lavish entertainment and show biz superstars, such as the Sinatras and the Martins and the Hacketts who earned in a week for their acts what most people don't make in a lifetime. But then almost overnight, in 1966, Howard Hughes became the town's biggest industry. Once he began to buy up the state, this invisible billionaire emerged as a Las Vegas folk hero.

Gambling and tourist income increased more than twenty-five

percent a year, twice the rate before he came. Suddenly, more people *trusted* Las Vegas. The place was damned near respectable. As a public relations man, privy to the conversations of his inner circle of executives, I learned quickly about his likes and dislikes. For one thing, he didn't like hookers.

"Chase those girls," were Bob Maheu's orders to his hotel people. "Mr. Hughes wants them out."

Soon each of the Hughes hotels became a Mom-and-Dad joint. The only problem is, you don't make money in Las Vegas with a Mom-and-Dad joint. The prospect of meeting a lady of the night at the bar, or in the cocktail lounge, is what made some of the Vegas hotels. Clean is nice, but I have always believed that anyone in business in Las Vegas should not stray too far from the Sin City image.

But you had to respect Hughes for ordering the hookers off his premises. In Vegas, that took nerve. It also confirmed, I think, a theory of mine—that there is no one more pious than a reformed hell raiser, after age has quieted the glands. In his heyday, Hughes had boasted of deflowering two hundred virgins in Hollywood (he must have got them all). According to my calculations, by 1974 he had not been laid in eleven years, including the six in which he did not sleep with his wife, Jean Peters.

Still, I admired Hughes for the reclamation job I saw being done. For nine years the Landmark Hotel tower had been a Las Vegas joke. Unfinished and unopened, it represented failure. To the people who had financed it and those who worked on it, the hotel represented a big loss of money.

"Mr. Hughes is buying the Landmark," Bob Maheu told me. "He thinks it's an eyesore."

Hughes could have bought it in bankruptcy for thirteen million dollars. But he wouldn't do it, knowing, I suspect, that a lot of small contractors would have been ruined. He paid 100 cents on the dollar, a total of 17.5 million dollars. He did the same thing when he bought the Frontier, which had been shaky.

It isn't easy to analyze a phantom, but the evidence suggests to me that Howard Hughes had a conscience. He pledged six million dollars for a Nevada medical school, a gesture not unrelated, I thought, to his own near brush with death in 1947. He was obsessed, of course, with aircraft. Long before he was rediscovered by the public as the world's richest hermit, he had established speed records in planes he designed. He flew around the world in 1938 and received a ticker-tape parade on Broadway that rivaled Lindbergh's.

But in 1947, Hughes was nearly killed test-piloting one of his own planes. He crashed it in the street in Beverly Hills, avoiding any homes. His face was burned and cut and he had broken more bones than the doctors could count. He grew a moustache to cover some of the scars and he began to retreat from people.

I knew this story from a pretty good source—Cans Jones, my old Steubenville pal whose younger brother John was the doctor who put him back together. Jonesy's money helped put John and another brother through medical school. The money he won gambling.

The day Hughes was released, after months of surgery and treatment, he handed Dr. Jones an envelope with a check in it. The doctor put it in his desk without looking at it. The next day he handed the envelope to his secretary and said, "Here, you better deposit this." He still hadn't looked at it.

A moment later the secretary walked back into his office. She looked puzzled. "Dr. Jones," she said. "There's no amount written in. It's just a blank check, signed by a Mr. Hughes."

How much would *you* have written down? Dr. Jones filled in an amount of one hundred thousand dollars and donated it to charity.

Anyone exposed to the Hughes organization soon develops a thing about doctors and medical care. Once, around New Year's 1969, I left the office feeling puny and went home to rest. Minutes after I got there, Dee Coakley, my secretary, phoned.

"Do you feel better?" she said.

"Not really," I said. "Worse, if anything."

"Let me talk to Joannie."

"She's not here. She must be out with the kids somewhere."

"I'll be right over," Dee said, slamming the receiver in my ear.

By the time she arrived I was stretched out on the couch in the living room. She phoned Bob Maheu for advice. "Just stay there with Jimmy," he said.

In a few minutes, one of the two Hughes company physicians, Dr.

Robert Buckley, arrived in an ambulance. "We're going to Santa
Barbara—now," he said.

With its sirens screaming, the ambulance roared down the Strip to
the private hangar at McCarren Field, where a Hughes plane, a
Cessna 402, was waiting with its twin engines running. I was loaded
into the plane. When we touched down in Santa Barbara, California,
another ambulance was waiting to take us to College Hospital. There
more doctors were waiting for me. In my room, the bed sheets were
even turned down.

My problem was diagnosed as an abdominal obstruction. I needed
immediate surgery. Later, in the recovery room, I had just come out
from under the anesthesia when one of the doctors leaned over me.
"We got that thing out," he said, "but we have to send it to be
analyzed, just in case. You understand."

"I know," I said. "In case it's cancer."

"Don't worry," the doctor said. "I doubt that it is. I doubt it so
much I'll give you a hundred to one it isn't."

"I'll take it," I said, smiling. Who could resist the odds?

Luckily for me, I lost that bet. Either way I owed my comfort to
Bob Maheu, a fellow I had grown to like. I could relate to him. I *saw*
him. I got in the habit of calling him "Uncle Bob," and it was the
kind of thing he enjoyed. What his inner feelings were about Hughes
I couldn't tell, but he seemed to me to be as loyal as an old bird dog.

Every now and then I would get orders to set up the Hughes
private jet to transport a critically ill child to a hospital hundreds,
maybe thousands, of miles away. Once I asked Bob about one of
them.

"Did he know the child?" I asked.

"Not that I know of," Maheu answered.

"That's a good story," I said.

"But you can't put it out. Mr. Hughes doesn't want any publicity.
You know that."

I knew that. It was one of the ground rules the day I was hired. In
fact, the key part of my job was to keep his name *out* of the news.

How I came to be hired in the first place had to do with my talent
for running into people at the moment they had a problem. In 1968,
Hughes, through Maheu, was negotiating to purchase Air West, an

airline with sixty jets that fanned out from Nevada to seventy-three cities in eight western states, Canada, and Mexico. I had known Bob Maheu slightly, but crossed paths more often with his son, Peter, a sociable fellow in his late twenties. They were near my table one night at the Sands, and Peter invited me over. Bob began to talk about the problems that had developed in the Air West negotiations.

"Do you have any ideas?" he asked me.

"Give me twenty-four hours to put a pencil to it," I said, "and I'll give you a prospectus. If you like my suggestions, you take credit for them. If you don't, throw them away."

"Send me your ideas, Jimmy."

I went immediately to the office, leaving behind a pouting wife and some puzzled dinner guests. What the hell did I know about airlines? That night I telephoned an airline executive in Los Angeles, a friend, who flew in the next day and helped me prepare a prospectus for Air West. It included a list of political and business leaders who might support a Hughes takeover. It must have been a decent prospectus, because a few minutes after Bob Maheu received it he was on the phone to me.

"Can you produce on this?" he asked.

"If I didn't think so," I said, "I wouldn't have suggested it."

"All right. You've got four months, through January, because by then our offer for Air West will have expired. How much do you want?"

I said, "Fifty thousand dollars."

Maheu hesitated. Instantly, I moved in. "If you're worried," I said, "I'll play you double-out."

"Beg your pardon?"

"Look," I said, "we're talking about fifty thousand dollars over four months. I'll play you double or nothing. If we win Air West by that time, I get double—a hundred thousand dollars. If we lose it, you don't owe me a penny."

"You mean you'd *do* that?"

"Try me," I offered.

There was a long pause. "No, let's do it at the fifty-thousand-dollar figure," he said, "win or lose. I'm sure that won't affect your dedication to the project."

"You'll get a full and total effort," I said.

And he did. He also got Air West, or Hughes Air West as it was soon known. Whereupon I went on the payroll, full time. Not long after that I was in Bob's office when Peter Maheu showed me a report on the underground atomic testing in Nevada with megaton-plus explosives.

"Can you do anything about this?" he asked me.

"I can do anything about anything," I said. "What do you want done?"

"All we can tell you is that Mr. Hughes doesn't want megaton-plus testing in Nevada."

"What else?"

"That's all."

"What do you mean, 'That's all'?"

"That's all we can tell you, Jim."

"Nothing else?"

"Except that Mr. Hughes's name is not to be used in any way."

"You always make it easy," I said.

It was a touchy assignment. Hughes's companies enjoyed a lot of government contracts, so it wasn't just modesty that prevented him from taking on the Atomic Energy Commission. On the other hand, Hughes was an ecology nut before it was fashionable. He preached the conservation of air, land, and water as far back as the forties, and that was at the heart of his fight with the AEC.

Still, it *was* the United States government, and if you're going to battle them it helps to have your own army. I had a small revolt in my own office. "I won't do it," said Dee Coakley. "It's unpatriotic. I refuse to work on this."

"Maybe it is," I said. "Or maybe Mr. Hughes is right. Why don't we research it before we judge it?"

We didn't have to dig very deep. Radiation had affected some cows, ruined their milk, poisoned some babies. Measurable amounts were found in the water. There was concern about an earthquake. The more we researched it the more we came to believe in our opposition to the testing. But since we couldn't connect Howard Hughes with it, we had to make our point indirectly. We flooded science writers with copies of newspaper and magazine stories that had supported our viewpoint. In no time we were sending out packages as thick as a phone book. Within six months, the Atomic Energy Commission announced that it was halting its megaton-plus testing in Nevada. Bob Maheu was pleased.

I never heard from Hughes. Only once did I ever get what I might describe as a personal reaction from him. It was the result of what I considered one of my more brilliant ideas. My office was preparing a feature story, a roundup on Hughes's first four years in Nevada, to offer the wire services. The usual PR mix: the growth of Vegas, new residents, higher employment, the increase in tourist traffic.

The last photograph anyone had ever used of him was taken in 1946, when he was forty. I knew it was impossible to produce a new photo of him. But I had a brainstorm. I gave a print of the last Hughes picture to artist LeRoy Neiman, and I said, "I want you to age this face. Show me what he should look like fifteen years later."

Neiman did a masterful job. Gray at the temples, a little salt and pepper in the moustache. A few lines for character. It was a handsome portrait and I was delighted. We delivered it to Peter Maheu for the approval of Mr. Hughes. Pete said, "I'll let you know."

Days passed. I was holding up the feature, in hopes of being able to offer with it photographs of a Neiman painting of the elusive Howard Hughes. What editor could resist that? I kept asking about the portrait. Finally, Pete said, "Come on over. I have your answer." I went to his office and there, on his desk, was the painting, with an original comment by Howard Hughes: an X slashed across the face.

Of course, my standing in the company was secure enough to sustain small setbacks. The last time my advice was ignored had been in the matter of an *Esquire* magazine piece promoted by Dick Hannah, of the Carl Byoir office, which had handled PR for Hughes for years. (He later arranged the famous telephone conference call, during which Hughes libeled Maheu.) Hannah was strong for the *Esquire* story, which was to deal with the Hughes Nevada operation.

We were having a meeting on it, and Maheu tapped a pencil and said, "What do you think about it, Jimmy?"

"Ben Gazzara," I said.

They all looked at me blankly.

"Run for your life," I said, which was the title of a TV series popular then, starring Gazzara. "Stay away from this story. They'll cut you to pieces."

The story ran in an issue that featured a fake photo sequence on the cover supposedly showing Hughes himself chasing a photographer into the trees around his pool. You can imagine what a hit that was. But from then on nothing that had to do with public relations moved in or out of the Hughes office without being bounced off the Greek.

With Hughes there was a new cause every week. We lobbied against dog racing in Nevada, and won. We kept a rock festival out of Las Vegas. And when a mechanic at the Hughes private airport pumped the wrong gas into a small plane, which crashed, killing three, I kept it out of the papers while the lawyers settled with the families.

One of the more curious assignments began on a January morning in 1970, when the ringing of the phone roused me from a sound sleep. "Jimmy," said Peter Maheu, "stay close today. We're going to have something special for you to do."

In my daily routine, I stopped by the Hughes Nevada offices about nine and stayed there for maybe an hour, on the way to my own office. But that day I was there by eight-thirty.

"What's up?" I asked Peter.

"We're waiting for something."

"For what?"

"Something."

I should have known better than to ask. But it was hours before "something" materialized. Finally, I was handed a typewritten statement:

> This is not a decision reached in haste; and it is done only with the greatest of regret. Our marriage has endured for 13 years, which is long by present standards. Any property settlement will be resolved privately between us.

As I read those brief sad lines, Pete sensed what I was thinking: this is a front-page story in every newspaper in the land. "The order," he said, "is not to change one word of this statement, and deliver it to the two wire services. Just the two wire services."

Looking back, Hughes's problems seemed to grow—his investments suffering, his distrust of everyone deepening—from the day of his divorce statement. He was now more alone than ever. Some of his Nevada interests were losing big money—Air West, it was reported, had dropped thirty-two million dollars in 1970. There were rumors that he developed pneumonia, but I had heard that Hughes had a strong heart, a young man's heart.

Other rumors began to circulate, as early as August, that Bob Maheu was about to be fired and Hughes was bound for the Bahamas. Maheu asked me to deny them and that was enough for me. The fact that Hughes didn't deny them meant nothing. He never denied or confirmed anything.

At that time, I believed I knew as much about Howard Hughes, his history and his habits, as anyone alive. Or, at least, I knew where the information was. One of my first acts had been to direct my staff to find, copy and compile clippings of every story written about him from his years in Houston and Los Angeles. It made for a dossier five hundred-pages thick, and I had it distributed on a very limited basis to the higher Hughes executives.

Passages from that file turned up years later, as source material for Clifford Irving's non-book about Hughes. He claimed it was from a computer print-out. I didn't know whether to be pissed off or flattered.

I had assembled the file for the usual good reason: to let my bosses know I was on the job and, also, because there was something I needed to know about Howard Hughes. His pattern. Everybody has one. And I discovered his.

Hughes picks up and leaves every four years. You could set your calendar by him. This item was of no small interest to me. I was in the PR business and I had only one account. So I went to Bob Maheu and told him that my research indicated Hughes got itchy feet after four years, and where did that leave me?

Bob was amused. "Jimmy," he said, reassuringly, "Mr. Hughes is going to spend the rest of his life right here in Las Vegas. Your job is secure."

As secure, it developed, as Maheu's. For Bob the difference between winning and losing was the fact that the purchase of the Stardust fell through. Hughes, who had been prepared to pay forty-two million dollars for it, backed off when the Justice Department threatened to bring a monopoly charge. There was no objection to his buying the Landmark, which was bankrupt, and he did.

Instead of owning the Stardust, which showed a profit of over twelve million dollars a year, Hughes now had a hotel that was losing seven. That's a difference of around twenty million per annum. When an investment goes badly, wealthy men get unhappy. It's a very short step from there to calling someone a thief. But I was a kind of firefighter for the company, and if Bob Maheu had been one, sooner or later, I would have known it. He wasn't a thief.

There was another small but enlightening fact I had discovered about Howard Hughes. He sat behind a desk that was specially made, one with special wiring so that any phone could be placed on it and the sound magnified. Hughes was hard of hearing. Wherever he went, the desk went. I seriously thought that he might have been kidnapped, until I heard that his desk was gone. It was part of his pattern, just like the four-year cycle.

On the eve of Thanksgiving 1970, exactly four years to the night that Hughes had arrived in Las Vegas, I had dinner at the Frontier with Governor Laxalt. As we left the hotel I looked across the Strip, up to the top floor of the Desert Inn, and nudged the governor.

"Excuse me," I said, my hands clasped as if in prayer, "I've got to say hello to God up there."

"It won't do you any good, Jimmy," the governor said. "There's nobody up there tonight."

His remark went right over my head. I mean, I don't know what the hell I could have been thinking, but it went right by me. It hit me a few hours later, and I intended to phone him the next morning. But then it was Thanksgiving Day and I didn't bother.

When I walked into the Hughes Nevada offices on Friday morning it looked like a Marx Brothers comedy. Everyone was running in and out of doors.

"Hughes is gone," someone told me.

"Where did he go?"

Nobody answered. I guess at that moment no one really knew.

"How did he leave?"

No answer to that one, either. It was obvious that the power struggle between the old-timers in the Hughes empire and the Maheu faction was in the open now. From where I stood, Bob had represented Hughes well. But he was like a successful football coach who had snubbed the board of regents. Aligned against him were Raymond Holliday and Frank Gay, executives of the tool company in Houston, and Chester Davis, the Hughes attorney. They had been with Hughes forever. Gay started out as one of his original Mormon helpers.

I had Bob release a statement expressing his concern for the safety of Mr. Hughes, hinting that his sudden departure may have involved duress. Maheu had the sheriff's office break into the Hughes penthouse. It was empty.

With nothing else to do, I left a day or so later to keep a business trip to Chicago. I was having dinner with friends when I was paged. (When you worked for Hughes you left a number where you could be reached *at all times*.)

Bob Maheu was calling. "They're trying to move us out, Jimmy," he said. "They came in like the Gestapo. But we're not going to give up. We're going to do the best we can to protect our people."

I said, "Bob, you mean Mr. Hughes. Protect Mr. Hughes, don't you."

"Yes, yes, that's right," he said. "Mr. Hughes."

I felt that Maheu had to take the position that he was the one looking out for Howard, baby. But there was another point. As far as I knew, I still worked for Howard Hughes. But to me, Bob Maheu *was* Hughes. When I boarded a plane back to Las Vegas that night, I thought to myself, "Greek, you sure got yourself into a sweet one this time."

The battle lines could not have been clearer. The old guard had been around Hughes for twenty-five years. I never saw so many people on a payroll with jobs no one knew anything about. But whatever else people might say, Hughes was loyal to anyone who had been loyal to him in his younger days.

I suspect that to a point Hughes enjoyed a little intrigue among his executives. He liked to pit them against each other. A little infighting kept them honest, kept them on their toes. He often challenged his people by giving them an assignment right on a deadline, to see how they executed under pressure.

There was no doubt that the old soldiers had viewed with suspicion the growth of Maheu's power. In a sense, Bob had gone into business on his own. He had unlimited use of the company Cadillacs, helicopters, and an airplane. He had bought into a housing development in Los Angeles, and was partners in several consulting firms with the Hughes security chief, Jack Hooper. He had a yacht, and he had the trappings of power.

Davis and Gay led a task force of auditors and security cops swarming into the hotels and casinos and Hughes Nevada offices. They publicly announced the firing of Maheu.

There was a meeting at Bob's home, on the grounds of the Desert Inn, beside one of the golf fairways. There was no small irony to that. It was a home Hughes paid for, and when it became apparent that construction costs were running fifty thousand dollars over estimates, Maheu sent Hughes a memo, offering to pay the extra costs.

Hughes sent him a memo back: "You're going to live in it the rest of your life. For another fifty thousand dollars, don't worry about it."

So there Bob was, more or less evicted from his own office. Outside, we could see plainclothesmen from Intertel, the security agency hired by the Tool Company executives. Among those at the meeting were the Maheus; Dick Danner, who managed the Frontier Hotel; Al Benedict, the liaison with all the hotels, who now runs MGM; their attorney, Tom Bell; and Jack Hooper. I asked Hooper the key question again:

"How did he leave?"

Hooper still didn't know. Neither did anyone else. To this day, no one can say for certain. One theory is that he walked down an interior fire stairs nine floors to the parking lot. Another was that the Mormons carried him down. But who knows? Maybe he just walked out through the lobby. Who the hell knew what he looked like anyway?

The point of our meeting was to devise a game plan to counter the takeover of the old guard. Both sides filed an injunction, Maheu claiming that their power of attorney was forged and only Hughes could fire him. Both sides hired so many detectives they spent most of their time trailing each other.

But it was all over for Bob when Paul Laxalt reported that he had received a call from Hughes, from Paradise Island in the Bahamas. He said Hughes confirmed that the Tool Company executives were acting under his orders: Maheu was fired. As one of the few who had talked with him directly, Paul was convinced that the voice he heard was that of Howard Hughes. Among the first to be fired with Maheu were the Greek, Hooper, and Danner, who had delivered to his friend, Bebe Rebozo, the Nixon campaign money.

There was no way I could disbelieve the governor. He was a friend and tennis partner of Maheu's. Bob was out, and so was Jimmy the Greek. There was still a matter of money owed for past services, specifically a bill I had submitted for 121,000 dollars. When it got to Chester Davis, the portly, crusty old lawyer roared when he saw it. "What the hell did you do," he demanded, "to earn all this money?"

I said, "In twenty-four hours I'll have a memo on your desk, listing some of the things I did. With copies to all the other attorneys and Hughes himself."

Two days later I had a call from Hughes's man in New York. "We're going to agree to X amount of dollars," he said, "but we're going to deduct twenty-eight percent from that. You would win if you took it to court, but it would take two years and attorney fees."

Why the twenty-eight percent? I never did figure that one out. I settled for 74,000 dollars and closed the account. I never did knock Hughes, which surprised a few people. Can't you see it? Jimmy the Greek shaking his fist and threatening, "I *made* you, Howard, and I can *break* you." Someday, maybe, I'll do another book about my three and a half years "with" Howard Hughes.

My philosophy is simple: he who pays me has the right to fire me. And I was well paid (six figures a year). On paper, Maheu won big—but so far it's still on paper. In December of 1974, a jury awarded him punitive damages of 2.8 million dollars in his libel suit against Hughes, who in that ill-timed telephone conference with newsmen had referred to Bob in language not recommended for general audiences. Liar, thief, and son of a bitch were among the gentler descriptions.

How long the settlement could be delayed by the Hughes attorneys remained to be seen.

My own last brush with the Hughes experience came some three years after I had left his employ. Questions were still being raised about the purchase of Air West, and on three separate occasions I was called to testify before the Securities Exchange Commission. I was suspected, I found, of having driven down the price of Air West stock—before the sale was closed—by spreading unfavorable statements. It just wasn't so. Poor management drove down the company's stock. In California it was known as Air Worst.

A joke about the airline quoted one of the Air West hostesses praying on takeoff: "Our Father who art in heaven, Howard be thy name. . . ."

On final reflection, I would have to say that it was one of the more interesting periods of my life. Working for Hughes, in some ways, was like putting a message into a bottle and casting it out to sea.

You would not exactly describe him as consistent. He didn't hire Jews or blacks, but I know that he donated generously to charities—the list was seven pages long—that provided for Jews and blacks.

He did prove this: few things capture the imagination of the American public faster, or assure a larger fame, than someone who craves privacy and goes to great lengths to obtain it. For more than a year you couldn't pick up a paper or a magazine without reading about him. There was the Clifford Irving hoax. Fantastic rumors. And all the gags. You know the kind:

"I just got a call from Howard Hughes."

"How do you know it was him?"

"Had to be. When I picked up the phone, no one was there."

CHAPTER

11

Oddsmaking:
Sometimes a Wrong Number

For the last six weeks of the 1968 season, I created a mild panic in pro football because of something I didn't do. I didn't establish a line—a point spread—on the Kansas City Chiefs. In betting parlance, they were "taken off the board."

Now, it is true that people in sports panic more easily than those in other fields, with the possible exception of high fashion. But the details of the story I am about to tell will explain why the odds are made, and sometimes not made, what moves them and to what purposes they are used. It gets close to the core of the sports experience in this country.

That is, we can enjoy our games and fall in love with a team, so long as we believe them to be honest and above suspicion. Always, the alien presence is *gambling*. People bet. And when they bet they tend to do two things: (1) look for an edge, and (2) justify their losses by screaming "fix." Both ways can spread alarm and sometimes, in rare and dramatic instances, there is reason.

I did not bar Kansas City in 1968 because of any suspicious behavior by the players. I barred them because what gamblers call "unnatural money" had begun to show up on their games. I should say, unnaturally *big* money. It was winding up in Las Vegas gambling shops, but not directly. The bets were being laundered, sent in from cities other than the source of the original money.

I began to check around, and what I learned was that the names of three Kansas City players were being misused by some unsavory characters. The full story would take a year to break—ironically, it would break the week of the 1970 Super Bowl, before the Chiefs met Minnesota. But for now what I knew was this:

Lenny Dawson, the quarterback, one of the straightest arrows in the league, was getting phone calls from a Detroit gambler named Donald (Dicey) Dawson (no relation of his). I doubt that Lenny had any idea what the other Dawson did for a living.

Johnny Robinson, the halfback from LSU, was thinking about opening a restaurant and sports club in a building thought to be owned by the Mafia.

And a third player—sorry, his name I just can't use—was mixed up with a crowd in Kansas City suspected of stealing cars and dealing dope.

There it was. And now I knew what was happening to the line. Say, the Chiefs were favored by seventeen over Denver, and Dicey Dawson takes the points. His friends, the people around him, tell each other, "Dicey talks to the quarterback. He *knows* something." The line drops to sixteen and *their* friends start betting, and soon it was down to thirteen.

That was when the suckers came in, and when the line fell to eleven the fellow in Detroit would bet that—take Kansas City and lay the points—and now he had the game middled. He was on both sides with maybe a six-point spread. Beautiful. For him.

He was *using* the public, and that was why I had to bar the Chiefs. The point spread is there to protect the public. It's a barometer. You can read it, measure the teams, test the winds of sentiment, see where the money is flowing and how fast. Some weeks it's like a novel.

Pete Rozelle, whom I admire, and others in high places in professional sports take the position that betting is not an essential part of team games. Fan interest does not depend on it.

Absolutely true. If all gambling somehow disappeared tomorrow, pro football and the rest would still exist. Unfortunately, I live in the real world. In the real world people bet ten billion dollars each year on pro sports. It wasn't a question of something funny going on with the Chiefs. Hell, they only lost twice all season. But, the *suspicion* of guilt can be as deadly as the real thing.

I'd bet my life that Len Dawson and Johnny Robinson were clean—and lie detector tests later vindicated both. As for the third fellow, I only know that he got in with bad company and, other factors aside, became an unsettling influence on the team.

The first week the Kansas City game failed to appear on the line, the calls began flooding in from all over the country. What could I tell them? Pete Axthelm of *Newsweek*, Dave Anderson of *The New York Times*, and Mort Sharnik of *Sports Illustrated* wondered if I had heard any rumors. I said that it was impossible to handicap them now because of their injuries—they had some—and why didn't we leave it at that?

The Chiefs won their last five games that 1968 season, then were blown out by Oakland in the playoffs.

Each week there were more calls, more questions. When I barred them, everyone did. The National Football League office, which doesn't like to acknowledge that people bet on games, was having convulsions. It became a suspense story: Would this be the week that a point spread appeared on Kansas City?

Later that winter, I heard that the NFL had investigated the rumors and asked several of the Chiefs to submit to lie detector tests. Len Dawson was the first to volunteer. The case was quietly closed, we thought.

When the 1969 season was about to open, I got a call from one of my favorite sports columnists, Bud Furillo of the Los Angeles *Herald-Examiner*. "An old friend of mine," he said, "is wondering if you're going to put the Chiefs on the board this season. He'd appreciate it if you did."

Bud didn't identify his old friend, but I knew it was the commissioner. Rozelle had been the general manager of the Rams in the early fifties, when Bud was covering the team. Pete understood that when a team was kept off the board, it was performing under suspicion. He wanted that suspicion removed.

The Chiefs were back, and there the matter rested until Super Bowl week 1970. Suddenly, with tens of thousands of football fans congregated in New Orleans and the press hovering like fruit flies, an FBI gambling investigation broke wide open. It centered in Detroit, and there the name of Dicey Dawson was publicly linked to the Kansas City quarterback.

Rozelle's office moved quickly to reveal the results of its own tests and to clear Lenny. But the timing had to be hellish for a team preparing for the biggest game of the year. The strain, the pressure, the distraction. That was all you could hear that week. The average fan had to figure that it would blow Kansas City right out of the game.

Immediately, I moved Minnesota from a three-point favorite to nine, for two reasons, neither of which had to do with Len Dawson's frame of mind. I moved it because the fans *thought* he would be affected, and because the Chiefs had a cornerback hurt (and that is where those big sixes are scored). The gamblers closed the game at thirteen, which shows you that the money was still coming in on Minnesota.

There was, thankfully, a lighter side to Super Bowl IV. The Chiefs were proving all the amateur psychologists dead wrong, with Len Dawson giving an inspired performance. They led at the half, 16–0, as I sat there in the company of Phil Iselin, owner of the Jets, his coach, Weeb Ewbank, and Governor Paul Laxalt of Nevada, doing my arithmetic: the Vikings had to score five touchdowns to beat my handicap.

I was only half paying attention as the half-time show unfolded below us, a noisy, extravagant reenactment of the Battle of New Orleans. Cannons were exploded. Horses bolted. Costumed soldiers were firing rifles and crumpling to the ground. ". . . And when the smoke cleared," the voice on the stadium loudspeaker was saying, "the British had lost nineteen hundred and seventy-five men, while the American casualties were six killed."

Out of the Kansas City section in front of us, a heavy voice boomed out, *"And one Greek."*

I had to laugh at that. So did everyone around me. After the Chiefs had finished polishing off the Vikings, 23–7, I caught some more of it. "Wrong again, eh, Greek?" strangers greeted me as we filed out of the stadium.

The year before I had made the Baltimore Colts a seventeen-point favorite over the New York Jets, in what has become the most historic of all the Super Bowl games. Before witnesses, in the middle of the week, Joe Willie Namath had "guaranteed" that the Jets would win. He did it at a banquet with a glass of Scotch in his hand. That is, he made the prediction there. The game came three days later, and the Jets won, 16–7.

I wasn't there, nor did I watch it on television. The day before the game I underwent surgery for the removal of a stomach obstruction, a final repair of the condition that had troubled me during my years with Hughes. I was under sedation all day Sunday. On Monday morning a nurse walked in, flicked on my TV set, and in my first conscious moments, just coming out of the fog, I heard Joe Garagiola on the "Today" show, saying, ". . . And even Jimmy the Greek was wrong."

So when the Chiefs surprised the Vikings, I had missed twice, or so most people thought.

Well, we all have our little identity problems. Mine has been to make people understand that I'm an oddsmaker. I don't pick winners. I'm not a sportswriter trying to match wits in the weekly "guesspert" competition. I establish favorites, odds, and point spreads—that is, the margin necessary to *equalize* the two teams.

Making the odds has become a hobby with me, a kind of loss leader for my public relations business. I spend over fifty thousand dollars a year to get the information that goes into the odds, and I give them away—to the sports press, and to such political reporters as Walter Cronkite, Harry Reasoner, and Jack Anderson. But it keeps my name out there.

It no longer vexes me when people conclusion-jump about my work or my style. But I do get the feeling that some expect me to appear in a frock coat and twirling a waxed moustache. It amuses me now to recall how Howard Samuels, who was then organizing Off-Track Betting in New York City, invited me to that city to pick my brains. I asked what time. "Why not Saturday night, in my office?" he suggested. "That's the best time."

I thought nothing of it, until I walked through the deserted lobby of the OTB offices in the old Paramount Building, on Times Square. My footsteps echoed through the halls. Then I understood. All the other offices were closed. There was no one around who might recognize Jimmy (the Greek) Snyder, notorious Las Vegas odds-maker and sinister influence. I can only guess what Howard expected. Maybe he thought I would arrive with four bodyguards carrying violin cases.

But what he met was a businessman, who happened to be an expert on odds and the science of probability, subjects he needed to know more about.

As we talked in Samuels's private office, to one side quietly stood Dick Aurelio, then the deputy mayor under John Lindsay. After maybe fifteen minutes, Aurelio glanced at his watch and broke in, "Howard, I have to go. Whatever you want to do with this guy, it's okay." With that he was gone.

I agreed to act as an unpaid consultant. My projections on the OTB handle for the first three years proved to be off by only one and a half percent. My estimate of their operating cost was low by only a point. But then, I should have remembered that it always costs more when the government runs things.

We hit it off instantly, Howard Samuels and I. There was no more secrecy. We stopped at his apartment, had dinner later at "21." The next week he put me on display, proudly, in a press conference in the OTB offices.

I was impressed with Samuels. In 1974 he had everything he needed to be elected governor of New York—distinguished looks, wealth, brains, and exposure—except for one thing. He couldn't get the nomination.

Everything in life is a betting proposition. You can get odds on whether you'll wake up tomorrow (don't worry, you're a heavy favorite). I've quoted odds on games, fights, elections, races, the Academy Awards, California falling into the sea, and when the cherry blossoms would bloom in Washington, D.C. I don't make them on matters involving life and death, although I did once, in 1960, on Caryl Chessman going to the gas chamber (he was a four-to-one favorite to go, which he did).

It is possible to quote a price on any situation. The biggest gamblers in the world, of course, are insurance companies. The first time I ever boarded a plane, Pittsburgh to Baltimore, in 1937, I stopped at the insurance counter. I asked the young lady standing there how it worked.

"Well, sir," she said, "you get five thousand dollars' worth of life insurance for twenty-five cents."

"Give me a dollar's worth," I said, reaching in my pocket. "Twenty-thousand-to-one are the best odds I've ever had."

Insurance companies employ highly trained mathematicians, known as actuaries, to compute the percentages in any situation. With precise formulas, they arrive at rates based in part on age, job, and health.

My own formula isn't quite so scientific, but it works. At least, for me it does:

Knowledge × *Energy* × *Intuition* = *The Odds*.

Whether it's the Super Bowl or the World Series or a presidential election, the formula holds up. *Knowledge* means the information I collect. *Energy* means the money and time I spend analyzing all the key elements, in the same way a broker analyzes the stock market. *Intuition* means how I react to the intangibles, what kind of gut feeling I have when I look at the whole.

Intuition is often the most important factor of all. A computer can absorb the raw material, perform the tasks of knowledge and energy, and spit out a price. But it won't have the full picture, because computers can't handle the intangibles—a team's mental attitude or a politician's charisma. It starts there, with that visceral feeling, the one you get when you look at a game and you think, "The line ought to be six. Now why do I feel that way?"

I haven't found a computer yet that ever had a gut reaction.

You learn by experience. When you figured a team wrong—you made a bad number—you look at it, study it, ask why. Then you decide: it was the wide receiver, his speed. When I first began to

handicap football, speed was the first item I considered. Then it was
the quarterback, who came in with the T-formation, replacing the
tailback (in the single wing) as the key man on the field.

So now I had two categories: speed and the quarterback. Then I
discovered a third. I had a bet won when, suddenly, a cornerback
slipped and fell and the other team completed a touchdown pass
over him. Right then, I began to think about the cornerback and his
importance to the team.

At the start of the 1974 season, my system included nine
categories: 1) team speed, 2) defensive secondary, 3) the quarterback, 4) front defense, 5) running game, 6) kicking game, 7) special
teams, 8) home field, and 9) intangibles, which includes those cases
where I may be aware that one team has a better game plan.

It is a continuing process, slow changes over a period of years. It
was only in 1966 that I added the special teams as a factor. Suddenly,
my numbers on Cleveland and Green Bay were wrong. I just
couldn't understand it. The game has to play *to the number*. Their
games were not. I kept checking my figures, my categories, and
finally it dawned on me. Blanton Collier and Vince Lombardi were
beating people with their specialty teams, at a time when some
coaches considered such units to be cannon fodder. Later, along
came George Allen and Don Shula, taking pride in their special
teams.

By the end of the 1974 season I had added yet another category, a
tenth: *discipline.* I'll give a point or two for that, based on
information that comes to me about the player attitudes, habits, how
they practice, their off-the-field behavior, the black and white
problems. And what I see for myself in the stadium and on the TV
screen.

I used to lump this under coaching, which fell under intangibles.
(Lombardi, Shula, and John Madden of Oakland were the only
coaches to whom I awarded points, on their own, as a factor in the
game.) But discipline commands more attention now, in an age when
some coaches are permissive, some players militant, and some teams
caught in the middle. You seldom give points for coaching, since
most coaches are equal. What you do is take off points for *bad*

coaches, such as Otto Graham, when he was with Washington, Joe Kuharich at Philadelphia, and Joe Schmidt at Detroit.

All of which comes under the heading of research. When it is done, I name a favorite by the number of points I think will equalize the game for the public. The points are there, at least in part, to assure the fairness of a friendly wager. Okay, take the 1969 Super Bowl. To me, the Colts by seventeen figured to be the number that best reflected what the fans believed to be the difference in the teams. As it developed, the number went a little higher in Baltimore and New York, moving as high as twenty. The NFL sentiment was strong in both cities, and the Giant rooters—who detested the upstart Jets—were betting the Colts big.

The Jets were regarded as somewhat of a fluke, an average team—with only the third best record in its own league—carried by a theatrical but gifted quarterback. The AFL was not exactly held in universal respect. Its champions (Kansas City and Oakland) had been beaten badly by Green Bay in the first two Super Bowls.

In most of the country the number on Super Bowl III held at seventeen, which meant that approximately an equal amount of money was being bet on each side. It also meant that my opinion had been correct.

As an oddsmaker, whether I'm right or wrong is determined *before* a game starts—by how the public reacts—not by a final score. I don't expect people to understand that. When I name a betting favorite they relate this to picking a winner, which is why I still sweat out every result. I'm human. I like to be right, too, *in the public's mind.*

But in a way I'm just like an umpire. An oddsmaker only draws notice when the fans think he has blown one. Nothing I had done in my life had prepared me for the overnight fame—well, notoriety— that came with the Jets' victory over the Colts. This was the game, remember, that won me the Bonehead of the Year award in Dallas.

There is yet another factor that goes into the weighing of the odds, and that is what the public *believes.* I have, on rare occasion, made a number that went against my own instincts because to do otherwise would have resulted in an *unrealistic* number, and the fans would scurry, trying to find a place to bet. That's what we try to avoid.

For example, the Joe Frazier–George Foreman fight in Kingston, Jamaica. I thought Frazier was ready to be taken. He was not training well, tended to get high blood pressure in camp, and, at that time, might have had trouble passing the California physical test. We knew, too, that Joe was overconfident, and that Foreman was the type of fighter who could hurt him. George had a punch like a mule. And Joe's style, always coming straight in, was like giving Aaron a waist-high fast ball.

But I made Frazier a three-to-one favorite, and this was why: Joe was the champion. Undefeated. In the eyes of the public he *was* the favorite. It's one of the first rules of the craft: you have to make a figure the public thinks is right, too.

The same condition applied to the comeback of Muhammad Ali. Few would remember this, but the day after Foreman belted out Frazier, I made Ali a six-to-five favorite to beat George and regain his title—if they fought within a reasonable time. But two years went by, and the boxing picture turned upside down. Ali had his jaw broken by an unknown, Ken Norton, then struggled to win return matches from both Frazier and Norton. Foreman had demolished each of them in two rounds or less. Ali was over thirty now, the sharpness gone from his legs and fists, and it seemed to many that he just couldn't recover the skills that had been dulled by a three-and-a-half-year exile. So in the minds of the public, Foreman figured to be an easy winner.

Now an emotional thing happened. I made Foreman the favorite, but established the price as eleven-to-five, which tells the fans the fight isn't that easy. Nevada bookies carried Foreman at three-to-one, and the big gamblers backed him.

But the little guy, my people, wanted Ali to win. It was one of the damnedest things I had seen in sports. It had only been a few years since Ali was widely denounced as a traitor, a menace, a threat to the American way of life. To others he was a braggart, a pest, and a clown. He made more people mad than the income tax.

But I have rarely known of a more popular victory in sports than his, a comeback that saw him win the world heavyweight title ten years apart. If I had been betting then, which I wasn't, I would have taken Ali and the odds myself. I thought sure he would win if the fight went past five rounds.

It is not exactly what you would call an exact science. Sometimes, your judgment is right for reasons that turn out to be wrong. That was the case of Secretariat, the week of the Wood Memorial in 1973, winner of the triple crown, an unbeatable horse if there ever was one.

Except that I had an informant whose life was horses, who practically slept at the track. He told me what few people then knew, that Secretariat had an arthritic condition in his left knee. If he didn't work out three or four days before a race to work the stiffness out of the knee, he could not run at top form on race day.

Sure enough, Secretariat didn't work out the week of the Wood Memorial. Later, I learned why. There was a loose horse on the track when his handlers took him out. When they saw the other horse, his trainer and jockey pulled him off the track immediately. All they could do was get the horse hurt, and you don't take risks with a property worth six million dollars. My man was there. He had the binoculars on them. But he didn't see the loose horse, and we assumed the problem was the knee. In interviews before the race I said Secretariat would get beat. And he did.

After that, Will Grimsley of the Associated Press asked me about the Kentucky Derby, and I told him Secretariat would go to the post as a three-to-two or seven-to-five favorite. I told Will that the price was too short in Nevada, where the books were quoting Secretariat at four-to-five. This offended the trainer, Lucien Laurin, and when Secretariat won handily, it pleased him to say that "Jimmy the Greek was wrong." Well, I wasn't. I didn't say Secretariat would lose, only that the Nevada odds were wrong. And the track odds proved me right. He was indeed a super horse, the Mickey Mantle of the paddock. But he was not—because of his arthritic knee—a consistent horse to bet on, such as Native Dancer or Tom Fool.

I have a reverence for numbers, for the odds themselves. I read them the way some people read poetry. Writers have described me as "Oddsmaker to the Nation" and the "Wizard of Odds." Calculating, measuring, comparing, filling up the pages of a note pad with my own equations, I am addicted to it.

In my office in Las Vegas, I keep the sports wires. On weekends, watching the scores come in, checking the ticker, is to me like a doctor taking a pulse.

CHAPTER
12

Politics:
Girls Don't Like Moustaches

Given the slightest excuse, people will bet on the number of jelly beans in a candy store window. I mean, they will bet on anything. But the professionals will tell you that what they bet on most isn't pro football or the Kentucky Derby or the World Series. It's politics. The professionals will tell you that more money, big money, is wagered on a national election than any sports event you can name.

It's the biggest Super Bowl of all.

In the memory of living bookmakers, only one presidential election ever went against the odds. The year was 1948, the underdog was Harry S Truman, and the election—if not the course of history—turned on a point so unlikely that I would hesitate to mention it, if not for the fact that I have the evidence cold.

The boys who set the price and the scientists who made the polls missed something. What they missed was a moustache. On Tom Dewey's face. Because of that shrub of a moustache, I won a suitcase full of money in what has since become the most historic of all presidential elections.

It started in a way that had nothing to do with anything. I was at home in Steubenville, dressing to go out on a date. As I studied myself in the mirror and adjusted my tie, I said idly, "I think I'm going to raise a moustache."

My older sister, Mary, who lived with me then, was across the room. "Jim, don't do it," she said. "Girls don't like moustaches."

"I don't know about that," I said, heading for the door.

I thought no more about it until a few days later. The kid who ran my errands had left my usual supply of out-of-town newspapers on my desk. This day there was a New York edition on top with a picture of Governor Dewey making a speech, with his hand chopping the air. But that wasn't what caught my eye. I stared at his moustache. That neat, manicured little moustache. And instantly in my brain echoed the words: *"Girls don't like moustaches."*

Impossible.

Dewey was as high as thirty-to-one to turn Truman out of office. A cinch. No one gave the feisty Missourian a chance.

That same photograph of Dewey appeared in more of the next day's newspapers. Damnit, I thought, everybody assumes Dewey will win, but how do they know? Fifty-two percent of the voters were women. What if Mary was right?

I decided to find out. My first move was to call the priest at Holy Name. "Father," I said, "I need three women."

There was a slight hesitation. "For what reason, my boy?"

"I want to hire them to stand in front of the A&P store," I said, "and I want them to ask every woman who comes out one question: do they like men with moustaches."

"Jimmy, my boy," he said, "have you taken leave of your senses?"

I assured him that it was all in the interest of science, and the arrangements were made. Among them, for a fee of fifteen dollars apiece, the ladies questioned five hundred shoppers. Over the years, I have often regretted not saving the sheet of paper on which their figures appeared. It would have made a fine political memento, a piece of history. But the breakdown told me exactly what I needed to know.

347 said they did not like moustaches
122 said they did
31 said they didn't care as long as it was on a man

Now my mind began to spin. I was always looking for a long shot. Hell, anyone can find a favorite. But this is what makes a betting man's pulse race. This is where the real carbonation was. Finding an edge on a long shot.

I had learned the value of research from Jack Nolan, an old-line Democratic politician who ran the county. I remembered that Jack always polled two Ohio precincts when he needed a line on a race. For reasons no one really understood, they had never failed to vote for the winner in a national election. (To this day I still poll those two precincts.)

I sent out my ladies—I had already begun to think of them as my "crew"—and in a matter of days we had the figures. The technique we used wasn't what you would call sophisticated. I had them vary the places they went—grocery stores, an expensive dress shop, men's stores, a store in the colored district—but the question was point blank: Will you vote for Truman or Dewey?

It was dead even in one precinct. In the other, Truman led, 48 percent to 46, with the rest undecided.

I was floored. If a pivotal state like Ohio could be a toss-up then someone—a lot of someones—had made a colossal miscalculation. This election was no cinch.

That night I got a ticket on the Spirit of St. Louis when it came through Steubenville, and headed for New York. I had eleven thousand dollars, in cash, in my pocket. They loved favorites in the big cities—especially in the Big Apple.

My old friend Harold Salvey, who was loaded and living in Florida, came to New York to place my bets. That was the kind of friend he was, willing to act as my beard even though he disapproved heatedly of my tossing my money away in such a hopeless cause. Two nights before the election he was still trying to dissuade me. He had stopped off in Washington, visited with some important Democrats, and walked away with four tickets to the party's Victory Ball—if Truman won.

"But even *they* don't think he has a chance," Harold said.

"They just might be surprised before it's over," I said.

"You stick to sports, Greek. That's your game. You're just throwing your money away."

"Look, Harold," I said, "this is no twenty-to-one shot. This is pick 'em."

"Well," he said, shaking his head. "If I can't change your mind, we'll drop by Lindy's tonight and get it down." Lindy's was a sports and show biz haunt on Broadway, and some of the town's biggest bookmakers were patrons of the corned beef and cheesecake served there.

Harold quickly put out the feeler that he wanted to bet ten thousand dollars on Truman at the best price he could get. In no time at all we had the most popular table in the joint. We were offered odds up to twenty-two-to-one. Finally, Harold placed all of it with one fellow at seventeen-to-one.

I said nothing about his taking the shorter price, but Harold read my thoughts. "This guy pays off," he said.

I should point out that Salvey was no debutante when it came to matters of finance. He was a part of the *original* Miami syndicate, a group of six men who controlled all the gambling in Miami.

The next night, election night, we went to the Little Club for dinner where Johnny, the Philip Morris midget, worked. You remember: "Caaaallll for Phiiiillllip Moooorrris." We were ordering and Johnny, in his red-and-black uniform, walked among the tables, calling out the latest election results. Dewey was ahead. Across the table from me, Harold grinned. He was getting caught up in the excitement of the play.

"Johnny," he said, "you got a dollar in your pocket?"

"Yes, sir, Mr. Salvey," the midget said. "What for?"

"Tomorrow night, when we come back for dinner, you sign that dollar and give it to me, and if Truman has won I'll give you a thousand-dollar bill." He pulled one out of his wallet and held it in front of Johnny's nose. I thought the midget was going to wet his pants.

"You got a deal," Johnny said. "I'll take those odds."

When we said good night, Dewey was still leading, but not by the margin that had been projected, and I brimmed with confidence. Salvey was staying at the Waldorf Astoria, and I was across the street at the Beverly. At six o'clock in the morning my phone rang.

Harold's voice was a whisper. "Greek," he said. "You were right. You won."

"Yeah. I know," I said.

At four o'clock I had called Ohio to learn that Truman had carried the state. I knew then he had brought it off—we both had. The Greek had won 170,000 dollars betting against a candidate who looked like the little man on the wedding cake. I went to bed happy as a warm pup.

Harold picked up my winnings the next day and brought them to my room. I had a total of $180,022, including the ten grand I had put up and the change in my pocket. It was the most money, in cash, I had ever won. My next bet was on the U.S. government. I slipped the money—most of it in hundreds and five hundreds and a few thousand-dollar bills—into three brown envelopes, wrapped them separately, went to the Post Office, and mailed them home to myself, each package insured for a hundred dollars.

The odds against it getting lost in the mail, with any amount of insurance on it, were tremendous.

Later, we went back to the Little Club for dinner and Harold paid off little Johnny. Harold, who loved an upset, loved the unexpected, was jubilant over the outcome. My own pleasure was nearly as great as the midget's.

What that election proved to me was the power of the women's vote. It is beyond numbers. Long after I had stopped backing my opinions with money, through my later role as an analyst for the likes of Jack Anderson and Walter Cronkite, this was the key to our research. It is what separates us from other pollsters. I'm giving away a trade secret now, but seventy percent of the people we poll are women. Say we poll a thousand voters. My crews are instructed to include seven hundred women.

That may sound ridiculous to some, but my instincts tell me it's right. You begin with a basic fact: women today represent fifty-four percent of the vote. In most cases, if the husband is undecided his wife will sway him. She's the one who has been to the coffees and the rallies and sized up the candidate on television. It was once the other way around. In all the years since 1944, I would say that this has been the single most important change in our election style. The husband today is too busy or too preoccupied. The wife knows the issues and her mind, once made up, can rarely be changed. Also, if they disagree, she has the ultimate weapon: she can slam the bedroom door on him.

So when you poll the woman you not only have her vote but her husband's thinking as well. One clue to the trend can be found in the letters to the editor's columns, which are dominated by women during the heat of a political season.

This frame of reference led me, in late 1971, to establish Ted Kennedy as a much bigger underdog to Nixon than anyone else had projected in the early line for '72. I based this on a poll we had taken, in which sixty-seven percent of the women said they would vote against the youngest of the Kennedy brothers. After Chappaquiddick, there was simply a lingering suspicion, an uneasiness, especially on the part of women over twenty-seven, which Ted had not been able to overcome.

I believe he was wise to withdraw from the race, and I have no doubt that the burdens of his family obligations weighed heavily in his decision. Ted has led a mercurial life. He was the most open of the brothers. He lived a little, he took a drink, he enjoyed a wager. I happen to know that in 1960 he bet twenty-five thousand dollars at the Cal-Neva Lodge in Lake Tahoe on John Kennedy to win the presidency. The bet was placed with Wingy Gruber, one of the bosses at the Cal-Neva Club, but it wound up with me. Even if Ted would deny it, I was rather proud of him. Hell, a fellow should bet on his brother.

The playboy image dies hard, but tragedy and responsibility have changed and tempered him. It isn't in my nature to see people only as percentages. I often wonder what Ted Kennedy must feel. He's a senator of the United States, two of whose brothers were murdered in high office. I can picture Ted getting up in the morning and the sun is out and he thinks, "By God, this is the day I'm going to run for President." And then he hears a car backfire in the street and he thinks, "What the hell do I want with it?"

In one of the first columns I ever wrote on politics, in the *Las Vegas Sun* in 1963, I described Ted Kennedy as "the shining star of politics." I wrote that of the three Kennedy brothers he had the most exciting personality, and I predicted he would be President someday.

He still can, if he has the patience and doesn't lose the ambition. His time could be 1980 or later, when he is edging past fifty and showing gray at the temples. Women have a tendency to more easily accept and to trust a man with gray in his hair.

As I say, the cult of female voters I discovered for myself in a quirky way in the fall of 1948. Much of what else I learned about politics came from Jack Nolan, one of the great men in my life, an attorney who at the same time was the political boss and best-known gambler in Steubenville. All of which should give you a small idea of how wide open the town was.

Nolan was about five-feet-four, plump, partial to big cigars and fast horses, and as Irish as Paddy's pig. There were eleven thousand voters in Jefferson County when I first met Jack, and I would guess that he knew at least nine thousand by name.

Whenever anyone ran for a state office in Ohio, from governor on down, they came to Jack Nolan—a measure of his power. It was in 1940, a few weeks after the Democratic convention in Chicago, where he had been a delegate, that Nolan called me to his office.

Nolan was strong for Franklin Roosevelt, who was seeking a third term against Wendell Willkie. "Jimmy," he said, "what are the odds on Roosevelt?"

"They're betting two and a half to one," I said.

"Can you place a bet for me?"

"If you want me to."

"How much can you bet?"

"A substantial amount."

"Can you bet a quarter of a million for me?"

I tried not to gulp. "Yes, sir," I said. This was the most powerful man in the state. Whatever I had to do, I wasn't going to tell him no.

"You come up tomorrow. . . ."

"Mr. Nolan," I interrupted. "I can bet it, but I don't have that kind of credit. You'll have to put the money up. But if you do I'll see to it that the other party's money is also guaranteed."

"All right," he said. "Come by tomorrow and I'll have the money for you."

The next day he handed me five cashier's checks, each drawn for fifty thousand dollars.

As a matter of form, I began to clarify the bet. "You're betting two hundred and fifty thousand dollars," I said, "to win a hundred thousand dollars. You've got Roosevelt. In case of a death to either candidate previous to the election, the bet is off. In the event . . ."

"Stop talking, Jimmy," he said, smiling, "and get it down."

I started out simply to offer Nolan a little, shall we say, professional courtesy. I made my living gambling. It was my *career*. This was when I kept an office in the National Exchange Bank building, with the door labeled "B & F Commissioner." I had, by the way, just turned twenty-one.

That night, before I could place Nolan's bet, there was a major news break. John L. Lewis, the pugnacious leader of the United Mine Workers—John L. of the bushy eyebrows—had come out for Willkie, after supporting FDR for eight years. Talk about a lucky stroke. Republican money showed instantly and the price fell to ten-to-six.

All of a sudden I could bet Nolan's roll on Roosevelt with a chance to win back 135,000 dollars. The money was covered in Pittsburgh, through the help of Slim Silverheart (the greatest gambling name I ever heard). Roosevelt won in a breeze, Willkie carrying only ten states.

A few days later I was in Nolan's office, returning his five cashier's checks, plus the hundred thousand dollars he had won. The extra thirty-five grand I kept. I wasn't stealing. If the odds had shifted the other way, I'd have had to make good the difference.

"Jimmy, you did a great job," he said. He counted out five thousand dollars from the pile and handed it to me. "For your efforts, five percent. Is that fair?"

I did some fast thinking. I was now thirty-five thousand dollars ahead, on *his* money. This was no time to get greedy. "Tell you what, Mr. Nolan," I said. "This election must have cost you a bundle. Please take my five percent and donate it to the Democratic party, on my behalf."

A tear came to his eye. "Jimmy," he said, leaping from his chair,

"God bless you. That's a very thoughtful gesture. If you ever need a friend, you have one in Jack Nolan."

To this day, I have never met a man who better understood the psychology of politics. One year his candidate in a mayor's election, a railroad man, was a lopsided underdog. There was no way he could win, or so everyone thought. Except Nolan. He knew a way.

"Jimmy," he said, "do me a favor. Go up on Sixth Street tonight and offer to bet any amount, at even money, on my man to win the election."

"I'll bet you myself," I said, laughing. "I'll take that. Up there, I'll get faded like crazy."

"Don't worry about getting faded. This is the way we're going to do it. You take this"—he handed me two thousand dollars—"and there's more if you need it. You'll get some takers, but then it will dry up. You'll see. Now please do as I say."

That night I stopped at the street corner on Sixth, outside of Charlie Greenberg's joint. "All right," I barked, "I'm betting even money on the railroader, any amount."

In no time at all I had a crowd around me. "I got two hundred dollars," yells one guy. "I'll take three hundred dollars," another chimed in. Almost as quick as a finger snap, eleven hundred dollars was gone. Then, just as Nolan had predicted, the action stopped cold. "Come on," I said, waving a fistful of dollars, "I've got the Democrat, even money. Who wants some more?"

No one did. The next day it was all over town. By the end of the week the railroader had become the betting favorite at six-to-five. He closed at nine-to-five and won in a cakewalk. Nolan had turned the town around. He convinced them his man was going to win. Psychologically, everyone *wants* to vote for the winner.

I figured we were even now. I had used Jack's money, he had used my reputation. It was quid pro quo.

Jack and I became partners in a half-mile racetrack in Steubenville, which we planned in due time to convert into a dog track. I had only one small problem: dog racing was illegal in Ohio. But Jack was working on an annual coincidence, in which the law would close us down each year at the end of our ninety-day season, and we would remain closed until it was time for next year's opening.

We were still working on it the Friday night before the Democratic convention of 1944. Jack called to say good-bye. "I'm off to Chicago," he announced, his voice filled with the fever he always contracted at that time of year. "I'll be at the LaSalle Hotel."

"Okay, partner," I said.

This was to be a special convention. Jack was to nominate a congressman named Ferguson, from Ohio, for the vice-presidency. Roosevelt, having dumped Wallace, had thrown it open to the floor.

One of Nolan's theories, incidentally, was that you never bet on a candidate after his party's convention. You waited until the *other* party did its act, when spirits and loyalties were pumped to a high. One of the last things Jack said to me was, "We're not going to get our money down on Roosevelt yet," he said. "We'll wait until all this cools down. When the Republicans have made their speeches, that's the time."

Jack didn't live to bet again on FDR, who won a fourth term over Dewey. The night before he was to nominate Ferguson he turned on the shower in his room, was scalded by a blast of hot water, and died of a heart attack en route to a hospital. Had Nolan lived, and with Ohio's support, Ferguson might have been on the ticket instead of Truman. When Roosevelt died less than a year later, Ferguson would have been President.

And now I can't even remember his first name.

With Jack's death I lost a friend and a mentor, not to mention a dog track. My interest in politics began with Jack Nolan. To this day it excites me as no other subject. It has all the drama, detail, color, and *meanness* of sports—but the stakes are out there where the meter doesn't register.

But my interest is purely as an analyst, as a spectator. Only once in my life did I ever actively involve myself in a political campaign, and that was for the best of reasons—revenge. In 1963, when I was forced to close my Vegas Sports and Turf Club by the Justice Department, I had three opportunities to sell, to pay off my debts and walk away with a little dignity. The office of the then governor of Nevada, Grant Sawyer, disapproved each of the prospective buyers. I was broke, and into bitter times.

I took it upon myself to work for the election of Sawyer's

Republican opponent, Paul Laxalt, whom I had never met. I went to the hotels and casinos and talked to the captains on each shift. Most of them I knew from Steubenville. There is a kind of Steubvenville ex-students' association in Las Vegas, maybe four hundred of us who learned the gambling business there. The captains talked to the dealers, and the wives to the neighbors, and we got out the vote.

Laxalt won. When we met for the first time, a few weeks before the election, Laxalt remarked that he had heard about my efforts. As Rick said to Louie at the Casablanca airport, it was the start of a beautiful friendship.

I made my last election bet in 1960, on the Kennedy–Nixon race. And lost. I was settled in Las Vegas by then and arguing politics almost daily with Wilbur Clark, who owned the Desert Inn and had helped put Vegas on the map. Wilbur was a silent partner of mine in the Vegas Turf and Sports Club but when it came to elections he loved to test me.

That year I didn't think John Kennedy could even win his party's nomination.

"He's a living cinch to get it," Wilbur said.

"I'm not so sure," I said. "He has to beat Johnson and Stevenson."

"I'll bet you twenty-five thousand dollars," Wilbur said, waving a hand. "You can pay me when you get it."

I should have known better. On elections Wilbur had the surest instinct of any man I've ever met. He could *feel* the winner. And he knew John Kennedy, a personal touch that made his opinion even stronger. Kennedy had stopped in Vegas once. In those years, anybody important enough to have a Social Security number stayed at the Desert Inn, and Wilbur had his picture taken with the young senator. From then on he was one of Wilbur's favorites.

The morning after Kennedy had won the West Virginia primary, I walked into Clark's office.

"*Who* do you think just called me?" he asked.

"Who, Wilbur?" I said, innocently. I could practically see a canary feather flutter from his lips.

"The next President of the United States," he said, "that's who."

To make a long story terse, I lost the twenty-five-thousand-dollar bet on the nomination. But as the election neared, my figures showed it to be a toss-up. Kennedy was a big favorite. After the famous television debates he had moved out at two-to-one, then eleven-to-five, and was now holding at two-and-a-half-to-one. But no matter how I figured it, it kept coming out a toss-up, a photo finish.

Wilbur disagreed. "Kennedy's a cinch," he said. "A living cinch."

"Wilbur, I've gone over this thing a hundred times and I'm telling you, this election is a coin flip."

"If you really think so," he said, his eyes lighting up, "I'd like to make a bet. A big one. I'll bet you a hundred thousand dollars and lay two-and-a-half-to-one."

"Okay," I said, "your hundred thousand against my forty. And even if it's my last forty thousand dollars I'm going to take it, because I know this race is even money."

"You might think it is," Wilbur said, "but I think it's ten-to-one."

In other matters of chance, Wilbur Clark couldn't pick his nose. He had horses, but they won when he didn't bet them and lost when he did. In the casino he was a cipher. But he had this *feel* for politics.

"Are you going to lay this off, Jimmy? Or are you going to keep it all yourself?"

I never lied to Wilbur. "I'm keeping it myself."

He nodded. "All right," he said, "you'll be paying me off at ten thousand dollars a month for four months."

I laughed. "I paid the twenty-five thousand dollars that way," I reminded him.

On election day we began to get the results from the eastern states. Kennedy was leading, but according to my state-by-state breakdown everything was developing the way it should. In some states it was even closer than I had thought it would be. But Wilbur just kept grinning.

"I told you," he said. "Jack's a living cinch."

"Listen, baby," I said, "this ain't over yet. You got a long way to go."

"If you want it," he said, "you can have twenty-five-to-one for another thousand dollars."

"You're damned right I want it," I said, "and on this one we'll pay off tomorrow."

"I'm glad I thought of it."

I just shook my head. "Wilbur, believe me, you're overlaying it."

The next morning we still didn't know who the President was. Nixon had come on strong in the midwest and in the west, just as I thought he would. I have a chance at winning $125,000, and the TV boys are still hedging.

I called Wilbur. "Mr. Clark," I said, "would you call this pick 'em?"

"Pick 'em, schmick 'em," he said. "Get my money ready."

It had never dawned on him that he might lose. When the votes were in, Kennedy had won it, by a plurality of fewer than 150,000 votes out of the nearly 70 million that were cast.

For the next four months I worked for Wilbur Clark—at ten thousand dollars a month. That whole year went to Wilbur Clark.

But at least I felt vindicated in one respect. My figures had been correct. By the time the 1964 election rolled around, even Lyndon Baines Johnson was aware of my figures. In October of that year the President was to appear in Las Vegas on a Sunday, on a campaign swing through the western states. To coincide with Johnson's visit, Hank Greenspun, the publisher of the *Las Vegas Sun*, suggested that I publish my state-by-state analysis for the weekend paper.

I was all ready for him. According to my forecast, Johnson would win forty-four states, Barry Goldwater would take four, and two were undecided. As far as I was concerned, the election was off the board. When I wrote that Johnson should be ten-million-to-one, it made headlines in other newspapers around the country.

Johnson was flying into the city when Howard Cannon, the senator from Nevada who was in his traveling party, handed him a copy of the *Sun*, with my column prominently displayed on page 1. Johnson, who liked favorable polls only slightly better than his left eye, was euphoric. "We spend all that money taking our own polls," he said, "and for a quarter I can find out all I want to know in the Las Vegas paper." Then he turned to Cannon. "Does this fellow Snyder know what the hell he's talking about?"

"He better," the Senator assured him, "because it means whether he eats or not."

Johnson folded the paper and put it in his coat pocket. "Well, Howard," he said. "If he's right, we've got to send him a button."

Completing the term of the slain John Kennedy, Johnson wanted desperately to be elected by a margin convincing enough to establish his own presidency. He won with what was then the largest popular vote and the widest popular margin in the nation's history.

A few days after the election, I received in the mail a small box from the White House. In it was a gold LBJ lapel pin.

Politicians, of course, do not respect neutrality. If you print results favorable to their cause, they react with gratitude, as though you had somehow recognized the rightness of their position. Polls are pure and simple a form of research, and my system differs from those used by the Harris or Gallup agencies. They base theirs on national percentages. I find that faulty. We break ours down state by state, according to electoral votes. That's where the elections are won. A candidate can win a state by three or three million, he still gets X number of electoral votes.

In 1968, when the other polls had Nixon and Humphrey too close to call, I made the number on Nixon four-to-one. I predicted he would get three hundred electoral votes. He got 301. On election night, Walter Cronkite's people at CBS kept phoning to check my figures, and I stood by them. The only state I really missed was Texas, where George Wallace slipped in. My people had contacted 164 political writers in Texas, and 163 thought Nixon would carry the state.

The work that has, in retrospect, pleased me the most took place that year, 1968. It was a tough year to be right. The nation had suffered continuing spasms of guilt, over the deaths of Martin Luther King and Bobby Kennedy, a war that wouldn't end, and riots on our college campuses. It was a bad year for politics. A bad year for anything.

At least ten days before any convention, I correctly predicted all six places on the three presidential tickets: Nixon and Agnew, Humphrey and Muskie, Wallace and LeMay.

As early as 1966 I had described Richard Nixon as the strongest candidate the Republicans had. Even my publisher, Hank Greenspun, thought I was nuts. We bet a box of cigars on it. But it was obvious to me that Nixon was picking up brownie points all over the country. The Republicans had been butchered in '64 with the

Goldwater candidacy, after a bitter convention fight against Rockefeller. Nixon was the only one out in the field fighting for the party's candidates in the midterm elections. There was no way Goldwater's people would let Rockefeller have the nomination; George Romney had eliminated himself with his famous "I was brainwashed" quote after a trip to Vietnam, and I could see no one else emerging.

Picking Spiro Agnew as Nixon's running mate was something else. I had listed him among six possibilities, including Jimmy Rhodes of Ohio, Gerald Ford, Chuck Percy, John Volpe, and Romney. It was clear that the Nixon ticket would be best served by a vice-presidential nominee from one of the midwest or border states. Nixon's strength was west of the Mississippi and in the south.

Rhodes, Romney, and Agnew were either uncommitted or had been leaning toward Rockefeller, with the convention two weeks away. I decided that the fellow who jumped first, who declared his support of Nixon, would get it. Within a day or two Agnew, displeased by Rocky's indecision, announced for Nixon.

My next column in the *Las Vegas Sun* declared that Spiro Agnew, governor of Maryland, would be Nixon's choice as Vice-President—and Nixon hadn't even been nominated yet. The ironic thing was that until he landed on the ticket in Miami, I didn't even know Agnew was Greek. It had never crossed my mind.

Picking Ed Muskie was a little easier. If you paid any attention to the speeches of Hubert Humphrey—it's surprising how many people didn't—you would have detected certain flattering references to the gaunt senator from Maine. Muskie was a New Englander, and a Catholic, a good balance for the ticket. I had projected Humphrey as the favorite from the start (one-hundred-to-one after the death of Robert Kennedy). Had Bobby Kennedy lived, I believe he would have been persuaded to accept the second spot on a Humphrey-Kennedy ticket.

As for Curtis LeMay, the darkest shot of all as George Wallace's American Party choice, frankly, that one was a tip. The night before he accepted Wallace's offer, LeMay called his old friend Charles Barron, the retired Air Force general who was then an executive with the Sands Hotel. I had good information going for me.

By and large, as I have said, the people in politics are not much different from those in sports. You project them to win and they interpret this to mean you are on their side. And the reverse is equally true.

During any election, after any poll, I receive my share of crank calls. Out of every 100 that came into my office in that 1968 election, 98 would be from Wallace supporters. I had made the odds five-hundred-to-one that Wallace couldn't be elected, even though he had from eleven to sixteen percent of the vote at different times and people were speculating that he could throw the race into the electoral college.

One day my secretary buzzed my line, her voice a bit amused. "It's somebody from the south," she guessed.

I picked up the phone.

"Yew Jimmy the Greek?"

"Yeeessss."

"Yew sumbitch. What raht you got sayin' Guvnah Wallace is five-hundred-to-one? What the sheet do yew know 'bout it? Would yew care to make a wajuh?"

I explained to the gentleman how the odds and the projections worked. Patiently, I told him that it was impossible for the governor to win the election, even if he forced it into the electoral college.

He said, "I tell yew what ahm gonna do. Ahm comin' up there with a hunnert thousan' dollahs and we'll see what kind of a gambler yew are."

I said, "Sir, I don't gamble. It's against the law, you know, to bet on a presidential election."

"Well, then," he said, "yew just a lot of bullshit."

Now I'm mad. "Sir, I'll tell you what. For me to cover your bet would be illegal. But if you'll bring the money here, you bring it to the state of Nevada, and I'll see that it gets covered." And I hung up.

Dee Coakley, my secretary, stared at me. "Mr. Snyder," she said, "do you know how much money that is, a hundred thousand dollars at five-hundred-to-one odds?"

"That's all right, Dee," I assured her. "If he wins the bet I'll just make him a partner." Of course, neither the caller nor the money ever appeared.

CHAPTER
13

Nixon:
A Thousand-to-One
Against Impeachment

On the wall in my office in Las Vegas hangs a framed cartoon by Jim Berry, which shows John Mitchell leaning over the shoulder of Richard Nixon. "I don't care what Gallup or Harris says," reads the caption, "tell me what Jimmy the Greek says."

It was the original cartoon, inscribed by both the artist and the thirty-seventh President of the United States. Herb Klein, Nixon's press secretary back in the Ike days, later his "communications" director, mailed it to me. Klein was my contact at the White House.

I could be the greatest odds maker in the world—and I am—and I would not have wanted to quote you odds in the spring of 1972 that Richard Nixon and Spiro Agnew would resign from the two highest offices in the land, shamed and broken men. Would anyone?

I am often asked, almost accusingly, if polls influence elections. As events of that period unfolded, I would have to suspect that they influenced a good deal more. Let me back up a bit, to July of 1970, to a meeting in Chicago with Jack Anderson, who wanted me to establish odds and provide the polling for his syndicated political column.

"Greek, we've followed you closely and, damnit, you're always right," he said. "I want you with me. And we'll pay."

I made Jack a counterproposition. I would furnish the polls to him exclusively, but my odds would continue to be available to any paper or any newsman asking for them. That was a rule I wouldn't bend. Even when I agreed, later, to write a column of my own for Publisher's Hall Syndicate, it was on the condition that I wouldn't hold back the odds. In other words, if a paper in opposition to one that carried my column called and asked for a number, I was free to give it to them. I assure you, that represents one helluva concession in the publishing business.

There was one other thing. I wouldn't accept his money. I never had, not for any work I might do involving politics. This was to avoid the risk of being compromised. Let's face it. I've got a touch of larceny in me. Show me a man who hasn't and I will make arrangements for him to be stuffed and mounted and shipped to the Smithsonian, because he will be one of a kind.

Jack said, "However you want it. But let's do something on the potential candidates in '72 as quickly as possible."

I said, "I'll have one for you in sixty days."

Two months later Anderson released our poll. It showed Edmund Muskie comfortably in front for the Democratic nomination. But more than that, we had established Muskie as *a seven-to-five favorite over Nixon to win the Presidency*. The figures left no question.

Nixon was beatable. The stock market was in trouble. Unemployment was still rising. The war in Vietnam had widened, causing more grief. In May, Kent State had exploded.

Not long after Anderson's column appeared, I ran into Herb Klein in Los Angeles. He seemed cool. "Herb," I said, "don't be peeved with me because I made the President an underdog to Muskie. That's the way it figured. If anything, I was light. The odds could have been a little higher."

What I didn't know, had no way of knowing until much later, was the wild reaction that poll had caused in and around the White House. A Nixon aide would testify before the House Judiciary Committee that the Dirty Tricks Squad was organized soon after, to stop Ed Muskie, harass his campaign, and neutralize the lead that a poll—my poll, in Anderson's column—showed him holding over the President.

Dirty Tricks begat the Plumbers, and the Plumbers begat Watergate.

I really don't want that, any of it, on my conscience. But it raises a point that people kept missing throughout the long ordeal of Watergate. Time and again I heard people ask, Why? Why did they do it, when Nixon could have beaten McGovern by staying in bed (which he practically did)?

But it was the Muskie candidacy, not McGovern's, that caused the Committee to Re-Elect the President its nervous moments, and led the President's men to bury him in the saddest political scandal the country has ever seen. They wanted to head off Muskie's nomination, if they could. It was to that purpose that all the funny games were first directed.

It started with a form of espionage not unfamiliar to the American political system. But somewhere along the line, it burst out of control. Money was spent, lies were told, power misused on a scale the American public had never before imagined.

The phony letters, the fake stories, the sabotaged schedules, who can really measure how much those damaged the campaign of Ed Muskie? But there is no question that the people at CREEP wanted McGovern. And McGovern they got.

It is a law of politics that where you match two candidates who are middle-of-the-road, the election will be close. As witness Kennedy–Nixon, and Nixon–Humphrey. In fact, even though events were running Nixon's way by 1972, had either Muskie or Humphrey been the Democratic nominee, the race would have been tight. It is when a party selects a candidate from the edges, the far left or the far right, a Goldwater or a McGovern, that it gets stomped.

That first presidential sampling of mine seemed to have been more widely read than *Confessions of a French Secretary.* In December of 1970 I was in Washington, and Senator Cannon from Nevada invited me to drop by. He said someone wanted to meet me. He led me through the halls and downstairs and, finally, he opened an office door; sitting there behind a large desk was this Lincolnesque figure, the lanky senator from Maine.

Ed Muskie smiled and thanked me for having made him the favorite. I started to explain that the numbers, not Jimmy the Greek, did that. But before I could he said, "I want you to know that we printed fifty thousand copies of the Anderson column, mailed them out, and raised nearly four hundred thousand dollars."

"Well, that's fine, Senator," I said, with a grin, "but where's my end?"

We chatted about the coming Democratic primaries, and I was startled to hear Muskie say the important one was in Florida.

"What's important about it?" I said.

"I've got to win it to knock Hubert out."

"Senator," I said, "neither one of you is going to win down there. Wallace is going to win it."

He flashed me a tolerant smile and said, "Ohhh, we're going to win it, all right."

I said, "Senator, you better get up to New Hampshire. Play the ones you've got. Stay cool to Florida."

Jack Anderson had told me that, whatever else we did, he needed the Florida outcome badly. In January of that new political year, my staff got on top of it. Florida was a beast of a race that discouraged most of the other pollsters. There were eleven candidates. We called it in the exact order of finish, right down the line, with almost the exact percentages. It was Wallace, Muskie, and Humphrey, with Jackson a close fourth. Anderson went out of his skull.

I have refined our research considerably since 1948, when we picked Harry Truman to win on the basis of Dewey's moustache. We break down our polling today into three categories: issues, image, and support. Under them are twenty-seven criteria. For example, we had Nixon a hundred-to-one over McGovern—it could have been more—on a line that looked like this:

NIXON   *McGOVERN*

Issues

10	Foreign Affairs	2
10	Business	2

7	Military	1
9	Law and Order	7
7	Busing	3
7	Economy	6
7	Welfare	7
8	Farm Subsidy	10
7	Federal Spending	7
3	Revenue Sharing	3
6	Vietnam	4
81		52

Image

10	Recognition	8
9	Politician	4
7	Credibility	3
7	Charisma	5
7	Intelligence	4
9	Religion	8
49		32

Support

10	Foreign Support	1
8	Financial	3
10	Republicans	½
4	Democrats	6
10	Big Business	2
6	Jewish-Americans	4
6	Independents	3
6	Labor	4
5	Youth	5
3	Minorities	6
68		34½

No President was ever elected with a larger mandate than Richard Nixon appeared to have, from every corner of American life. If ever a man's fortunes seemed to be ascending, if anyone's future ever looked golden, it was Richard Nixon's. By the time the election was over, Jimmy the Greek was known as the President's favorite pollster. And occupying the second highest office in the land was another Greek.

Hey, my future didn't look so bad, either.

Then came the self-destruction of Spiro Agnew. I had already established him as the favorite for the Republican nomination in 1976. There was no doubt in anyone's mind that he would head the party's ticket. He was the living embodiment of the great American dream sequence. Nowhere else in the world can a fellow fall out of bed one morning and find himself a star. And having achieved that, disappear as quickly or completely.

My information was that Agnew resigned for reasons other than his tax problem or the charge that he accepted graft from Baltimore County contractors. I am told that he was willing to fight that, and he felt he could win. But he had attended certain motel parties while he was the governor of Maryland, and he didn't want to put his family through the gossip that would be made of that.

Has there ever been a more ill-fated pair in the history of American government? I guess not. Agnew's downfall coincided with the rough beginnings of Watergate and, suddenly, the country felt as though it were on a road never traveled before, taking us we knew not where. And not a comfort station for miles.

I don't think I felt much different from most Americans during that time. I exclude the partisan or the ideologue, who always prefers someone else. I think most of the public wanted to believe that their President wasn't guilty of anything.

My own feelings were complicated by the fact that I had met Julie Nixon Eisenhower, through friends at the *Saturday Evening Post*, and I was taken with her. I had, however, kept my distance from the President, for reasons that had to do with the integrity of my polls. I try like hell to avoid the appearance of taking sides.

I remember meeting Hubert Humphrey at a party in my honor in Minneapolis, shortly after I had made McGovern a two-to-one favorite for the '72 nomination. He arrived late from a speech in

Youngstown, and the guests, everyone, rose when he walked into the room. "Well," I cracked, "I'm glad to see the Senator has arrived to find that he's a two-to-one underdog."

Humphrey grabbed my hand and pumped it. "Jimmy," he said, "at this moment I know your odds are absolutely right. But I'm going to upset them, because I intend to work hard enough to win it."

I said, "Senator, I hope you do."

A few weeks later I was sitting in the box of Bob Strauss at the convention, when Humphrey appeared on the floor. Everyone converged on him. After a while he looked over and noticed me sitting alone, and I waved. Suddenly, I realized he was going to walk over and shake hands. I just wasn't sure that he should, at that particular time, so I bounced out of my seat and met him halfway. I wished him luck and told him—and I believed it—that I considered him one of the great Americans.

I have an enduring affection for Humphrey. He is one of those politicians who overdosed on goodwill and good humor, qualities that the people consistently reject. But he would have been a superior President.

At the time, there was no reason to believe that Dick Nixon wouldn't be. He had wound down the war in Vietnam, opened a bridge to Russia and Red China. The stock market had recovered. The campuses were cooling down.

Watergate had been characterized by Ron Ziegler as "a third-rate burglary," and not many rose to argue with that. It attracted only scattered paragraphs in the papers. No one was paying much attention to it.

But all through 1973 it wouldn't go away. It was like living in London right after the war. Every other week some damned half-buried bomb, some forgotten war souvenir, would explode in your yard. The first inkling of unrest in the Nixon administration had been evident to me when Pete Peterson resigned as secretary of commerce. He said, "I got tired of clicking my heels." I didn't know what he meant at the time. Later, when the stories about Haldeman and Ehrlichman began to surface, I did.

The first time anyone was curious enough to raise the question, I made the odds a thousand-to-one that Nixon wouldn't be impeached.

Art Buchwald, among others, had a dollar on that. I gave a few of my other writer friends—Shana Alexander, Pete Axthelm, and John Merryman—odds of a hundred-to-one for a buck that he would finish his term. I had them sign their dollars for my collection, a practice I picked up from Harold Salvey the night he bet the midget.

Then in January of '74, as soon as the football season ended—first things first—I decided to take a hard look at Watergate. I could see it turning uglier, but I had the gut feeling that Nixon would survive, even though he could no longer rally the country with his dramatic travels. "Nixon," I told a friend, "is plus six abroad and minus twelve at home."

I put my office to work finding out what Congress thought about impeachment. It couldn't be ignored now. The speculation leaped with each new disclosure, with each move. The eighteen-minute gap in the tapes. The firing of Archibald Cox. The transcripts. The sparring with Leon Jaworski. For the first time in centuries people had stopped talking about sex.

We polled Congress. It was 91 against impeachment, 64 in favor, with 105 undecided. That projected to fifty-to-one that Nixon would not be impeached.

For months Jack Anderson and I argued constantly. He knew that I felt some sympathy for the President. But Jack was convinced of his guilt, and certain that Nixon's presidency was doomed. Let me tell you about Jack Anderson. From a moral standpoint, he is damned near a saint. He's a Mormon, has nine kids, doesn't smoke or drink, and I've been around him enough to know that away from his wife he never looks at another female. He probably has more information in his files than the FBI, but I have never known him to use it maliciously. He doesn't knock people for mischief, he won't hurt anyone intentionally, unless it involved an act or deed that affected the way the government worked. He is totally honest.

With me, Jack knew that it was a case of math, not politics. Just a month before the last tape showed—the "smoking pistol" tape—I insisted it was still two-to-one that Nixon wouldn't be impeached.

"Jimmy," he said, "you're crazy. You're dead wrong."

I was looking beyond the obvious. He was by then a slight underdog in the Congress, but there were three other factors that figured into Nixon's future: (1) he could be censured, set down by Congress for ninety days; (2) he could volunteer to step aside for an indefinite period; (3) he could resign. I wasn't saying he was guilty or not guilty. But when you added the four *possibilities*, it boiled down to simple math: two-to-one that he wouldn't be *impeached.*

But in public I had stopped quoting odds. For months Watergate had been a rich new vein of material for nightclub and television comics. One joke had Nixon calling in three immortal ex-Presidents to confer with him. Washington advised him not to tell a lie. Jefferson urged him to follow the Constitution. And Lincoln suggested that he go see whatever was playing at Ford's Theater.

When the jokes stopped, I stopped. It became much, much too serious. A man's existence was at stake. His family was demonstrating, almost daily, a large capacity for public suffering. In such cases the odds often became a part of the results. And as a matter of policy, I don't set odds on moments of urgency or life-and-death situations.

I was still in touch with Herb Klein, who had been squeezed out of the White House some time before by Haldeman and Ehrlichman. But the President had called him back when the trouble got thick. Herb was the guy who supervised the preparation of the transcripts, who put the books together. The Wednesday before it all blew up, I asked Herb, "How about these tapes that are going to Jaworski? Will they kill Nixon or what?"

Herb said, "No, there isn't anything on there they don't know already."

Klein believed that, I'm sure. But in my business, you are only as good as your information, a point I can't make too often (and will probably make again). I was certain Nixon would quit if it appeared that he lacked the votes in the Senate to turn back impeachment. The day the last tape was exposed—and with it Nixon's early knowledge of the cover-up—he still had thirty-nine senators who favored acquittal, enough to win. But it didn't matter now. They had found the smoking gun, without which Wiggins and Sandman and the other Republicans on the Judiciary Committee insisted there was no case.

A few hours before the news broke on television, I received a phone call from Julie Eisenhower's publisher at the *Saturday Evening Post*, Dr. Cory Cervas. She was sobbing, almost incoherent. "Jimmy," she said, "I want you to send a telegram. Tell the President not to resign. This cannot happen. It must not happen."

I couldn't think of a damned thing to say. I knew there was nothing I could put in a telegram that would change anyone's mind. But I knew what the call meant. She kept insisting I should send the wire: "He mustn't quit. He mustn't. He mustn't. Jimmy, we still have time."

I knew she was reflecting what Julie felt, what Julie must have said to her a few minutes earlier. All I could say was, "Cory, I'm sorry. I'm so sorry." She was still crying when I hung up the phone.

It was all over. Within the hour I had heard from two close friends, Jack Kemp, the Buffalo congressman and former quarterback, and Senator Howard Cannon. I did what I'm sure millions of Americans were doing that afternoon. I turned on my television set and listened to a statement by Wiggins, Nixon's staunchest defender in the House, calling for the President to resign. And a few moments later, a TV newsman was reading the letter of resignation that carried the signature of Richard M. Nixon. The date was August 8, 1974.

I reflected on the bitter irony of politics, of life. Two men who might have been President, Ted Kennedy and Spiro Agnew, were out of the picture, Kennedy for now, Agnew forever. And a man who had been President left it in dishonor.

In a curious way, my reputation as a political analyst had benefited from the career of Richard Nixon: through his close defeat to John F. Kennedy, his comeback from the political tombs, his election in '68, and his landslide victory over McGovern.

I'm not a moralizer, and I have no profound point to offer from all of this. If I have learned anything, it is that politicians are the biggest gamblers of all. And no one ever gambled for higher stakes than Richard Nixon.

CHAPTER
14

The Track:
Where Windows Clean You

Late in 1953, not long after my Saudi Arabian fiasco, I was still hanging around New York, suffering a bad case of the shorts and at loose ends, when a friend introduced me to Charlie White. He was an Atlantic City bookmaker, very active, an intense little man with the look of custom tailoring. When he dressed for an evening, he used three different colognes.

"Greek," he said, "I've heard about you, that you know how to bet, how to book, everything."

I blushed attractively and said, "I haven't been active lately. I'm looking for oil. I've been away from betting."

But Charlie had a proposition. He was barred from the track at Atlantic City, but he had a little action going the next day and he needed someone reliable to handle it. Why not? I had planned to go out anyway.

He handed me an envelope containing six thousand dollars, in hundreds. He told me to watch for a certain jockey, in three races, when his horse was in the paddock. "If he takes off his cap and smooths his hair with his hand, you bet him a thousand dollars to win and a thousand dollars to show. If he don't take his cap off, don't bet the race."

I stared at him. "You *got* to bet it," I said. "Either way."

"What do you mean?" he said. "How can you bet it either way?"

"Look. If he doesn't take his hat off, he's telling us he doesn't think his horse can win, right? Then that eliminates one mount. Now, it depends on the price of the horse. If he's sitting on anything up to a six-to-one shot, and he doesn't give us the signal, I think we should bet the favorite, because his chances are now improved by fifteen percent."

"How do you know that," he said, "fifteen percent?"

"Here," I said, taking a pencil and a scrap of paper. "It's simple. Six plus one equals seven, and seven into a hundred is almost fifteen."

I was amazed that an experienced bookmaker didn't know percentages, but I figured he may have been testing me.

"All right," he said, "do it your way. But keep an eye on him. Watch him every second he's in the paddock. He knows somebody will be watching him."

"Do you want me to wear anything special?"

"No," he said, "that don't make no difference."

Now this, I thought, was a great system. *The jockey doesn't know me. I don't know him. He doesn't know who he is signaling, and he doesn't know who is looking for it.*

The next day at the track I checked the prices on our jockey's three mounts: they were six-to-one, four-to-one, and five-to-two. His first appearance was in the third race, and when he moved into the paddock I was on the bridge between the grandstands, looking down. The jockey never moved. I went to the favorite and placed the bets, including two hundred dollars of my own, which constituted most of my worldly assets.

The favorite won and paid five dollars. I was ahead a couple of thousand with Charlie's money and I had won three hundred dollars for myself.

On the jockey's next race the cap came off and he brushed back his hair and I bet everything. His horse dropped from five-to-one to three-to-one. He charged out of the gate like the Light Brigade and won it, wire to wire, and paid eight dollars.

For the last race, he was on the favorite, the five-to-two shot. My eyes never left him in the paddock. He edged up in the saddle, he fixed the stirrups, he adjusted the bridle. I was leaning over the rail of the bridge. He went under me without touching the cap.

It was like candy for the soul. Man, oh man, I thought. Look at this, and I've got somebody else's money on top of it. Charlie had told me to bet a thousand to win and show on each race. But if ever a guy should plunge, I thought, this was it. I didn't really know him well enough to take the chance. Hell, I had had to explain the percentages to him to begin with. But if we lost, at least I'd have the tickets to show him. So I pressed the bet.

With the favorite out, I went to the second choice, a three-to-one shot. On the way to the hundred-dollar window the price dropped to two-to-one, and the horse our jock was on moved to four-to-one. It looked to me as though maybe some other people had the same information I had. Which made it all the stronger.

Everything was all right until the eighth pole, with my horse in front by two lengths. Now who do you think came roaring up? Yeah. The jockey whose horse wasn't supposed to win. That didn't keep him from trying. He was beating the hell out of his horse, laying the whip to both sides, and closing fast. I was about to croak. The finish was a photo . . . but we won.

That night I went around to Charlie White's house. His eyeballs did a pirouette when I handed him his winnings, around fifteen thousand dollars, and a breakdown on the bets and payoffs for each race. He pressed a bonus of fifteen hundred dollars into my hand and asked for a favor. "I got all these betting slips here," he said, nodding at a cardboard box on his desk. "You got the winners of today's races, you know what they paid. Do my bookkeeping for me, Greek, just tonight. As a favor."

When I finished the books I told him he had cleared about twenty-two thousand dollars for the day, including his own bets.

"How about staying on?" he said. "You stay, you got two hundred dollars a day and a piece. Everybody knows Charlie takes real good care of his people."

I found out later that Charlie had to struggle to read or write. I thanked him, but told him I had other plans. I didn't even stick around for a party he was having that night in his home, and a lot of beautiful dolls were going to be there. Charlie was a lady-killer.

Two days later, back at my apartment in New York, there was a knock at the door. Two fellows walked in, blue suits and rotary club faces, and flashed a badge. The FBI. Did I know a Charlie the Blade, a bookmaker in Atlantic City?

I thought fast. "I knew a Charlie White," I said.

How did you know him?

"I'm a handicapper," I said. "I offered him a deal for my services, but he thought the price was too high."

After a few more questions they left, and that was the end of it. How long the FBI had been tailing Charlie, or why, I didn't know. I didn't want to know. Years later I heard he had opened a successful gambling house in London with George Raft, the actor, briefly involved.

I have always considered the racetrack a kind of sanctuary. I never bet the horses *professionally*, as part of my livelihood. Racing is my recreation, my therapy. Other guys go out and get drunk. I go to the track. It is my spa, a place to relax and have fun.

There is a grace and leisure, a mellowness, around a racetrack that doesn't attach to other sports. They take your money just as fast, of course, and that's the trick. It helps your enjoyment if you assume at the start that, sooner or later, the track will end up with your money. It's fun, and it isn't hard-core gambling, *if you don't bet more than you can afford to lose.*

Of course, it doesn't exactly dilute your pleasure to win. Some of my gayer afternoons were spent in Miami, when my ex-father-in-law, old man Miles, had his horses running there.

One morning I rode out to Hialeah with him to time a workout by Rush Act, a gelding he owned. Rush Act had finished out of the money his last six starts, but there was a reason for it. The old man had caught his trainer playing games with his horses. He changed trainers, and no one really knew how to handicap Rush Act. Now he was down to seventy-five hundred dollars claiming races, and was entered the next day at seven furlongs.

In the workout, he breezed three-quarters of a mile in a minute, twelve and two-fifths. The computer in my head began to whir. The horse was ready, and the next time he was a cinch to be at least twenty-to-one on the morning line, off his record.

Rush Act opened at forty-to-one. As I watched that mercury thermometer at Hialeah, he went to sixty, eighty, finally one hundred-to-one. My adrenaline was pumping. The favorite was a horse named Johnny J., owned by a clique out of Canton, another wide-open Ohio burg. Johnny J. was six-to-five, and a couple of busloads of tourists from Canton were betting him like crazy. Quietly, I began buying tickets on Rush Act, twenty dollars across, ten dollars across, five dollars across. To condense a long story: I made a fairly substantial bet, maybe two hundred dollars across the board. His price came down only a little, so I bet another fifty dollars across.

By the time the field went off he was thirty-five-to-one. Johnny J. broke in front and led until right at the wire, when Rush Act—apt name—came on to win. I let out a yell that turned every Flamingo in Hialeah white. The horse paid seventy-seven dollars to win, thirty dollars to place, and thirteen dollars to show. It took me *four* days to cash all the tickets at the two-dollar, five-dollar, and twenty-dollar windows. But it was one of the most memorable periods of recreation I have ever known. Won something like twenty thousand dollars.

Around that time, old man Miles had claimed one of Alfred Vanderbilt's handicap horses, Speed to Spare, and was running him at Tropical Park, with Don Meade the jockey.

Meade was a lively character, whose usual riding style reminded you of a Cossack in heat. In close quarters he was known to use both the whip and an occasional half-nelson. Donald had led the nation's riders in winning mounts in 1941, but he was later suspended in Florida for betting on horses that happened to be competing with his own.

But no one could ride a horse any better than Don Meade, if Don Meade wanted to ride that horse, especially coming out of the gate with a speed-burner. I went down to the saddling path with Mr. Miles, who was a beautiful old fellow, but so tight he squeaked. He just wouldn't give anybody anything.

"Don," the old man said, "you got a good horse. You've got a good chance to win."

"I'm sure that I do," Meade said, "but it would be nice to have something going for me."

With Meade there was no bullshit. I loved him for that. I waited until Miles stepped away and I whispered to Meade: *"I'm betting two thousand dollars. You got a piece of mine."* His face was expressionless. I wanted Don Meade on my side. The old man didn't seem to understand him. But I read him perfectly.

"You're going to get seven hundred and fifty dollars," Miles said when he came back. "Ten percent of the purse. I think that's pretty good." I kept my eye on Meade. Finally, he nodded, just once, without looking at me.

Meade broke Speed to Spare in front and had him three lengths in the lead coming into the stretch. He was starting to shorten his stride, but Meade held him together to win by a half length. The win was worth a grand to the jockey, plus his ten percent of the purse. Don Meade may have been the best rider ever lifted onto a horse.

Bookmakers were not always so sporting. What you have to accept is the fact that bookmakers do not like for other people to make excessive sums of money, at least not on bets that they book. Their position is that this leads to inflation, gout, and other unpleasant human conditions. Whenever possible, to shelter their own losses the boys indulged in a practice known as *laying off.*

The best I ever knew at this art, as it applied to racetracks, was Jimmy Carroll of St. Louis, the very cradle of horse books. Sid Wyman and Charlie Rich had large offices there, furnished somewhat spartanly with a desk and a couple chairs. In those days, people could wire their bets to St. Louis, and many did. Jimmy Carroll was then the official price maker on horses, though not the extravagant gambler many assumed he was. Carroll would take a sizable wager, but he would dump a percentage of it into the racetrack pool to lower the price on the horse he was booking, thereby reducing his risk.

No one really knew what Jimmy was doing, but quite by accident I discovered one day where, and how, he managed to lay it off. I knew a trainer at Oaklawn Park, in Hot Springs, Arkansas, named Red who was a heavy bettor. I mean, he wasn't running horses for the improvement of the breed or even to win purses. He ran them to bet. He phoned me one afternoon at my office in Steubenville.

"Greek, I got some horses down here, and they're ready to run. Can you bet for me? If they knew it was me it would kill the price."

"How much are you thinking about?"

"Up to three thousand dollars across," he said.

"That's no problem, Red, so long as I get the total bet. I don't want you giving it to me and then give it to somebody else, too."

"You got it all," he said.

See, if you're running a betting stable—that is, betting your own horses—the object is to get the biggest possible price. If you give out the horse to everybody, you're just not helping your cause. The fewer people who know about it, the higher the price. I phoned Jimmy Carroll in St. Louis. He agreed to take up to five thousand dollars across the board from me. He also assured me that he wouldn't dump any of the bet into the track itself.

"But," he told me, "I want the bet at least half an hour before post time."

A few days later Red phoned in the morning from Hot Springs with a horse. I waited until the afternoon, half an hour before the post, and called Carroll. I placed the five thousand dollars across. After the race Red called, boiling mad.

"We won it," he said, "but I only got two-to-one."

"What the hell happened to the price?"

"With a couple minutes to post," said Red, "the horse was six-to-one. All at once three thousand dollars hit across the board— just like that, three-three-three. The horse only paid $6.00, $3.20, and $2.40. Greek, the son of a bitch musta dumped it. What do we do now?"

I didn't want to go off half-cocked. "Let's give him another chance," I said. "Maybe it was somebody else."

The next time Red phoned, he had a long shot. We went through the same procedure. His horse lost by a head on this one, but the money showed again. We got a very poor price for place and show. When Red told me about it, I knew for sure that Carroll had dumped the money at the track.

"I'll have to find somebody else to take the bets," I said.

To my surprise, Red didn't agree. "No, stay with Carroll one more time," he said. "I got an idea."

I decided not to argue with him. They were his horses and his money. Besides, I knew Red as a cunning fellow, slightly unpolished, but not easily used. A few days later he called with another horse. "Do it just like you always do," he said. "Only this time see if you can get down for another thousand dollars across."

I asked Jimmy Carroll if he could press the extra thousand for me. "Make it six across," I said. "We can handle it," he said.

This time Red was late in calling back. I was curious as hell. An hour and a half after the race my phone rang. Red was laughing.

"What happened?" I asked.

"We won it," he said, between whoops. "We got eighteen dollars to win, nine dollars to place, six-eighty to show."

"No money showed?"

I had to wait a moment while Red composed himself. "*Nobody* showed," he said, finally.

Then he told me the story. It seemed that across the street from the entrance to Oaklawn Park was a drugstore. A couple of clerks from Carroll's office would park in there between races, waiting near the phone booth. Jimmy would call, give them their instructions, and they would trot across to the track and bet whatever he had told them.

This day the scenario had been a little different. Red had staked out the store and he was ready for them. When the runners started across the street, a car swung up to the curb and three guys piled out. One of them shouted, "Hold it right there." He flashed a badge and ordered the two stooges into the car. They drove aimlessly around Hot Springs for an hour, during which time Carroll's men offered the cops a bribe—a hundred dollars apiece, probably—to let them go. They took the money and finally shoved them out the door, knowing the race was long since over. The phony cops, of course, were hired by Red. But you couldn't have disproved it by looking at them. They had the dark suits, the plain brown shoes that needed a shine, the Dick Tracy hats.

One way or another, justice was served.

I know of only two ways to win consistently at the races: with research, or by backing a great horse. If you're one of those people who thinks he has a system that can't lose, the track will send a car and meet you at the airport.

In the years when Native Dancer and Tom Fool were running, I practically supported myself by betting on them. *Big* bets. I once put up fifty thousand dollars on Tom Fool to win ten thousand dollars, that's how sure I was.

In 1959 I could have darned near retired from what I stood to win on Sword Dancer in the Kentucky Derby. I had taken odds up to fifteen-to-one in the Winter Book at Caliente, on down to three-to-one, and by the day of the race I had bet a total of nearly twenty thousand dollars across. In the stretch, Sword Dancer lost by a nostril in a photo finish to Tomy Lee. Though I made out on place and show, clearing ninety thousand dollars, I had figured to win fifteen times that much. The kicker was that while Sword Dancer went on to be chosen the Horse of the Year, Tomy Lee was to win only one more race in his career, an overnight in California.

All of which recalls the old horseplayer's lament, "I hope I break even; I need the money."

It takes patience to develop a great horse. It doesn't happen in two or three races. But when it does happen, it can be money in the bank for those along for the ride. Of course, inside information is the coin of the racetrack. And sometimes even that can backfire.

In 1949 I was at a dinner party in Fort Lauderdale, attended by Jimmy Jones, son of the legendary Ben, the trainer for Calumet Farm. The year before they had won the Triple Crown with Citation. Now they had the Winter Book favorite for the Kentucky Derby in Blue Peter.

But at the party that night, Jimmy Jones let a bomb drop. "Blue Peter won't be ready for the Derby," he said. "He hasn't been running up to expectations."

Now Fred Hooper had a horse called Olympia, and with Blue Peter out of it I knew Olympia, listed as ten-to-one in the Winter Book, loomed as the favorite. The price figured to drop to maybe three-to-one.

"We'll have Ponder ready," Jimmy Jones said, casually, "but it will be June before he's even close to his best stride." I sympathized with Jimmy, but when he said that I mentally scratched Ponder. After dinner I couldn't get back to Twenty-third Street in Miami Beach fast enough, rubbing my hands all the way. Everyone there had an opinion on the Derby. Twenty-third Street was a supermarket for people wanting to bet horses. That night I must have laid fifteen thousand dollars on Olympia for the Derby, with odds of up to twelve-to-one.

I watched the odds drop on Olympia with the inner contentment of a man who had put his money in gold bullion shortly before the market crash of '29. Olympia went to the post as the favorite, at four-to-five, with Eddie Arcaro in the saddle.

Olympia broke out in front, stayed there for a mile, and finished sixth, barely in time to hear the last chorus of "My Old Kentucky Home." Naturally, you will never guess which horse won: Ponder.

History tells us that Ponder paid thirty-four dollars to win, and I did not have so much as a bus token bet on him. It is trying to understand such matters that keeps a horseplayer's brain, and also his belly, lean and hard.

But to demonstrate how racing luck really works, one of the best days I ever had at the track I forgot to bring any money. I had gone to Gulfstream Park with a friend, Peter Van Vaks, and while he bought the tickets I dropped the car at the valet parking. It wasn't until I was inside that I realized I'd left my cash at home, on my dresser. Pete was already off, wandering through the stands, blocking an aisle someplace.

I reached in my pocket and scooped up the change and counted it. I had $2.80, enough for a two-dollar bet in the first race. English Bid, I think the horse's name was. He won and paid fifty dollars. Here we went. A trainer I knew, F. W. Martin, had three horses running that day. I happened to land on the first two, then I parlayed everything on Martin's horse in the last race. This one came in and paid nine dollars. I would have to say that at that moment my physical tone was splendid. I just cashed in and took home the package.

When I walked in, Charles, who worked around the house for me then, was waiting at the door. "Mr. Snyder," he said, "you forgot your money."

"No, I didn't, Charles."

"Oh, yes, you did, sir."

I reached in my pocket and pulled out a roll that would have choked a rhino. It contained seven thousand dollars. "Then where," I said, grinning at him, "did this come from?"

Charles scratched his head. "I don't know, Mr. Snyder, but the money you had here, it's still here."

When I go to the track, I still bet, but that isn't what pulls me. A light lunch, a little wine, good company, fast horses and slow judgment, that's my idea of a day at the races. I enjoy challenging the board, knowing that in the long run I can only finish second.

And, believe me, many another time I wish I had forgotten to bring my money.

CHAPTER
15

Nick the Greek:
Freeze-out at the Fremont

"The greatest experience in life is winning a bet, and the second greatest is losing one."

—NICK THE GREEK, said many times

There was a kind of faded elegance about Nicholas Dandolos in the final years of his life. He was like a once-rich European aristocrat, living in an empty mansion. The servants were gone. Drop cloths covered what was left of the furniture. The electricity had been turned off. But he still dressed for dinner every night.

He was Nick the Greek, once the biggest name in gambling and, in a way I didn't always enjoy, an important figure in my life. He was the stereotyped movie gambler: a smooth, almost oily charm, complemented by a mean, suspicious mind.

He died broke in 1966 at eighty-three, owing me money and hating me. By then he hated the world, because it wouldn't let him be Nick the Greek forever.

I spent most of my first fifteen years in Las Vegas trying to outgrow being confused with Nick by strangers. But the pros never confused us. "I bet fifty thousand dollars on a football game once," I remember Nick boasting one night across a card table. *"Fifty thousand."*

I let it pass. But a bookmaker named Pittsy Manheim didn't. He winked at me and turned toward Nick. "Hell, that's nothing, Nick," he said. "I know a Greek who once bet a *quarter of a million* on one game."

The boys at the table laughed. Nick glared at me and the space above his collar reddened. We were not of the same generation, but our roots were one. I had respected Nick at one time—Greek kids are brought up to honor their elders. But to him I was a counterfeit. He was the big Greek, the only Greek, and he *was—once*. He didn't like the idea of anyone moving in on his territory.

I'm quite sure that his fame as Nick the Greek didn't hurt me when I came along. I don't take that away from him. His legend enveloped me. It even prompted me to make him a business offer, in 1951, five years before I moved to Las Vegas to stay.

I was friendly with the Goulandris family, the Greek shipowners. (The six richest men in the world were Greek, maybe still are. Does that tell you anything?) I was trying to persuade them to build a hotel in Vegas, which was just starting to boom. The Sands hadn't been finished yet, it was that long ago. We looked at land where Caesar's Palace now stands. The idea was for Nick to be the front man for the hotel, the general host. Nick the Greek, a name that said gambling like a neon sign.

I had suggested to the Goulandris family that Nick deserved a hefty salary, plus five points in the hotel. That's five percent of the profits. Over the years it would have been worth *millions*. But for Nick it wasn't enough. "I can get more points than that," he told me, "from any gambling house in zee vorld. Forget it, kid."

That killed the deal—and a five percent cut I would have collected, too. Maybe, deep down, that's why I didn't try harder to get along with him after I settled in Vegas.

We had first met in 1950, in Florida, where I was in the oil business with Ray Ryan and swapping football games with H. L. Hunt. Nick breezed in one day with Tom Whalen and Murph Calcatura, friends of mine out of St. Louis. They brought him out to my home that winter and introduced us. I was fascinated by him. *Nick the Greek.* He told stories by the hour. He recited poetry. He had a deft touch with a phrase and said things like, "I would rather fall from a mountaintop than die of boredom on the plain."

We drank good wine together. Memory can be a con man, but that night I think I wanted to like him. I mean, I didn't need his patronage. It wasn't a schoolboy thing, the student hoping for the professor's approval. There was just a certain amount of honest admiration for the *name*, for a fellow who had prospered at the business of living by his wits. (I was out of it at the time, being engaged at the witless profession of trying to take oil out of the ground.) And, of course, he was the—more or less—original Greek.

It was remarkable, really, to watch him in action. He attracted people like fish to a flashpan, people who begged him to play with their money. It was the legend and the charm and, no doubt, the idea of sharing winnings with Nick the Greek. He was beautiful with women. He made Omar Sharif look like a truck driver.

He was at the peak of his fame then. He had an entertaining personality, and he bowed to ladies and kissed their hands. This and other odd mannerisms led to a popular belief that he was a very cultured article. But he also had a reputation, in the trade, for running games that were less than pure. In the old days he often traveled with two or three other guys, moving into a town and maneuvering a poker game with the local star or the local money. The star seldom had a chance. Two or three players against one represents almost impossible odds. Whenever one of them had a good hand, he got help in raising the pot against the town pigeon. That's how Nick went around winning all those big pots.

Not that he won them all, but he was invariably promoted as the big winner. He may actually have been among the best, once. But when Vegas hit its stride, he was in games that were on the square, in with younger, sharper cats who knew the percentage on every card that was turned up.

I always suspected that his skills, and his nerve, never really caught up with his publicity. A magazine writer once described a scene in which Nick, sitting with kindred spirits in a parlor car of an eastbound train, passing through a light drizzle, made a bet on which raindrop would hit the bottom of the windowpane first. The bet was for around five hundred dollars. By the time it reached print, the figure was up to fifty thousand dollars.

In Miami, at the racetrack one day, Nick got me alone. "Jeemmy," he said, in his thick, old-country accent, "you got to do me favor. I got to play Ray Ryan again."

Nick and Ryan, it developed, had been in a poker game in Las Vegas, a 250,000-dollar freeze-out. In a freeze-out, you can't quit until you have *all* of the other guy's money. Under the rules, if you quit you forfeit fifty thousand dollars automatically. Now there ain't nobody who's going to kiss off a fifty-grand forfeit. That night, Ryan won it all, the $250,000, but Nick had another reason for wanting to try him again.

"Ryan had a peek on me," Nick insisted. "From behind me, he vas getting signals."

I learned later that Nick played poker like a sucker. He never looked at his cards the way a real player should: low and quick and turn them down. He held his cards high, fanned out. Nick was convinced that Ryan had a peek on him, that is, a conspirator reading Nick's cards and tipping Ryan off. But I knew Ryan better than that. They never had another freeze-out, which didn't exactly surprise me. Neither of them would play unless he thought he had an edge. But at least Ryan used his own money. Nick always had somebody else putting up the bankroll.

A couple of days later Nick asked me to help him cheat Ryan. Yeah. Not just arrange the game. What he had in mind—he soon made clear—was my giving *him* a peek on Ray. For half the winnings. "It voud be easy, Jeem," he pointed out. "He ees your friend, and everyvun knows you are honest man."

Sure, Ray trusted me enough to open his hand to me. The rest would have been a cinch. A certain card, a certain signal—you light a match, touch an ear, a hundred ways of doing it. I refused, informing Nick that I found his style of larceny a bit crude, and that I meant to tell all to Ryan (which I did). Nick was offended. "I vas mistaken," he said. "I thought you vas a gentleman."

That was the beginning of the tension between us. At the time, Nick the Greek was sixty-seven and on his way down. The old ways didn't work any more, but he couldn't let go of the past. He was getting bankrolled less and less. His judgment grew more erratic.

In a curious offshoot to all this, Nick was arrested by the FBI in 1963, along with two or three others, on charges of conspiring to extort money from Ray Ryan.

The problem was that to some people Nick was still a kind of elder statesman, and they believed him. He kept yelping that Ryan owed him; he still thought he had been cheated. The word went down, and one day a couple of young toughs set out to collect on Nick's behalf.

They held Ryan for maybe a day, but Ray was cool enough to get some people on the phone who could straighten it out. In the meantime, they had made the error of driving across the Nevada line into California, and the FBI got interested. Later, the charges against Nick were dropped, but the two young guys who had muscled Ryan were put away for a year, as I remember it.

But back in 1959, by which time I had settled in Vegas and resumed gambling, I couldn't avoid Nick. We sat in on frequent card games and our contacts were polite. Then one night, at the Fremont, we were playing lowball poker. I had never liked cards, but when I moved to Vegas I knew I had to learn to play at least one game well, because it was practically the town sport. (It was like an executive learning to play golf.)

I picked lowball: you take the five lowest cards of the six dealt. Two down and one up. Then three more up, one at a time. I went into a complete study of it. I even put lowball hands on a computer in Santa Monica. I learned the value of the hand according to what was in the pot.

This night we were playing 160-320—the minimum bet was 160 dollars on the first three cards, 320 dollars on the fifth and sixth. The betting got to Nick, who had a nine up, and he raised it 160 dollars. I was to the left of him, the last man, with an eight up and a deuce-trey in the hole—the better hand in three-card. My hand actually called for a raise, but I decided to slow-play it, figuring that Nick might try to steal the ante. I just trailed in.

On the fourth card he drew a nine. I got a jack. Now I was low, because he had the two nines. I bet 160 dollars. He saw it. On the fifth card he caught an off card, a six. I caught an eight, which gave me two eights with the jack up. Over our heads, the cigar and cigarette haze was so thick a plane couldn't land in it. But at the table not a facial muscle had moved.

Nick had the two nines with the six up. He appeared to have the better hand now, because it looked as though he could be low with a nine against my jack. He laid out another 320 dollars, the maximum. There was now nearly seven thousand dollars in the pot. On the last card, he caught another nine—for three nines and a six—and I caught a second jack to go with the two eights. But now I could throw away one of the jacks, which left me with two eights for low. The best Nick could do was throw away one of his nines, which left him with two nines for low. I had him beat. Across the table, the dealer nodded at me.

"Jimmy, you're low," he said.

But alongside me, Nick was shaking his head. "I'm betting another 320 dollars and raising 320 dollars," he growled, biting his cigar. Around the table, a couple of chairs scraped.

I didn't want to embarrass him. In Greek, I asked, "Do you know what you're doing?"

"Bet you hand, punk," Nick snapped. "Who you think you are? Who you think you play with?"

I shrugged. "You asked for it."

Very deliberately, I slid three black hundred-dollar chips and two tens toward the pot. Nick matched them, pushing his chips to the center of the table. "I vill keep raising you," he said, "vit all I got."

Soon it was all out there, nearly thirteen thousand dollars. We were down to the cloth. Nick turned over his other cards, but he still had the two nines. I turned over mine: two eights for low.

"Jimmy wins," the dealer announced.

Nick jumped to his feet. "I vant a house decision," he shouted. "I'm low. Jimmy not low. I vant a house decision on this."

The dealer called over Paul Wyerman, one of the Fremont managing partners. "Paul," said Nick, showing him his cards. "Lowball. Who vins?"

"Well, Nick, Jimmy has the two eights, you got the two nines. Jimmy wins."

Nick whirled toward me, his chair clattering to the floor. "You bastid," Nick snarled. "You punk bastid."

I walked away. I wasn't going to lose my temper with him. Hell, he was older than Moses. If anything, I felt sorry for him. I saw Nick as an almost comic figure, hustling other people's money in the casino. It was his one sure way of showing a profit. He was in for half of what he won; in the meantime he pocketed whatever he could steal while he was playing it.

If my name had been Jimmy the Italian, or Jimmy the Hungarian, it wouldn't have bothered him, I think. But to lose to some hot dog named Jimmy the Greek, that incensed him, it just wrecked him.

Beating me became his obsession. There was no pretense now of being sociable. From then on we were bitter enemies. A few days after the lowball scene, Nick challenged me to a series of freeze-outs, twenty-five thousand dollars each, the money on the table. I beat him the first. He won the second.

The third game—this was happening over a three-month period—took place at the Fremont the night of the first heavyweight title fight between Floyd Patterson and Sweden's Ingemar Johansson. Our competition had not gone unremarked in Las Vegas, a town that dotes on the eternal triangle—two players and a pile of money.

Nick was winning—I was down to about seven thousand dollars—and he couldn't conceal his glee. He grinned. His eyes danced. A little tobacco juice stained the corner of his mouth from the cigar he was always chewing.

The fight was coming on soon, and Paul Wyerman brought over a radio. They were in the middle of the ring introductions. Across the poker table, Nick sat back, shifted his cigar, and threw me a long look. "What price the fight?" he asked.

I said, "Six-to-one, Patterson."

"Who you like?"

"I don't care," I said, "as long as I get the price."

In his head he was counting the money on the table. He wanted to clean me out quick. "You got seven thousand dollars," he said. "I give you six-to-one. You got the Swede."

I nodded. We're betting for the whole pile, or damned near. He has forty-three thousand dollars in front of him. He kept out a grand, and we moved all the checks to the center of the table.

No one had really known what to make of Johansson. He was a

blond, dimple-chinned playboy whose training camp featured Swedish beer and a cupcake named Birgit. By contrast, Patterson lived like a monk. But I liked the price. And I thought Floyd had a chin made of fine crystal.

Ingo put him away in the third round, using a combination he called "toonder and lightning." The world had a new heavyweight boxing champion, and I had rebuilt my holdings into a fast forty-nine thousand dollars.

Nick was down to that last grand. In no time I had taken that, too. He was tapped out. But with gamblers, such a condition is only temporary. As test pilots love to put it, "There's always another dawn."

"Vait, vait," he said, "I come back. I go to the Sands and get money. Ve keep playing."

I was stacking the chips and handing them to Paul to be cashed. I shook my head. "Not tonight, Nick. Let's make it tomorrow. We've had a long day."

I stayed away from the Fremont all that week. Nick showed up every night, looking for me. That was fine. I wanted him to be steaming. This went on for a couple of months. I always meant to give him another round, but I heard other music and I got involved in other things, and we never played freeze-out again. I had won the rubber game and finished twenty-five thousand dollars ahead.

The months and the years rolled on, slow, painful ones for Nick, a fine old clock running down. He had always been a handsome guy, tall, with the wavy black hair and the chiseled Grecian profile. Now he was fleshy, stooped, the face lined, and his disposition was always crabby. But he still walked into a room as though someone had blown a trumpet. He played the role, he was still Nick the Greek, and though I hated to admit it, I felt a grudging admiration for the old son of a bitch.

A year or so after the freeze-outs, when I was operating the Vegas Turf and Sports Club, he dropped in to see me. "Jeemmy," he said, "I got a proposition."

"What is it?" I asked, wary of it already.

"I got a couple Japs in Los Angeles," he said. "I tell 'em how to bet. I have 'em call you on baseball. You know, I say, bet on

Vashington against Yankees. You don't have to lay no three-to-one [the Yanks were big favorites in those days]. You lay 'em seven-to-five, you cut the price way down. They don't know no better. They bet ten, fifteen thousand."

It was a scam. What he was doing was probably bullshitting altogether, trying to set me up. Whatever the odds, he had a free ride for, say, a ten-thousand-dollar bet. If the Senators won, he stood to collect fourteen thousand dollars. If they lost, he probably didn't intend to pay off anyway. He'd just tell me his Japanese friends had stiffed him.

I had to fight back the hairy bear in me that stirs when I know I'm being used. I took a deep breath and said, "Nick, I don't do things like that. I have to quote my prices the way they are."

Nick gave me a look that would exterminate head lice. Then he turned and walked out.

I'll say this for Nick. He was irrepressible. Six months before he died he was still scheming. This was 1966, during my own cold attic period. I had been sat on by the Justice Department and the IRS, I wasn't gambling, and I had to scrape to meet the six-hundred-dollar monthly payment on my Federal fine. That's how low I was.

A good deal of sympathy existed for me around Las Vegas then, and at the hotels and casinos I was still accorded special courtesies. No matter where, I was allowed inside the velvet ropes that always marked off the *big* poker games. I was allowed in, even though I no longer was in a condition to play. I could sit next to Sid Wyman or any other high player, it made no difference.

Nick knew this. He also knew that I was in bad shape. One day he phoned me. "Jeemmy," he said, with his standard opener, "I got a proposition."

It developed that Nick had lined up a wealthy sucker from Tucson for a poker game, and he wanted me to sit next to the fellow and spy on his hand. Any time the two of them were in a big pot, I was supposed to tip off what the other guy had. "Everybody know we don't speak," Nick said. "It vill be perfect."

"Nick," I said, "all I know is that you owe me five thousand dollars," and I slammed the receiver down on him.

I had made him a loan when the Turf and Sports Club was still going strong. I couldn't explain to myself why I gave him the money, knowing we detested each other, and that it was damned unlikely I would ever see a dime of it again.

A few months after the phone call, Nick the Greek was dead. I felt nothing, not elation or sadness or regret. I only wondered if now, at last, people would stop calling me Nick. (The answer was no. In November of 1974 I was at the desk of the Madison Hotel in Washington, getting my key, when a party of maybe four slightly tipsy couples moved through the lobby. They stopped, whispered, and sent over one of the husbands. "We just made a bet," he grinned foolishly. "My wife says you're Nick the Greek." "She loses," I said slowly. "My name is Jimmy Snyder.")

The morning after Nick died I got a phone call from Hank Greenspun, the editor of the *Sun*. Hank had always been fond of Nick and had pushed him in the early boom years as a sort of public relations front for Las Vegas.

"Jimmy," he said, "I think you should be one of the pallbearers."

I almost choked. "You have to be kidding," I said. "Nick and I never got along, you know that. We were enemies."

"I don't care what you were. At least be at the funeral."

I attended the services. And when I arrived at the Greek Orthodox church I lit a candle. But that was it. I mean, a guy who was a son of a bitch in life doesn't become any more lovable just because he died.

CHAPTER

16

Gambling:
There Are No Good Systems

Now and then a friend who hasn't known me very long will ask, "Jimmy, why did you start gambling?" This has come up a hundred times and it always stumps me. To me, it's like being asked, "Why did you start breathing?"

A lot of things go into the answer; some of them I may not be aware of. My environment for one thing. I grew up in Steubenville, where it was wall-to-wall gambling. But basically what drew me to gambling was the challenge of it, the challenge of matching my wits against the other guy's. It was my information against his information, and if my research was better than his, I beat him.

That's why I never cheated anybody. There's no fun to cheating to win. It takes the challenge out of it. The great thing about gambling, my kind of gambling, was the satisfaction in the aftermath of a win. When you've stolen the money, what do you have except the money?

A few of my friends have accused me of having a total disregard for money. It's true I made a single football bet of 250,000 dollars, a sum of money many men spend all their lives to accumulate so they can bank it and live off the interest. When I was a kid starting out and betting one of my first bookmakers, Chuck Deemer, in Steubenville, he would say, "Greek . . ." He would say it with three e's and repeat it twice to get my attention. "Greek, you got to take it easy. Always remember to pinch your last bet. Hold something back for tomorrow." But when I liked something, I would bet it *all*. Let tomorrow take care of itself.

What few people noticed was this: When I made a big bet, it was because I was winning! When I was losing, I cut my bets back.

That was the key to my philosophy as a gambler. The size of the bankroll had nothing to do with it, except to scale the size of the bets. My usual custom was to make single, double, and triple bets. If I had a ten percent edge, say, I'd bet a single unit. If my edge was fifteen percent I'd double it. Over that, I'd place a triple bet. On occasion I did bet it all, but experience taught me, as Chuck Deemer said it would, that the smart gambler managed his money.

If my units of play were ten, twenty, and forty, and I won, over a period of three weeks I'd move it to twenty thousand, forty thousand, and eighty thousand dollars. But if I lost, I'd cut it back to five thousand, ten thousand, and twenty thousand dollars.

A part of that philosophy is the thing that separates the gambler from the sucker. The smart professional gambler, when heads comes up four times in a row, will bet that it comes up again. A team that's won six in a row will win seven. *He believes in the percentages.* The amateur bettor will figure that heads can't come up again, that tails is "due." He'll bet that a team on a losing streak is "due" to win. *The amateur believes in the law of averages.*

From the time I started betting at age fourteen, I was always looking for an edge. Betting against Chuck Deemer, I made him change almost every rule he had on the board. I would sit up nights thinking up new angles. One day I bet one dollar to place on a horse, "if-come a dollar to win." Chuck took it. I have made thousands of bets since then, but I remember the horse and the rider, White Legs with Paul Keester up, at Arlington Park, Chicago. White Legs won, and when Chuck added up my payoff he had a fit. "You can't do this," he said. "It's not right."

"You don't have anything on the board that says I can't if-come it," I said. "What if the horse had run second? You would have been able to take a dollar off for the if-come bet."

"I'll pay you this time," he said. "But it's not right." A new rule went up on the board.

In searching for the eternal edge, let me look at the three biggest betting sports.

FOOTBALL

In making a football bet, I always have to believe I know something about the game a lot of people don't know. The point spread on a game is a reflection of opinion held by the general public, the great mass of bettors. It is the number designed to get the most action, to split opinions right down the middle. Maybe I will look at one team's strength and see that it is matched head on against the other team's strength. Alabama's strength is running, Notre Dame is number one in stopping the run, and Alabama can't pass. This will lead me to bet on Notre Dame. But it's tough to bet on the Irish, because they are a national team with hordes of backers who like to back them with money. This led to Ara Parseghian's retirement, which he said was spurred by a 14–6 victory over Navy. "After the game," he said, "you would have thought we lost." Hell, yes, he "lost"—or the people who bet on Notre Dame did. The Irish didn't beat the point spread.

I missed one of the biggest killings I could have ever made, betting on Notre Dame, simply because I was greedy. This was August 1946, and the previous year Army had humiliated Notre Dame, 46–0, with Blanchard and Davis and Arnold Tucker. But the Cadets had been playing against students. Now Frank Leahy was holding tryouts before he'd let anybody on campus. He had virtually a pro team. I went to Mel Clark's in Chicago and asked Charley McNeil to quote me a money line on Army–Notre Dame.

He said, "Okay, I'll give you a point line. How much do you want it for?"

A "point line" is nine-five and one-two, or six-five and seven-five, only a point different between what they're laying and what they're taking. I thought, "Oh, Jesus, if he's going to give me a point line that means he's going to make it under two-one."

I said, "Okay, a point line under two-one is what you're talking about."

Mac said, "Yeah, but the regular spread if I go over two-one. How much?" He didn't know who I was going to bet.

I said, "Oh, twenty or thirty." He said twenty was enough, but Jakie Summerfield, his partner, said, "That's okay. Let him bet thirty. We'll put it up now and do a lot of business on this game."

So Mac made it two and a half and three. I could lay three-to-one and take Army or take two-and-a-half-to-one and Notre Dame. I took the Irish for thirty thousand dollars from Jakie and Mac, and some other fellows around Clark's that day laid it to me for ten more. I finished up betting forty thousand dollars (to win a hundred thousand).

When the game rolled around that fall, it came up dead even. The week of the game, Army came up a half-point favorite, and I pressed my bet for twenty-five thousand dollars more on Notre Dame. The game ended 0–0 with the ball on the fifty-yard line. Back in August, if I had taken any points at all, instead of being greedy for the odds I would have won the whole bundle.

On many occasions when I had information about a game, I made damned sure "my team" got hold of the same information in some way. With my contacts on the campuses, through an assistant coach or a player or an ex-coach who saw the practices, I would know how one team was preparing to play the other.

Before one bowl game in 1959, I learned of a certain team's game plan, offense and defense, and had a complete report on their practices. I called one of my scouts, who had a good friend on the other staff. I gave him what I had and he relayed it. The coach knew he could believe him. I liked the favorite to beat the point spread, anyway, but this was additional insurance.

My team, the favorite, scored two touchdowns in the first quarter and another in the third. The other team didn't get on the board until the fourth quarter.

How immoral or unethical was this? The coaches were doing it themselves whenever they could. When Army used to "upset" Michigan every year, it was because Red Blaik had a guy who could watch Michigan's practices. Every night at West Point, Blaik knew what had happened that day at Ann Arbor. I know this, because Herman Hickman was on Blaik's staff then and he told me about it.

There are two reasons I no longer gamble. One, it would hurt my credibility as an oddsmaker, and, two, the laws are bad. It's against the federal law to make a phone call across state lines for purposes of betting or even to convey betting information. I should know.

Consequently, you can't gamble like you used to in those days, when you could match your wits against everybody in different cities, get different points, different ideas. You don't have the percentage going for you. If I liked a Chicago team and it was playing a team from Atlanta, I'd call Atlanta to bet on Chicago. If Fordham came to Pittsburgh to play Pitt, I'd call Slim Silverheart at the Amorita Club in Pittsburgh to get a half point more. I did that once: got Pitt and half a point in New York, and Fordham and half a point in Pittsburgh. It came 0–0 and I won both sides.

Today in Vegas, from one sports club to another, you won't find more than half a point difference. On occasions, you can buy in early on the first line on Monday and find there's movement by Friday. Then you can buy in on the other side. Every experienced gambler knows this. It is called "catching a middle." The average bettor is either too lazy or too unaware to do this. All you are betting is the "juice," the one point to win twenty. The wider the "middle" the more beautiful is twenty-to-one.

BASEBALL

Football is a numbers game. Baseball is an odds game. If you get the right odds, it doesn't matter if Sandy Koufax is pitching. If it's two-and-a-half-to-one and you get three-to-one, you take it. You don't bet on the team, you bet on what the odds are.

Consider the 1974 World Series between Los Angeles and Oakland. I made it a toss-up. We sent it out eleven-to-ten Dodgers just to make somebody the favorite. The reason we said eleven-to-ten Dodgers was because the Dodgers get most of the publicity. The World Series belongs to the public, not to the smart guys, the bookmakers. This is one betting proposition that runs away like crazy. The player, the outside guy, takes the team that he *wants* to win. My opinion was eleven-to-ten. With the bookies it went to eight-to-five Dodgers, way out of proportion.

That used to happen in the heyday of the Yankees, too. Everybody wanted the Yankees. And they were not often disappointed.

One of the great Series I should have done well on I didn't, because I was a Cleveland fan at the time. That was my *Ohio* team. I was in the Hickory House Restaurant in New York. Between the Hickory House and Gallagher's in those days, 1954, you could bet a quarter of a million dollars, because all the gamblers loafed in there. This was early, the moment it looked like the Giants were going to play Cleveland, and I wanted something ahead of time. I ran into Manny Kimmel, one of the smart people of the world. He owned the Kinney Parking lots and finally sold them out. I bet Manny eleven thousand dollars on Cleveland to his ten thousand dollars. I knew the public was going to bet on Cleveland, because it had one helluva pitching staff—Lemon and Wynn and Garcia—and it was getting all the publicity. Cleveland opened a seven-to-five favorite, but the public sent it to nine-to-five.

I went to the opening game, when Willie Mays made that catch on Vic Wertz in center field and Dusty Rhodes hit a pinch homer in the tenth. Al Rosen, the Cleveland third baseman, was hurting. I said to myself, "I'm in trouble. I'm going to go in and get rid of this." Because I had made such a good bet originally, it was still only eleven-to-ten with Cleveland losing the first game, so I laid eleven-to-ten on the Giants so I could get off. Now no matter who won I had to lose a thousand dollars—*but*, at least I wasn't going to lose eleven thousand dollars. Because I liked Cleveland at the start, I stayed away from the Series altogether, and the Giants won four in a row. Every day the public made Cleveland the favorite, and the last game was eight-to-five. The public kept saying, "The Indians can't lose another one."

Now, I do *not* like systems. I hate systems with a passion. But there *is* one system that does exist in baseball, which I've checked on and followed from a statistical point of view. As follows:

If a team has won four in a row, bet on it until it loses. If a team has lost four in a row, bet against it until it wins.

Here's what happens: There's a cycle of four in baseball with every team. They have four starting pitchers. There are a lot of four-game series. Four is the basic structure of baseball.

And you will from time to time have a *double* bet going for you, when a team that has won four or more in a row is opposing a team that has lost four or more in a row.

A great advantage in this system is that you can't get hurt with it. What does happen is that you'll find yourself overlaying almost a nickel a hundred on these games, or two and a half percent a hundred, because the bookmaker will increase the odds. Instead of a thirteen-to-ten favorite, the team that's winning will be seven-to-five. The team that's losing, instead of being a three-to-two underdog, they'll be an eight-to-five underdog. Sometimes even the guy making the odds will hold them down. It's amazing that otherwise-smart betting men don't realize this. They bet the other way.

Of course, in baseball, you are often betting on or against a certain pitcher. You study them, learn their habits, file away odd pieces of information and look for trends. Warren Spahn, through most of his great career, had problems in the early innings—on those days when he had any problems at all. I always liked Spahn, but that became one of my gimmick bets. I'd take odds that the other team would score on Spahn in the first inning.

In 1947, I had already picked the Boston Braves as a team on the move—they would win the pennant the next year—even though they appeared to have only a two-man pitching staff. The Boston battle cry was Spahn and Sain and a day of rain. In June of that season I stumbled into one of the most unusual betting opportunities I *thought* I had ever known.

The Braves were in Cincinnati for a series with the Reds, a mediocre team kept alive by one great pitcher, the late Ewell (The Whip) Blackwell. He was to win twenty-two games that year, sixteen of them in a row, with a sidearm motion that came by way of third base and drastically increased the laundry bill for National League hitters. They were forever flinging themselves into the dirt, as the ball snapped over the plate for another stirke. The Whip was a joy to watch.

This night was even better, because I was watching him from the next table, in a club across the river in Covington, Kentucky, where all the gambling was. Three of us were having dinner, me, Nate Linnett and Sleep-Out Louie Levinson, who owned the place we were in, the 606 Club.

Sleep-Out was the best of company. He knew the lyrics to every song ever written, or so it seemed. He was a great gambler, ambidextrous, and could throw a silver dollar against a wall with either hand and make it land on its edge. Once he stopped a crap game, took two wheel balls off the table and we played marbles for five thousand dollars a shot. He beat me, too. Louie was rolling them and I was playing fat lady style, like a jerk. I lost twenty-five thousand dollars.

When Blackwell walked in with a doll on his arm, light brown hair and built, Sleep-Out got very excited. They sat down at a table just behind us. "My God," he said, "get a load of the barracuda with Blackwell."

I had never before heard the expression. It meant, in the deep, natural sense, a man-eater. Sleep-Out said, "He may not know it, but there won't be nothing left of his pecker when she gets through with him tonight."

Blackwell was to pitch the next night, June 18, 1947, against the Braves, who were starting a righthander named Eddie Wright, one of the pitchers they had to use on days it didn't rain. The Reds were favored, I knew, by eleven-to-five.

I began to get an idea. "Sleep-Out," I asked, "will she take money?"

"Doesn't everybody?"

I reached into my pocket and fished out four $50 bills. I said, "Look, sooner or later, one of them has to go to the rest room. When it happens, catch her alone and slip her the two hundred dollars. And tell her, all she has to do to earn it is give you a report on what she did with Blackwell and what time she left him. Nothing more. If she takes him to bed, how many times. Now, get this straight. You're not paying her to *do* anything. She's not getting paid to sabotage Blackwell. Make that goddam clear."

Sleep-Out nodded, but I made him repeat it back to me, every word. He was an intelligent fellow, but I wanted nothing said that might sound—later—like a fix had been attempted. I told him the Barracuda was to call us, no matter what time it was that she and Ewell parted company.

After a while she got up and headed for the powder room and, very smoothly, Sleep-Out rose and crossed her path. When he returned to the table he said it was all set. Now, keep in mind that this was 1947, and $200 wasn't candy, and all she had to do for it was make a phone call.

At a quarter after eight the next morning, the phone rang in my suite at the Netherlands Plaza. It was Sleep-Out: "Well, the Barracuda just called. She left him fifteen minutes ago. *Five* times."

I wasn't wide awake yet. "What do you mean, *five* times?"

"She says she went down on him five times."

I said, "Let me get this straight. Are you telling me she says she took him off five times?"

"Greek, that's what she said, and there's no reason for the girl to lie. She don't know what information we wanted, or why, and we already paid her. Why would she lie?"

"My God," I repeated, "five times." I was impressed, if only from an aesthetic standpoint. Forget the gambling angle. Twice, maybe three times, might not mean much. But those extra two turns, I figured, had to take something out of a guy. Most fellows who get off five times in a night would wind up in a jar at the Harvard Medical Laboratory.

It began to look to me like a six-inning game. Between the three of us, Sleep-Out, Nate and myself, we bet one hundred thousand dollars on the Braves. In those days, the late forties, with black market money still in circulation, gambling was the national pastime. You could call five places in Covington alone and get down a hundred grand in an afternoon.

I have seldom anticipated a baseball game with more glee. And that night, before a home crowd that cheered every delivery, Ewell

Blackwell pitched the only no-hit, no-run game of his big league career. The victory was the ninth in his string of sixteen straight, and the Reds breezed, 6–0. In his next start, against Brooklyn, The Whip came within two outs of a second straight no-hitter.

Thank the Lord, I had no inside information riding on that one.

HORSE RACING

I was reminiscing one day about Jack Nolan, the political boss of Steubenville when I was growing up. Nolan liked to bet very big at the racetrack, and he would bet a horse ten thousand dollars to win and twenty thousand dollars to place. A friend interrupted me. "Is that a good system?" he said. And I almost shouted my answer: "There is *no* good system to bet horses."

Horse racing is a different thing to me. Even though the track finishes up with all the money, racing is my recreation, which I love. In my opinion the moment you look upon a racetrack as a place to make money—rather than a place to have fun and enjoy—you are going to get hurt.

But there are occasions, what are called "spot" plays, where you can have the parimutuel odds working in your favor.

I was at the track when Riva Ridge won the Belmont. For some reason or another Riva Ridge never got the credit he should have gotten, as good a horse as he was. I would rather bet on Riva Ridge than Secretariat, Penny Tweedy's next horse. Riva Ridge was actually overlaid most of the time he ran. Secretariat took the country by storm, and his prices were far shorter than they should have been.

This day in the Belmont, I start looking at the board where Riva Ridge was three-to-two to win and I looked at the place price and, holy Moses, he's thirteen-to-ten or seven-to-five to place! I said to myself, "Oh, gosh, that will change." But New York tracks today get a tremendous impact from the Off-Track Betting shops around the city, with something like a million and a half dollars on a big race. Most of the OTB players played Riva Ridge to win, and the pie-in-the-sky bettors played the long-shot horses to place. A price of three-to-two to win and thirteen-to-ten to place is something like a three hundred percent overlay. He should have been three-to-five to place, returning sixty cents on a dollar. Here he was returning $1.30 to a dollar.

I had five thousand dollars in my back pocket, so I gave it to a friend, Mike Pearl, and sent him to the hundred-dollar place window with instructions to buy fifty tickets on number 3 (Riva Ridge). The horse paid $4.60 to place, and I won sixty-five hundred dollars, more than double what the horse should have paid. I *had* to go for the overlay.

When I go to the racetrack these days, I haven't been following the horses. I'm not going to take a racing form and try to figure it out, except on a big race. I'm not going to handicap the claiming races and the allowance races. I'll handicap the big stakes races, because it's all there. There are too many intangibles in the other kind of races.

But there is a way of playing so that I may not have any of the worst of it. I want to overcome the seventeen or seventeen and a half percent take-out by the track and the state, at least for the fifty or two hundred dollars I'm going to bet per race.

So what do I do? The handicapper at the racetrack should know more about these horses than anybody, right? That's what they hire him for. He makes the morning line, and that line is right there in the track program.

What I do then, a minute or so before post time, is compare his odds in the program with the odds now on the board. Now I am going to bet two horses:

1. The horse that's an overlay on the handicapper's line.
2. The horse that had the money for it.

I'll bet, say, fifty dollars on one, and thirty dollars on the other, the "money" horse.

But it has to be a certain figure. If a horse is three-to-one in the handicapper's line and now he's six-to-one on the board, I have got to take it.

If another horse was four-to-one in the handicapper's line and now it's two-to-one on the board, I know there has been a lot of money bet on it.

This saves me the time of studying, because I know the track handicapper has done all the studying. So if it goes from three-to-one to six-to-one, well, hell, the handicapper has been there since the racing date started. This is just a logical way of playing. It doesn't mean you're going to beat the track. It's a way to have some fun—because you've always got a "live" horse, one with a lot of money going for it, *and* you've got an overlay. When those overlays win, baby, you really get your money back.

I'm talking about the first, second, and third choices only. I'm also not looking for a money horse being the favorite, like a horse going from three-to-one to eight-to-five. I'm talking about a ten-to-one shot coming to five- or six-to-one. Or a six-to-one shot coming to three-to-one.

If you like favorites, the stakes races are the only place to play. They're solid. I bet thousands and thousands of dollars on Native Dancer and Tom Fool. They were horses you could trust. I'd get three-to-ten or one-to-two or two-to-five, but that is forty cents on the dollar. Where the hell else can you make forty cents on the dollar in two minutes?

CHAPTER
17

Casino Gambling:
A Nonprofit Sport

I was never turned on by Las Vegas, or I could have owned interests in a dozen hotels, one or another, the first time I came out. The reason is, I hate casino gambling. I despise it. It's a killer. It's working on the weakness of people.

Gambling, and most of all *casino* gambling, is a disease. Forget me, forget the certain small percentage of guys who could make a living gambling because they were smart enough to research it.

Nobody makes a living betting in casinos.

That was never my game, but it was more to my taste in the heyday of the Mounds Club, in Cleveland, and the other great old casinos that belonged to another America. It was the America of black Packards, evening dress and orchestras with violins. They were still going strong until the late 1950s, these casinos tucked away in the woods or on a hill, somewhere back off the highway.

The Mounds Club was like a castle, completely surrounded by a high iron gate. You had to identify yourself to a guard, and you couldn't get in without a reference. Inside it was elegant, tasteful, like the homes of people who have been wealthy a long while and have no further need to prove it. I mean, there was no French whorehouse decor, just expensive lamps and chandeliers and old leather furniture. There would be one big act, say, Hildegarde or Joe E. Lewis, and it was the beginning of an idea that would come to flower in Las Vegas. The Mounds Club was among the first to pay top money for entertainers, up to ten thousand dollars a week, starting in the forties.

It was accepted routinely that, for such places to operate, they had to have the sheriff on their side. That was just part of the overhead and no one thought much of it, either way. The big politician in the area usually had a cut too. When his side lost an election, someone else took over.

The times and ambitious lawmen eventually wiped out the grand old gambling houses. I never subscribed to the theory that the casinos were linked, or backed, by a national syndicate, what conspiracy fans have sometimes called "The Organization." We're talking about casinos, not take-out taco parlors. You didn't franchise them. They were owned by tough men who bought whatever polish big money could give them, and some had reputations several pages long. But, as a rule, the casinos were privately owned by men who didn't believe in chain stores.

Crime has always struck me, an observer of the passing scene, as notoriously disorganized. If it were not, if there really was such a thing as "Organized Crime," it would run the country. There isn't much to keep your business from growing if you don't mind killing people.

In the matter of simple larceny, gambling has a long tradition, although the advantage keeps shifting. In Nevada, gambling was legalized in 1931, because the state had little other income, and in the early stages cheating was rampant. In those days, around the time Hoover Dam was being built, they would erect tents and operate games of chance inside them, mice running into holes, three-card monte, all the hustling carnival stuff.

Casino gambling grew out of that era, and for a long time no one could or would do much about improving it. Almost anyone who wanted a license could get one. The state *wanted* them to come in, needed the investment and the people gambling would bring. The governors had no jurisdiction.

All that began to change ten years ago, during the second term of Governor Grant Sawyer, and continued under Paul Laxalt. They cracked down, cleaned it up, created order and discipline and appointed impeccably honest men to the Gaming Board to keep it that way.

Today the pendulum has swung the other way. What the house has to do is protect itself. The cheating is done by the customers. They'll mark cards, copy the dice, slip some gadget into the slots. Three to four million dollars *each year* are stolen from the casinos. Any day, you can visit the office of Sheriff Ralph Lamb, and you will see on his walls a rogue's gallery of cheaters, identified by their specialties—slots, craps, cards. They're on posters, like the FBI wanted list, only these people are gambling cheats.

A hotel will allow one percent leakage for thievery by their own dealers, in the course of a year. But the casino people are always looking for it. They have what they call the catwalk, and the peep—hidden mirrors—through which someone is looking down at all times at the dealers. A fellow would need super quick hands to get away with anything. And he won't last. In time they'll catch him and fire him and, if the word gets around he's a thief, he won't work again. No, they don't break his fingers. That went out with high button shoes.

The boys were more likely to go into business for themselves and do a little skimming, in the days when they could play where they worked. Today the state laws forbid any employee from gambling in his own casino—including owners, dealers, bellhops and entertainers. Especially entertainers. In the first place, no owner wants his star to gamble, in the belief that they don't perform as well when they are *losing*. The owner doesn't want his money; he wants his talent, which brings in other people's money.

The late Joe E. Lewis used to blow at the tables whatever he earned on the stage, usually seventy-five hundred dollars to ten thousand dollars a week. (In salary, he wasn't up there with the heavies.) When he worked for Belden Kattleman at El Rancho,

Belden tried to protect his pay by calling the other casinos and asking them to limit Joe E.'s credit, or bar him completely. He did it because he loved him, everybody did, and wanted him to leave town with something in his pocket besides lint.

Eddie Fisher was another who often ended up singing for nothing, or a little less than that. But the grand champion was Frank Sinatra, who played like a crazy man. The difference was that the Eddie Fishers had to pay off, and Sinatra's markers, most of them, were usually torn up. That, in fact, was what started the feud between Frank and Howard Hughes.

The background was this. When Sinatra played the Sands, before it was sold to Hughes, he drew such enormous crowds that whatever he lost at the tables they just canceled it out. Playing for free, or next to it, was his bonus. He brought in the big gamblers.

Under Hughes this practice was discontinued, and Bob Maheu instructed Jack Entratter to inform Frank. Entratter was the entertainment director of the Sands, a booking agent on the side for a few select clients—namely, those who appeared most often at the Sands—and a guy with the burly build of a onetime bouncer.

But Jack was afraid to tell Frank, and so he didn't.

What happened next was that Frank was in the casino, losing, and he had reached whatever limit Carl Cohen, the casino manager, had put on him. I think it was twenty-five thousand dollars. Carl, of course, was under the impression that Entratter had advised Frank he would be playing with his own dough.

Sinatra asked the pit boss for more chips and was told, in front of the table, "I'm sorry, Mr. Sinatra. I can't give you any more credit. I have to call."

It is like playing with gunpowder to put down Frank in front of other people. He exploded. Steam came out of his ears. Instantly, Carl Cohen appeared and tried to calm him. Sinatra got really nasty, with a torrent of hyphenated words, the mildest of which was cock-sucker. Then he heaved a room service cart through a glass partition, turned to Cohen and squared off. Now *that* was a bad move. Carl shot a right hand to the side of the face, point blank, and decked him. It was instant anesthesia, the only way Carl knew how to end the scene before it got even more out of hand.

And that was how Frank Sinatra happened to drop the Sands, and move over to Caesar's, in 1970.

Now, it is part of his charm that Frank won't dislike a man just because he got hit by him. Chances are he would like him no less, and no more, than before. My understanding was that Sinatra didn't stay mad at Cohen, who slugged him, or Entratter, who deceived him, but at Howard Hughes, who cut off his credit.

Carl Cohen doesn't exactly fit the gambling stereotype, if there is one. A refined and educated man, he speaks half a dozen languages. Carl was one of that breed of executive gamblers—along with the likes of Benny Binion, Eddie Torres, Sid Wyman, Al Benedict and Charlie Rich—who learned the ropes young, grew up with it and became businessmen, not adventurers.

Whores and gamblers are supposed to have hearts of gold. Sometimes they do. And that calls for a Sid Wyman story.

In Vegas, Wyman is one of the gods when it comes to running a casino. Big and heavyset, Sid has a kind of corporate smoothness. He's a fine storyteller out of his own experiences.

He was playing poker in The Dunes one night when one of his staffers came over and said, quietly, "Sid, one of our busboys is very ill. It looks like he's got cancer. He's going into the hospital and we're all pitching in. You want to put in something?"

Sid looked up from his cards. "Whaddaya mean, put in something? Here," he said, scribbling a name on a scoresheet. "Call this doctor in Los Angeles, send him there and tell them to bill me for whatever he needs. I'll take care of him."

Sid had never met the boy. To this day I doubt if he remembers his name. But a year and a half went by, the bills came in, and Sid paid them all.

One morning—that is, by his clock—Sid ordered breakfast from room service. It may have been three in the afternoon. A bachelor, he always ordered breakfast at whatever hour he met the day. It depended on when he got to sleep, and what he had to do.

The waiter wheeled in the cart and set up the table and Sid barked, "Take five dollars for yourself off the dresser." He signed the checks, but made it a point to pay his tips in cash.

The waiter hesitated, then said, "Mr. Wyman, if you don't mind, this one is on the house."

Sid snapped, "What? You so rich you won't take my money?"

"No, sir," the waiter said. "I'm Rico, Mr. Wyman. The guy you sent to California a year and a half ago. I'm well now and I just came back to work, and I got no other way to thank you."

Gratitude always made Sid nervous. He muttered something like, "Gee, that's great, kid," and watched him back out of the room. He had never seen him before, didn't know his name, and had probably spent $15,000 on him.

When I told that story in my column in the *Sun*, Wyman, who is probably one of my five closest friends, didn't speak to me for three weeks. It wasn't all modesty, of course. He was deluged with phone calls and sad letters from people wanting handouts.

Of course, it might not be easy to convince anyone who hasn't been back since the fifties that Las Vegas has a heart. Until twenty years ago, the town still had the soul of a bus-stop joint. And the people who ran the casinos cheated *everybody*, including each other. But not now. Those elements have been bought out and chased out. Of course, the casinos have never needed to cheat; and I'm not talking about house percentages—I mean something more certain and magnifying than that: human frailty. *That* is the fuel that keeps the neon lights burning.

The people who live in Vegas actually do not gamble. Maybe two percent of them do. But that two percent would go broke on a punchboard in Allentown, Pennsylvania. They'd find a way of doing it. Gamblers Anonymous isn't going to help them.

There are a select few in Vegas who make a living gambling, by betting on sports events or perhaps playing poker. These fellows occasionally go to the casinos and play the tables. *But they play the games for entertainment.*

That's the oddity.

If you work it right, Las Vegas can be the greatest place in the world for a vacation or a convention. The glitter is contagious. It has a greater concentration of big-name entertainment than anywhere in the world. Year-round golf and tennis. And the world's most beautiful hookers go gliding by with a rhythm all their own—Sodom and Gomorrah, Sodom and Gomorrah, the rhythm goes. There is a hysteria in the air that leaps from player to player.

Oh, yes, Las Vegas can be a lot of fun, and you can have a swinging time at the tables, if you can stick to two simple principles:

1. *Never gamble with more money than you can afford to lose. When that's gone, walk away.*

2. *Consider that sum of money as an entertainment expense, and gamble for fun.*

The first rule is purely practical, dollars and sense. The second is important because it's psychological, and this is the rule that will help you walk away with your own money and perhaps some of the casino's, too.

The truth is, it's not the house percentages so much that you have to beat. You have to beat *yourself.*

The percentages against you, mathematically, are not that bad. At the dice tables it's one and a half percent. If you bet the line and take the odds back of the line, it's only seven-tenths of one percent. Over the long haul it will break you, but you are going to get in and get out, have fun, remember? The percentage at blackjack varies depending on the player, which explains why this is my favorite casino game, because the player has some control over his destiny, as we shall see. At roulette the house edge is 5.26 percent if you are playing numbers. At baccarat, it's one and a quarter percent on the bank, one and a half percent on the players, but I'm not even going to go into baccarat, where the minimum bet is twenty dollars and the players have no decisions to make. They have no control over the play at all. Keno has an advantage of twenty-five percent, and therefore you will avoid it altogether, except for reasons noted below.

Aside from keno, those numbers are not the kind to rely on if you are going to finance high-rise hotels and pay entertainers 175,000 dollars a week, while charging eighteen dollars for the dinner show. In 1973 the Las Vegas casinos reported a gross income from the games and tables alone of more than 586 million dollars. That's how much the players lost. They must be doing a helluva lot wrong, other than bucking the percentages. And they are.

Casino operators have their own language in discussing profit margin. They use words like "drop" and "percent." The *drop* is how much money is bet, as in "the handle" at a racetrack, and it is figured on a daily basis. The *percent* is what the house expects to make. This figure varies according to the game, but *not* according to the players. The casino knows it should average between nineteen and twenty-two percent at blackjack and craps. In other words, they have a calm anticipation that you, ol' buddy, will lose twenty cents on every buck that you bet.

Where do these extra percentages come from? They come from the average bettor who doesn't have the discipline to quit when he should. He won't walk away until he has punished himself to where it hurts.

Here's what happens when a visiting tiger is turned loose in Vegas: he's a successful businessman back home, and he has a two-thousand-dollar line of credit at the casinos. That's where the big numbers for the casinos are. Not in the five-, ten-, or twenty-thousand credit bettors, but in the two or three range. The first time Tiger comes to Vegas he gets, say, four hundred dollars ahead and he figures that's enough to cover his expenses, so he quits and then brags for a few months about his "free trip." The next time Tiger is in town, he may win another two hundred or three hundred dollars, and again he quits. On his third visit he hits nothing but losers and runs through all the money he made on the first two joyrides. Then he loses his two-thousand-dollar credit.

Everybody hits a streak of bad luck sooner or later. This is true, but Tiger compounds his troubles. He is going to get that money back. He goes to another casino and expends his line of two thousand dollars. When Tiger says good-bye to Vegas this time he is down seven thousand dollars. So what most customers do is lay Las Vegas ten-to-one.

And *that* is the built-in advantage that keeps the Vegas wheels turning. Most people lose ten times more than they win.

All the extra percentages disappear *if* the player sets a limited sum he knows he can afford to lose, *and* if he plays the game for fun. Because when you are playing for fun and not in desperation, you may be able to keep in mind a few tips to better your chances. As follows:

BLACKJACK

Blackjack is the only casino game in which the player has reasonably wide latitude to exercise his judgment. This is the only casino game other than poker in which playing skill as well as money management is really important.

Because judgment *is* important, the good player can bring the odds down, while a bad player will destroy himself.

One sophisticated approach to playing blackjack is based on counting the cards, and particularly the aces and ten-point cards that are out. At a certain point in the game, the counter is supposed to remember that with twelve cards to go there are two aces and six ten-point cards remaining in the deck, and bet accordingly.

But there are only a handful of people in the country who can keep track of the cards as they are played. It's tough to do with a single deck, and now that many casinos use a shoe with two, three, or even four decks it's virtually impossible.

The average casino player is not going to invest hours and hours of time in memorizing cards as they go by. I'm assuming he is going to play for fun. So here are some general observations on the game, and some basic guidelines.

The great advantage of the house is, of course, that you have the chance to bust before the dealer does. Even if the dealer has a lousy hand, he may beat you just because you bust first. That imbalance gives the house an advantage of nearly seven percent. That is, if a player follows the same rules as the dealer—hitting sixteen or less, and standing on seventeen or better—he will lose almost seven percent of the time.

But the player has four advantages. He gets paid three to two on blackjack; he may double-down; he may split a pair; and he always sees one of the dealer's first two cards.

The last point is crucial. It's the one that catalyzes all the others. Except, naturally, for the blackjack payoff.

That's simply a function of the rules of the game. The advantage—that the player gets three to two for blackjack while the dealer simply is paid even money from the players—is worth somewhat more than two percent. Subtracting that from the house's original edge of nearly seven percent, that leaves the house with an advantage of about four and a half percent.

That's the figure that you have to overcome in order to win at blackjack.

Okay. If you have a hard seventeen or better in the first two cards, you *stand*. No matter what the dealer has showing, you do not draw another card.

But suppose you have a stiff—a two-card hand that is more than eleven and less than seventeen, and that may bust you if you draw a card? The answer is, you hit a stiff or not, depending on what card the dealer shows.

If you have a stiff, and the dealer shows a strong card—a seven, eight, nine, ten, or ace—you hit your hand once.

If you have a stiff, and the dealer shows a bad card—two, three, four, five, six—you stand. (*Except* if you have a 12 and the dealer shows a two or three, hit your hand once.)

If you have a soft hand—one that allows you to hit without fear of going bust—you hit until the sum of the hand is governed by the rules above.

Everything I've said so far assumes that you either have a strong hand—seventeen, eighteen, nineteen, twenty, twenty-one—or a stiff. And because a strong hand plays itself, most of what I've said has been directed at making the best of a bad hand. It's the equivalent of playing defense in football. But as in that game, so in blackjack, there are times when you go on the offense. Such positive decisions can be made in two ways: through card strategy and through betting.

There are two distinct tactics in card strategy: doubling down, and splitting a pair.

When you have a two-card total of eleven, always double down. *Always*. If the dealer shows an ace, you'll soon discover whether he has blackjack. If not, you double down. If you have a two-card total of ten, always double down *except* when the dealer shows a ten or ace.

If your two-card total is nine, double down *unless* the dealer shows a strong card—a seven, eight, nine, ten, or ace.

All double-down situations require you to double your bet, and only allow you to receive one card. However, the percentages are such that, depending on the card the dealer shows, you are betting from strength. Because you are only permitted one card, you cannot go bust, and the dealer may. The best double-down situation is when you have eleven and the dealer shows a six. Anyone who doesn't double down in this situation should be led to the keno room.

The second part of offensive blackjack strategy is splitting pairs. Correctly done, this strategy will provide about twenty-five percent greater productivity than doubling down. However, such situations arise only about two percent of the time, compared with the approximately eight percent incidence of hands which permit you to double down. Thus the profit potential to the player from doubling down and splitting is about the same.

Splitting also brings us to one of the most common errors. A lot of otherwise sane people will notice that the dealer shows a six or other poor card, check their own hands, discover a hard twenty, and split their cards.

This is dead wrong. A player's twenty versus a dealer's six is as close to a lock as you can get—short of blackjack. Splitting a hard twenty does not give you two half-locks. Sure, it *can* be done, and *maybe* you'll get covered with an ace or a ten. But don't bet on it.

When you're dealt a twenty stand on it. Period.

Actually, the reason for splitting is to turn a stiff hand into a better one.

Of course you split a pair of aces. Always. Regardless of what the dealer shows. If they're covered with ten-point cards, dandy. If not, you play them as soft hands until they appreciate to strong hands. If they turn into stiffs, play according to the rules stated earlier, that is, value your hand against that part of the dealer's hand that is showing.

The best advertisement for splitting a pair is when you hold eight-eight and the dealer shows a seven. If you treat the hand as sixteen, the dealer has a strong edge. You must hit your stiff. But not happily, because the probabilities are, approximately, .27 to win, .06 to tie, and .67 to lose.

But if you split the pair of eights, you now have a light edge on the dealer. What you're looking for, of course, is an ace or a ten or a nine; or, a three, in which case you will, if the casino rules permit, double down.

There's no certainty here. But the probability is that you will have converted a loser to a winner. Again, not a sure loser but a likely one. And not a sure winner, but a likely one.

Because sixteen is the worst of all stiffs, always split a pair of eights.

Split nines except when the dealer shows seven, ten, or ace. (Your eighteen is a lock against dealer's seventeen, but is doubly disadvantageous as a split against a possible twenty or the flexible hand that includes an ace.)

Split sevens except when dealer shows nine, ten, or ace.

Split sixes except when dealer shows eight, nine, ten, or ace.

Never split fives, because the count of ten is a basic building block.

Split a pair of fours only if the dealer shows a five.

Split threes and twos unless dealer shows eight, nine, ten, or ace.

All of the preceding advice assumes that you have a hard hand. But if your two cards include an ace, your approach has to be slightly different.

Don't settle for a soft total of less than eighteen. If you have a soft nineteen or twenty, you always stand. If you have a soft eighteen, hit only if the dealer shows a nine or ten.

We come now to a gimmick the casinos love—when the dealer has an ace showing. He will ask if you want "insurance." This is an invitation to bet half your original wager on the likelihood that the dealer has a ten-point card in the hole. Insurance pays two-to-one, so the offer seems attractive. Particularly if you have a strong hand. Especially if you already have blackjack. Just ask any player. And you'd get a wrong answer.

Assume that you're playing with a fifty-two-card deck. The dealer's down card is drawn at random from fifty-one other cards. Of the cards that are out, sixteen are ten-point cards, thirty-five are not.

The odds are thirty-five-to-sixteen against the dealer's down card being a ten. But your payoff is only thirty-five-to-sixteen—two-to-one. So you're paying about six percent for insurance. At that price, the premiums are too high. Even if you check your own cards and find that neither is a ten, there's still a house edge of about two percent.

If you have blackjack, insurance is an even worse bet. The dealer will have blackjack only about one-third of the time. And since you cannot lose this hand, only push it, two-thirds of the time you will be giving away your edge.

Now, about betting—money management. If you can afford to bet a hundred a hand, that's fine. But whatever your unit of betting is, stick to it. Except as indicated below. And if you lose, get up and walk away.

Your unit of betting—two bucks or a grand—is the basis of your money management.

You may have a general sense toward the end of a deal that the deck is rich in ten-point cards. This favors the player, and you *may* want to increase your bet. I said *may*, because I don't have much faith in the average player's ability to keep track of cards. But if you can be generally aware of what is in the deck, that knowledge will help you for both insurance bets and general betting.

If your unit of betting is two dollars, head for the table with fifty bucks. That's enough to let you play, in theory, twenty-five hands. Plenty of action. But when that's gone, leave.

The basic error that most guys make at casino games is that they try to force a hot streak. When they lose, they bet heavier in an attempt to get even. That's the reverse of what should be done. Bet *light* when you are losing, bet *heavy* when you are winning.

If after a half hour you have doubled your money—your fifty bucks is now up to a hundred—increase your unit of bet by fifty percent. That is, increase your unit bet to three dollars. But as soon as you start to lose, decrease your betting to the original level.

If you win, set yourself a realistic limit for your profits already in hand, and don't dig into that. If you're ahead fifty bucks, and your unit of betting is two bucks, tuck twenty away, and if you lose thirty more quit.

You will have quit a winner which, in Vegas, is in mighty select company.

Finally, a word about shills. They are not designed to lure you into anything. The casino knows that a lot of gamblers don't like to play head-to-head with a dealer, so shills provide the social framework for a game. Some shills are men, others are women. Invariably the shills at baccarat seem to be women.

If you want to know if there are any shills at your table, ask the dealer. Nevada law requires that he tell you which of the players are house players—a gentler term than shills.

CRAPS

The velocity of this game is part of its attraction. That quality is also part of its danger. It is easy to become caught up in the pace of craps. And a gambler should never get caught up in anything—even when he's playing for entertainment.

The basic attraction of craps is the speed of the game and the opportunity to bet on various numbers during every roll of the dice. And unlike blackjack, which is played in relative silence, craps is noisy. That can be colorful, or it can be distracting.

The sprawling craps table offers multiple opportunities to bet. Prominently featured in the layout is "the field," which is what the house man is referring to when he intones, "The field, play the field, pays two-to-one."

Avoid it like the plague. Also shun the high payoff bets usually featured in the table center—Any Craps, eight for one, and associated bets. The house edge on these apparently lucrative wagers is high.

Craps does offer some good bets. The Pass Line pays even money when you bet with the shooter. The percentage against you is about 1.4 percent. Most important, the Pass Line bet entitles you to bet an amount equal to your original bet that the shooter will roll the specified number before he either makes his point or rolls a seven. This is called taking the odds, to wit:

Point	Odds Paid
4 or 10	2-to-1
5 or 9	3-to-2
6 or 8	6-to-5

These are the *right* odds. There's no house edge whatsoever. The only limitation here is that the amount of your odds bet cannot be more than that of your Pass Line bet.

You may also bet against the shooter, on the Don't Pass Line. The house percentage here is a few hundredths of a percentage point less than its edge on the Pass Line, but the difference is so small as to be practically meaningless. A bet on the Don't Pass Line allows you to Lay the Odds, the reverse of Taking Odds, but also a fine bet because the odds are correct. Your bet here is also allowed to be no larger than your Don't Pass bet.

Point	Odds Paid
4 or 10	1-to-2
5 or 9	2-to-3
6 or 8	5-to-6

The same proposition is open when the shooter has made his first roll and now has a point. Then, Come and Don't Come, each with the opportunity to take or lay the odds, is available.

If you get lucky, always increase the size of your bets using the house's money. Parlay your bets two or three times and then either drag half, or at least your original investment.

ROULETTE

Roulette is a pleasant, relaxed, and highly comfortable way to lose your money. The basic American wheel has thirty-eight possibilities, numbers 1 through 36, 0, and 00. The odds are thirty-five-to-one on an individual number which equals the house edge of 5.26 percent.

And it gets worse. There's one five-number bet you can make—o, oo, 1, 2, and 3. The house edge on this is 7.89 percent.

The only way to beat the wheel is to bet—whether numbers, colors, odd or even, or columns—and parlay your winnings and quit. Or bet a number a few times, hit it, and quit. Forget systems. There is no such thing, but it can still be fun to play the wheel. Remember that we are considering roulette as entertainment.

It's always relatively quiet and peaceful. You have a seat. The wheel man is pleasant. There's no rush. (There's even a pleasant inheritance from Europe of, well, style.)

And there is always the chance that you might hit a number— which will pay you seventy dollars for a 2-dollar bet, one hundred seventy-five dollars for 5 dollars.

The relaxed pace of the game is one of its principal attractions, but you can hit. When my wife and I went to Europe, we went to the casino in Rhodes and I bet Joannie's birthday—the 26th. It hit. And I bet the kids' birthdays, and a couple of them hit.

It can happen. But even if it doesn't, roulette is a gracious way to spend an evening, or an hour. For short money, the long odds are attractive.

THE SLOTS AND KENO

Don't sneer at slot machines. They are the single most profitable form of gambling in Las Vegas. Although not for you.

Of the 586 million dollars that Vegas casinos grossed in 1973, more than 165 million dollars came from slots.

For pure entertainment, nothing beats the slots—if only because they certainly can't be considered gambling. No one knows for sure what the house percentage is, but some reasonable estimates can be made. It is lightest at the big casinos. The casino people know that a low percentage—meaning relatively large payouts—will attract volume, and that's the name of their game. So expect casino slots to keep between eight and twelve percent of everything you deposit with them.

Slot players being a breed apart, many of them want to burn their dough at twice the normal rate, so they play two machines at once. In recognition of this, rumor has it that a high-paying slot will squat in between two miserly machines, set perhaps to keep fifteen percent of what you drop in them. But that's only rumor.

It does seem to be true that the slots in gas stations and other retail places are tougher, keeping as much as forty percent.

So, if you're going to play the slots, or if your wife is going to, play at the casinos. And don't sneer at them. They can be fun, in the same way that going to a shooting gallery or an amusement park is fun. But I can't see standing in front of a machine hour after hour. I mean, lots of people do it, but I don't understand it.

On the other hand, at some point during your visit, invest a buck in a dollar slot, or four halves in a fifty-cent slot. You might be the one to hit.

But then stop. The machine doesn't owe you anything. And there is no mechanical certainty that says that because you see a hundred people put money into a machine that it's overdue. When those wheels spin around, it's a fresh start every time.

Tell your wife or loved one to invest ten nickels in a slot, or an equivalent unit of speculation. If the machine doesn't cough up something, she should try another machine, because some machines do seem to pay better than others.

And at least once, throw a couple of bucks into one of the big slots. A guy did that with three singles in the monster slot at the MGM Grand. And he hit—for sixty-two grand. So it can happen. But don't chase it. It doesn't pay. Except, of course, as entertainment.

If you believe in miracles, head for the keno lounge. True, there is always the chance that you may hit for the twenty-five-thousand-dollar jackpot. But it is remote, to put it kindly. You get even money on a five-spot win, and your chances are one in twenty. An eight-spot ticket is a one in seventy-four-thousand shot. And to hit the ten-spot, you're bucking odds of one in nine million.

Play keno because the keno runner has nice legs. Or play because the seats in the keno lounge are comfortable, the drinks are free, or your favorite numerologist told you that this is your lucky day.

Don't play to win. But there is no harm in speculating with a couple of bucks just to see what happens.

POKER

Ever since the World Series of Poker began being played in Las Vegas, there's been a slow but steady increase in the visibility of house-run poker games.

They are generally stud, five, six, or seven cards. The stakes cover the spectrum from nickel ante, fifty cents to open, three dollars maximum bet, to quarter ante, two bucks to open, five-buck maximum, and on up to a rather stratospheric game at the Tropicana at two hundred and four hundred a card.

Most games are table stakes, and for the big ones you better have five grand or more to put on the table. But at every level, the players are probably better than the ones back home. Local people have more time to play, whether they're salesmen or professional gamblers, because the games go on and on.

The house cut is limited to the ante. This may seem trivial, but the inexorable gathering of "before" adds up, to the house's profit.

Shills are usually present in the smaller games, and often an off-duty dealer, or maybe a dealer who's on his break, will sit in. That's probably the ultimate tribute. You don't see stickmen from the crap table rolling, or blackjack dealers trying to beat the house. Only at poker, and that says it all about the fascination of the game.

I don't have any inside tips to offer. Poker has to be played for stakes that are significant to you without being fatal if you lose. There's no point in playing in a small game if your bankroll is a couple of grand. Purists will dispute this, claiming that the logic, the insight, the inherent excitement of poker is the same at all stakes.

Maybe so. But the bluff is basic to poker, as is the principle that you make guys pay if they chase. Both are sensitive to the willingness and therefore the ability of a player to pay. If a guy's wallet is choking on C-notes, he isn't going to run from a two-dollar raise.

Shills and local non-pro players tend to play a tight game. A table of seven players is usually cut to three, maybe four players after the first cards are dealt.

As it happens, I am nuts about poker. But about the only time I play is those four, five, or six times a year when Joannie and I have a war. In the wake of domestic argument, I play poker, in the biggest game I can find. Sometimes I come home exultant, and sometimes I come home chagrined. That's part of it.

Unless you are an excellent poker player, don't try the game in Vegas. Never play in a game you can't afford. Because of all the casino games, poker will exhaust the undercapitalized player faster than any other. There's just no way around the disadvantage of valuing the money more than the other players do. You'll start scared, and end skinned.

I have said many times that there is no system ever invented that can beat the casinos, but there is one exception to every rule. My wife has a foolproof system.

When we go over to the Strip to have dinner and see a show, she'll ask me, "Jimmy, are you going to play the tables tonight?" If I say I might, she says, "Well, here's two hundred dollars to bet for me." If I win, of course, she gets it all. If I lose, she just takes two hundred dollars off the dresser the next morning before I wake up.

Epilogue

A lingering cloud was lifted from my head on December 18, 1974. That cloud may have existed mostly in my own imagination, but that means it existed, nonetheless.

On that date I received a full and unconditional pardon, signed by the President of the United States, from my conviction eleven years before on charges of transmitting gambling information across a state line.

I had paid a fine and served my probation and, I'm reasonably sure, few people thought of me as a felon. But I *was*. I had lost my right to vote, not to mention my business, and a half million dollars in accounts receivable that were on the books and had to be written off.

That conviction was like a scar that always seems more visible, more unsightly, to the one who has it than to others. I lived in a quiet fear that it would come up at troublesome times, embarrassing my wife and children. Oh, I didn't go around wondering if people were whispering, "Pssst, he's a *felon*." But it was there, never very long out of my thoughts.

Twice it came up in instances where companies were considering me for their public relations accounts. Fortunately, they investigated deeply enough to determine the circumstances, and it was overlooked. Everyone seemed willing to overlook it but me.

I didn't then, and I am not now, stamping my feet and beating the floor with my fists and screaming "miscarriage of justice." But my attorneys have never been convinced that the charges against me could have held up in court. What I had done, remember, was give the odds on a basketball game, over the phone, to a fellow in Salt Lake City. But having lost my source of income I couldn't afford the cost of a trial, or the risk of one in a city where I had little chance of winning.

My defense had to be based on the fact that I was operating out of a legal gambling house, I paid taxes, and I owned a license issued by the state of Nevada. To the good Mormons of Salt Lake City, Las Vegas was awaiting the punishment of God.

We gave up and decided to plead *nolo contendere*, soon after we had checked out the presiding judge. Judge Christopher was a man who drank *no* stimulants. When he went hunting, on those cold, miserable mornings Utah is famous for, he carried cold water in his thermos instead of coffee. He didn't drink Cokes, preferring Dr. Pepper, a soda with a prune extraction content. He was an extremely fair man, but we didn't see how he could be *sympathetic*.

I had the distinction of being the first nationally known figure to be tried under the new gambling law, passed by the Kennedy administration in their big sweep against organized crime. A member of the Nevada Gaming Commission told me, with some regret, I think, that I was to be made an example. My timing had been horrendous. The Justice Department had just lost a big gambling case in New Orleans, involving Gil Beckley and others. Joe Valachi was singing about the *Cosa Nostra* and titillating the country with expressions like *the kiss of death*. In Las Vegas, the story had broken of an attempted shakedown of a wealthy gambler, who happened to be my friend Ray Ryan.

The headlines everywhere were about crime and gambling, and few people could separate the two. I guess I was lucky, in a way, that I didn't get the chair for that lousy phone call.

I have made light of it at times over the years, even boasted that I must have been a bigger man than I thought, if it was so important for the government to *get* Jimmy the Greek. But I wanted that pardon, wanted it with a passion, and my attorneys filed the application the first moment I was eligible in late 1971.

For the next two years I was investigated—it was standard procedure—by the federal and state law agencies. I didn't mind. They talked with more than a hundred people, friends, some not so friendly, business contacts, neighbors. But the local FBI office, the sheriff, and the U.S. attorney in Las Vegas gave me the most glowing recommendations of all. They damned near eulogized me. I later saw copies of the letters. You would have thought they had gotten me confused with Father Flanagan.

Now all I could do was wait. The request for a pardon went through the office of Senator Howard Cannon, to the Justice Department and, hopefully, on to the President. I was on the phone to Washington so much—"Where is it now?"—one of Cannon's aides had to cool me down. "Hey, Jimmy, take it easy," Chet Sobsey said one day. "We can't push these people too hard. There's a limit. It has to go through certain levels."

I could hear the wheels of justice turning, ever so slowly, inches at a time.

What I constantly feared was that something would go wrong at the last instant and wreck it for me. Something almost did. In the summer of 1974, I was told that the pardon was getting close. By August it would be on the desk of Richard Nixon.

About that time I had dinner with Jack Anderson one night in Duke Ziebert's, my favorite Washington pit stop. We were having a warm discussion, as we often did, on the honesty of politicians. I expressed the thought that those in Nevada, in my state, were more honest than most. I told Jack that I knew of cases where big money had been refused for special favors. Why, I had once heard a fellow boast he would pay a half million dollars if the governor would issue him a gambling license in Las Vegas.

That conversation was filed away in Jack Anderson's agile mind, and a few days later he mentioned it to one of his staff people and told him to look into it.

I had quickly forgotten it. That summer I had checked into the

Duke University clinic at Durham, North Carolina, hoping to shed a
few pounds on their famous rice diet. There a call reached me from
the U.S. attorney's office in Nevada. An Anderson column had
appeared in which the remarks I made showed the honesty of
Governor Paul Laxalt of Nevada, but in a way sounded as though I
had offered him a bribe.

At first, I treated the whole thing as a joke. Then it hit me that it
was serious, damned serious. I could just see my pardon being tabled
while this matter was resolved, and then never surfacing again. I
caught the first plane back to Las Vegas and went before the Gaming
Board. I even took a lie detector test.

I didn't blame Jack. I had probably made it sound less casual than
it was, and his staff had done the rest. What actually happened was
simply this: at a party one night I warned the governor about a
rumor I had heard, that a fellow was in town boasting he would pay a
half million dollars to anyone "who could get me a gambling
license." Laxalt knew him by reputation. So did I. Paul laughed it off.
"That fellow," he said, "could offer fifty million and it wouldn't make
any difference. He couldn't get a license to sell apples on a corner."

It quieted down, and I went back to my nervous vigil. Then the
first of August, with Watergate coming apart like a grenade, I
received word that my request for pardon was on Nixon's desk.
Great. It was still there on August 8 when Nixon resigned.

My only hope now was Gerald Ford, the new President. I had met
him once, years before, in the home of Bob Maheu. He was a
congressman then, and my impression of him hasn't changed. When
he took office, I told anyone who asked that the Ford Presidency
would be neither fancy nor tricky. "He played center on his college
football teams," I pointed out. "Centers only know to do one thing:
go straight ahead. They don't have room to maneuver." That was
Ford. That will always be Ford. Right or wrong, he will meet the
moment head on. He won't change.

I believe that was the case when he pardoned the former
President—*I've got to do it sometime; we can't put an ex-President in
jail; why not now?*

But the reaction that erupted around the country did not bode well, I thought, for getting my slate cleaned. I wouldn't make a price on my chances after that. For the next few weeks I moped around pretty good. Then in December, I was in my hotel room in Indianapolis, where I was doing a promotion film for a client, the Delta Faucets Company, when the phone rang. It always does when I'm in hotel rooms. But this was absolutely the most welcome call of my life.

"Jimmy," the voice said, "this is Paul Laxalt, and as my first official act as the newly elected junior senator from Nevada, I have the pleasure of informing you that the President has just signed your pardon."

Paul had been elected to the seat vacated by the retiring Alan Bible. The Senator had stepped down a few days early to give his successor a slight jump in seniority.

I don't recall now what I said or what I did, but I do know my heart leaped like a fawn. Then I called home and told Joannie, and after that I had room service send up some wine, good German wine, Bernkaestler Doktor at thirty-five dollars a magnum.

The stigma was gone, no more a threat to Joan or my kids, and I could vote again, a right we take all too lightly in this country and which some never exercise. Can you imagine the irony I felt? Here Jimmy the Greek studied the candidates like few others, did massive research, had a ton of information, and for eleven years couldn't vote for the candidates he thought most qualified. And now, again, I could.

I guess I was born with gambler's luck, hot streaks and cold, winning long shots and losing the sure thing, up one week and lower than a snail's navel the next. But it has been one helluva fine ride.

Testing yourself, taking a chance, being around people that do, there is the excitement in life. Not knowing from day to day if the sun will shine and, sometimes, not caring.

The last time I bet with a bookie was at Aqueduct, I won't tell you what year, and his name was Doc Connick, an old-timer I knew from Las Vegas. I bumped into him at the track that day and he offered to handle whatever I wanted to play. It happened that I liked four horses, and I gave them to Doc, three hundred dollars across on each of them.

I bet with Doc because, for one thing, you didn't have to carry that kind of money. Two, if I had bet a thousand dollars at the window it would cut down the price. And, three, I liked Doc. He was from an era when a bookie's word was as good as government bonds.

That day I beat him out of thirteen thousand dollars, and after the races we agreed to settle up when we both returned to Vegas. I didn't get home until three weeks later, and Doc showed up on a day when I was coming down the stairs, leaving to catch a flight to Chicago.

At the door he said, "Hey, here's your money," and he tried to hand me an envelope. I had a couple of thousand on me, and I didn't have time to go back into the office and put away the pile Doc was holding. "Look," I said, "give me three of it and hold the other ten. I'll be back Tuesday and you can pay me the rest of it then." I had no worries. Doc was a hundred percent.

I was at the Continental Plaza in Chicago this time when the phone rang. It was Bobby Berendt, a friend of forty years, a fine handicapper who helps me with the colleges. Bobby grew up wise on the east side of New York.

"Greek," he said, "I got good news and I got bad news. Which do you want first?"

I sighed. "Give me the good news first, Bobby."

"It wasn't you."

"What the hell is the bad news?"

"Doc Connick just dropped dead."

When I arrived back at the airport in Las Vegas, Bobby met me, and on the ride to the office he sympathized with me on the ten grand I would now never collect. Bobby had been with me when Doc had tried to pay off and, in fact, had driven me out to catch the plane to Chicago.

"You know, Greek," he said, "you could have given the money to me at the airport if you had taken it from him."

"The idea passed through my mind, Bobby," I admitted. "But to tell the truth, Connick looked to me like he was in better shape than you."

Actually, I had left the money with Doc because I couldn't embarrass him. If I had taken it and turned it over to someone else, it would have flat said that I didn't trust him.

Sure, it has cost me, trusting people, but I am able to live a little easier with Demetrios Synodinos that way. I even have, to this day, a grudging admiration for those whose larceny was of a gentle kind, who lived by their wits, who could maneuver you in a thousand creative ways.

One of the premier con artists of my time, and the time before that, was a gremlin of a man named Swifty Morgan. This was one of the great hustlers of the world. In fact, Swifty *was*, *is*, the Lemon Drop Kid, transferred to print and made immortal by Damon Runyon in his Broadway classic, *Guys and Dolls*. Bob Hope later played the part in the movies.

Runyon's fictional Kid was unpolished, corrupt and irrepressible, no more so than Swifty, who had balls of brass. He spent all of his life looking for an angle and, one way or another, he usually found it. In 1949, at Joe's Stone Crab in Miami Beach, I saw Swifty try to sell a gold wristwatch—hot, of course—to a man whose name was J. Edgar Hoover.

I was having dinner with Herman Hickman, the Yale football coach, when Swifty walked in and headed for our table. I was a benevolent customer of his, a buyer of ties, watches, cuff links, whatever he was hustling. Swifty sat with us only a moment when his eyeballs, which were always working, picked out Hoover a few tables away. "I'll see you guys in a few minutes," he said, pushing back his chair. "I got a bigger pigeon over there." And he nodded in Hoover's direction.

Hoover was in town to watch the ponies run at Tropical. I'll say this for him: J. Edgar was hip, bright and, at times, convivial. He wasn't then the stern old grouch he was pictured in later years.

Swifty sat down, uninvited, pointed to the watch on the G-man's wrist and shook his head. "Hoover," he said, "why don't you get rid of that piece of shit and buy yourself a really fine watch? Man of your stature, you ought to be wearing something in *gold*."

Whereupon he produced a gold watch and put it on the table. "Now, here's one that will give you some class."

Hoover turned it slowly in his hand. He nodded. "Give you a hundred dollars for it," he said, firmly.

Swifty looked at him with wounded eyes. "Goddam, J. Edgar," he said. "Look at that watch. The insurance reward alone is worth more than that!"

When I was living at the El Rancho, in Las Vegas, Swifty dropped by for seven straight weeks to sell me a pair of cuff links, one hundred dollars a pop. Every week. They were good links, and well worth the money, or would have been, except that I didn't wear French cuffs. I bought them anyway. You had to do something to help Swifty make expenses.

But when the eighth week rolled around I was begging for mercy. "No, Swifty, no," I said. "Please, no more cuff links. I'm up to my ass in them already."

Swifty gave me a look of complete innocence. "Who said anything about cuff links? I just brought you a jewelry box to keep them in." The price tag was $100.

The last I saw Swifty he was still going strong, living in a suite at the Beverly Wilshire, though he needed a wheel chair to help him get around. He was 83, a stocky, rumpled little man looking for a good bridge game. He was still complaining about his ex-wives and girl friends, of which there had been an abundance over the years. "I didn't mind spending my money on that bitch," he said, recalling one of his divorces. "But, goddam, I got tired of supporting the two boy friends she kept on the side."

Swifty had great connections. To this day, I'm sure Frank Sinatra helps pay his bills. Joe E. Lewis chipped in for years. And once or twice I tided him over, between capers. The one of which he was most proud landed him in a French jail for six months.

For three hundred dollars Swifty once rented a complete ward-robe—tails, top hat, gold-tipped cane, studs and pocket watch—and walked into a plush Paris gambling house. He took a position near the *chemin de fer* game, and waited until a big play came up. There was sixty thousand dollars on the table. When the dealer asked for bets, Swifty raised his gold cane—it alone rented for fifty dollars—and said, "Banco, m'sieur." He was covering the table.

The dealer looked at him, and took it all in, the tails, the cane, the watch, even a diamond ring he had borrowed. The bet was on. Swifty lost. When they discovered that he couldn't pay, hadn't a cent on him, the gendarmes were summoned and Swifty went to the bastille. Still, it wasn't a bad gamble—six months against sixty grand.

I heard him tell that story one night to Cheesecake Ike, during an argument over who was the better con man. Ike hadn't worked a single day since he was twenty-nine. Swifty recited his story about yelling "banco" for sixty thousand dollars but he made one mistake. He went first. That immediately makes you an underdog.

Cheesecake Ike curled his nose and gave him a look that passed for contempt. "You poor, phony, cheap little bastard," he growled. "Why, I laid down to Dunhill's for more than that in cigars." I moved on, leaving the two philosophers to argue it out.

Today, in his late seventies, Ike is one of the elder statesmen in Las Vegas. He will spend out his years there, as many old gamblers do, the way retired seamen so often hang around the docks. You can find him at the casinos, in the side rooms where the cards are played or at the California Turf and Sports Club, making a small investment on the daily double. It is a monastic life and Ike thrives on it.

No accounting of famous con men I have known would be complete without one more reference to Nate Linnett, also known as Nigger Nate Raymond. Nate was tall, dark complected, with kinky white hair. He was handsome in a vacant way. We saw a lot of each other, and I enjoyed Nate, though he wasn't a fellow easily trusted. He was in the room at Atlantic City, remember, when some of the boys set back my watch and cleaned my clock.

Gambling was Nate's trade and he was candid about it; about some of his sidelines, less so. He spent a long stretch in prison.

From time to time I lent him money, but always with the understanding that someday Nate would give me the full, inside and unedited story of what happened in the most famous card game in the history of American crime. He was there. He sat in on the card game that led to the murder of Arnold Rothstein.

Rothstein was a romantic underworld character of the day, a bootlegger who didn't drink, a gambler, loan shark and diamond smuggler. The game was held in September of 1928, at an apartment on New York's West Side. Others at the table included Nate, Sam and Meyer Boston, Abe Silverman, George McManus, Red Bowe and Titanic Thompson. All of them had big reputations as gamblers, bookmakers or horse players.

The story circulated that Rothstein lost over two hundred thousand dollars that night. On November 4, 1928, in Room 349 of the Park Central Hotel on Seventh Avenue, Rothstein was shot and killed by a gunman hiding behind a screen. The weapon was thrown to the street below.

George McManus, the brother of a New York cop, went to trial for the murder of Rothstein and was acquitted. Courtroom testimony brought out the fact that Rothstein, while losing two hundred grand to the others, had won fifty-one thousand dollars from McManus at high card. Who killed Rothstein, and why, what happened at the game and later, are a puzzle, the details known only to a handful of men who kept it that way.

I had heard, but never really believed it, that Nate fingered Rothstein. That is, he arranged to have him at that place at that time. I had planned to ask him when he told me the story, as he always promised, whenever he put the touch on me. We were going to sit down, with a bottle on the table, and Nate Linnett, aka Raymond, was going to spill the secret of Arnold Rothstein's killing. He took it to the grave with him, as I knew all along he would.

I last saw Nate on his deathbed. When I heard he was sinking I felt an urge to see the old rogue and not let him die unremembered in a hospital room in Vegas. He was well past eighty then, a hard eighty. His wife, Dale, stood quietly at the foot of the bed as we visited. When it was time for me to go, Nate raised himself slightly on his pillow and motioned me to lean down. "Jimmy," he whispered, "I'm a little short right now. Medical bills and all. Could you lend me two grand for a few weeks until I can pay you back?"

It was all I could do to keep from laughing, right there in the hospital. "Tell you what, Nate," I said, taking out my roll. "I've got exactly fifteen hundred dollars on me, and I'm going to give you half of it. And that way we're *each* gonna make seven hundred and fifty dollars."

We said good-bye and Dale walked out into the corridor with me. She was upset. "Jimmy," she said, "what did you do that for? Nate has plenty of money. He didn't need a loan. Let me get it back."

I patted her on the hand. "It's okay," I said, smiling. "I don't mind. Nate just had to make a score one last time."

To the end, Nigger Nate Linnett was a pro. I admired his competitive spirit.

We were speaking of gambler's luck. Twice in my life I have canceled out of flights that a few hours later crashed, killing all or nearly all aboard. The first time was in 1949 or '50, the date doesn't really matter, except that it was one of the half dozen times I decided to marry Joannie before we actually did. I was in New York with Harold Salvey and I confided my plans.

"You're crazy," he said. "She's still a schoolgirl. Her father is a respected businessman. You're a gambler. Believe me, Greek. It's not a good mix. It won't work."

"I'll make it work," I said. "I'm gonna buy her a ring."

"In that case," said Harold, "I can get it for you wholesale."

We went to Tiffany's first, found the ring I wanted, a marquise diamond, four carats, and priced it. It was thirteen thousand dollars. Then I followed Harold into a cab and we headed for the diamond market. It was a beehive. Shops and stores and vendors. People were practically selling out of pushcarts. The sight was so vivid to me. There were little Jewish men, with their full beards and yarmulkes, who had put their money in gold and diamonds and escaped from Germany before the war. The ones who were lucky.

We found a friend of Harold's named Sam, and in a few minutes he produced the stone I wanted, wrapped in tissue paper. The price was forty-five hundred dollars. I described the setting I wanted, platinum, with a baguette on each side, and I needed it in time to catch a flight to Miami the next morning.

Sam threw up his hands. "Impossible," he said. "You come back late in the afternoon. Ve haf it then."

"So you stay another day," said Harold. "What's the difference?"

The next afternoon we went back to pick up the ring. At the

corner Harold bought a paper, and as we drove away from the diamond market he said, "Greek, what was the number of that Eastern flight you were supposed to catch?"

I told him.

"Well," he said, "you're a dead man." And he handed me the paper. The Eastern flight had collided outside of Washington with a small plane, in which a Bolivian Air Force pilot was *practicing*. He bailed out. Everyone aboard the Eastern jet was killed.

The other missed death flight was in January 1969, two weeks after the Super Bowl, and after my surgery. The night I left the hospital in Santa Barbara, I caught a flight for Los Angeles, figuring to change planes there for Denver, where I was involved in a mining deal. We landed in Los Angeles on a foggy, dreary, miserable night and I suddenly realized how weak I was from the operation. I decided to cancel my connecting flight, take a cab to the Beverly Wilshire, get a night's sleep, and fly to Denver in the morning.

The United Airlines plane I would have been on went down a few minutes outside of Los Angeles, crashing into the Pacific. A few passengers survived.

I don't dwell on the whims of fate, or the deeper meanings of life, or *why me?* These were just another couple of cases where I beat the odds, good bets cashed.

But as I think back over all those years, all these pages, I realize how many of the people who brushed my life, who left an imprint on me in one way or another, are gone. It is like walking through a cemetery. Slim Silverheart, Billy Hecht, John Nolan, Nick the Greek, Wilbur Clark, Herman Hickman, Harold Salvey, Nate Linnett. All gone. And a saintly old man I met only once, Bernard Baruch.

I was in my twenties then, visiting New York for reasons long since forgotten, when I ran into Moan Anathan, a wealthy Jewish merchant from Steubenville, whose family owned the Hub Department Stores. He invited me to join his party for dinner that night, half a dozen of us, at the Plaza Hotel. One of the guests was Bernard Baruch, a certified genius in the world of finance.

He was also one of my boyhood heroes, along with Robert Young, the president of the Chesapeake and Ohio Railroad. It did not seem strange to me, as a boy, that my heroes were very rich men whose autobiographies I had read. Those were, in fact, the only books I read.

The morning after the dinner I dressed early and walked across the street from the Plaza and into Central Park. Within a few yards I found Baruch, sitting on a park bench, as everyone always pictured him. It was his front porch to the world.

I sat down and we talked for about an hour, Baruch treating me very seriously, as an equal, answering my questions with great patience. For years afterward I wished that I had taken notes, and that so many of my questions had not dealt with the subject then most on my mind, the making of money. I asked him about politics, the stock market, gold, metals, what he thought was the future of aluminum (I had recently bought my shares of Reynolds Metals). I spoke as quickly as I could get the words off my tongue.

He looked at his pocket watch and rose, and I took that as my cue to thank him for his time. I told him I felt honored to have met him. He said nothing as I stood there, not knowing whether I should offer to shake hands, curtsy, or just go. What does one say to a patriarch? Finally, he said, "Young man, you're going to be broke and rich seven times in your life. Be sure you watch the seventh."

I never saw or spoke with Bernard Baruch again, but I have thought of his prediction often. It's possible that I have approached, even passed, the seventh cycle. Sometimes, I wish I had kept score.